Survival

GLOBAL POLITICS AND STRATEGY

Volume 61 Number 4 | August–September 2019

'European populism may leave a lasting impression on social relationships. It has already changed political discourse in ways that allow greater scope for exclusionary language.'

Erik Jones, Populism in Europe: What Scholarship Tells Us, p. 20.

'It would … be imprudent to discount the emerging global trend of subversion and the necessity of rethinking statecraft in light of this trend. Liberal democracies need to reconcile their self-images with this new reality, and craft policies that carefully embrace it.'

Henrik Breitenbauch and Niels Byrjalsen, Subversion, Statecraft and Liberal Democracy, p. 37.

'All three big nuclear powers are sensitive to the danger of counter-nuclear command, control and communications cyber war. As a result, any interference with these systems could trigger fear of nuclear or non-nuclear attack, which could in turn threaten nuclear peace.'

David C. Gompert and Martin Libicki, Cyber War and Nuclear Peace, p. 57.

Survival
GLOBAL POLITICS AND STRATEGY
Volume 61 Number 4 | August–September 2019

Contents

On the cover
Brexit Party leader
Nigel Farage arrives at
an event in London on
27 May 2019 after his
party won 29 seats in the
European Parliament.

On the web
Visit www.iiss.org/
publications/survival
for brief notices on new
books on Politics and
International Relations,
Russia and Eurasia, and
Asia-Pacific.

***Survival* editors' blog**
For ideas and
commentary from
Survival editors and
contributors, visit
www.iiss.org/blogs/
survival-blog.

Survival
GLOBAL POLITICS AND STRATEGY

The International Institute for Strategic Studies

2121 K Street, NW | Suite 801 | Washington DC 20037 | USA
Tel +1 202 659 1490   Fax +1 202 659 1499   E-mail survival@iiss.org   Web www.iiss.org

Arundel House | 6 Temple Place | London | WC2R 2PG | UK
Tel +44 (0)20 7379 7676   Fax +44 (0)20 7836 3108   E-mail iiss@iiss.org

14th Floor, GBCorp Tower | Bahrain Financial Harbour | Manama | Kingdom of Bahrain
Tel +973 1718 1155   Fax +973 1710 0155   E-mail iiss-middleeast@iiss.org

9 Raffles Place | #51-01 Republic Plaza | Singapore 048619
Tel +65 6499 0055   Fax +65 6499 0059   E-mail iiss-asia@iiss.org

Survival Online www.tandfonline.com/survival and www.iiss.org/publications/survival

Aims and Scope *Survival* is one of the world's leading forums for analysis and debate of international and strategic affairs. Shaped by its editors to be both timely and forward thinking, the journal encourages writers to challenge conventional wisdom and bring fresh, often controversial, perspectives to bear on the strategic issues of the moment. With a diverse range of authors, *Survival* aims to be scholarly in depth while vivid, well written and policy-relevant in approach. Through commentary, analytical articles, case studies, forums, review essays, reviews and letters to the editor, the journal promotes lively, critical debate on issues of international politics and strategy.

Editor **Dana Allin**
Managing Editor **Jonathan Stevenson**
Associate Editor **Carolyn West**
Assistant Editor **Jessica Watson**
Editorial Intern **Jan Zdrálek**
Production and Cartography **John Buck, Kelly Verity**

Contributing Editors

Ian Bremmer	Bill Emmott	Jeffrey Lewis	Teresita C. Schaffer	Ruth Wedgwood
Rosa Brooks	Mark Fitzpatrick	Hanns W. Maull	Steven Simon	Lanxin Xiang
David P. Calleo	John A. Gans, Jr	Jeffrey Mazo	Angela Stent	
Russell Crandall	John L. Harper	'Funmi Olonisakin	Ray Takeyh	
Toby Dodge	Erik Jones	Thomas Rid	David C. Unger	

Published for the IISS by
Routledge Journals, an imprint of Taylor & Francis, an Informa business.

SUBMISSIONS

To submit an article, authors are advised to follow these guidelines:

- *Survival* articles are around 4,000–10,000 words long including endnotes. A word count should be included with a draft.
- All text, including endnotes, should be double-spaced with wide margins.
- Any tables or artwork should be supplied in separate files, ideally not embedded in the document or linked to text around it.
- All *Survival* articles are expected to include endnote references. These should be complete and include first and last names of authors, titles of articles (even from newspapers), place of publication, publisher, exact publication dates, volume and issue number (if from a journal) and page numbers. Web sources should include complete URLs and DOIs if available.
- A summary of up to 150 words should be included with the article. The summary should state the main argument clearly and concisely, not simply say what the article is about.
- A short author's biography of one or two lines should also be included. This information will appear at the foot of the first page of the article.

Please note that *Survival* has a strict policy of listing multiple authors in alphabetical order.

Submissions should be made by email, in Microsoft Word format, to survival@iiss.org. Alternatively, hard copies may be sent to *Survival*, IISS–US, 2121 K Street NW, Suite 801, Washington, DC 20037, USA.

The editorial review process can take up to three months. *Survival*'s acceptance rate for unsolicited manuscripts is less than 20%. *Survival* does not normally provide referees' comments in the event of rejection. Authors are permitted to submit simultaneously elsewhere so long as this is consistent with the policy of the other publication and the Editors of *Survival* are informed of the dual submission.

Readers are encouraged to comment on articles from the previous issue. Letters should be concise, no longer than 750 words and relate directly to the argument or points made in the original article.

ADVERTISING AND PERMISSIONS

For advertising rates and schedules

USA/Canada: The Advertising Manager, Taylor & Francis Inc., 530 Walnut Street, Suite 850, Philadelphia, PA 19106, USA Tel +1 (800) 354 1420 Fax +1 (215) 207 0050.

UK/Europe/Rest of World: The Advertising Manager, Routledge Journals, Taylor & Francis, 4 Park Square, Milton Park, Abingdon, Oxfordshire OX14 4RN, UK Tel +44 (0) 207 017 6000 Fax +44 (0) 207 017 6336.

SUBSCRIPTIONS

Survival is published bi-monthly in February, April, June, August, October and December by Routledge Journals, an imprint of Taylor & Francis, an Informa Business.

Annual Subscription 2019

Institution	£607	$1,062	€890
Individual	£153	$258	€208
Online only	£524	$917	€769

Taylor & Francis has a flexible approach to subscriptions, enabling us to match individual libraries' requirements. This journal is available via a traditional institutional subscription (either print with online access, or online only at a discount) or as part of our libraries, subject collections or archives. For more information on our sales packages please visit http://www.tandfonline.com/page/librarians.

All current institutional subscriptions include online access for any number of concurrent users across a local area network to the currently available backfile and articles posted online ahead of publication.

Subscriptions purchased at the personal rate are strictly for personal, non-commercial use only. The reselling of personal subscriptions is prohibited. Personal subscriptions must be purchased with a personal cheque or credit card. Proof of personal status may be requested.

Dollar rates apply to all subscribers outside Europe. Euro rates apply to all subscribers in Europe, except the UK and the Republic of Ireland where the pound sterling rate applies. If you are unsure which rate applies to you please contact Customer Services in the UK. All subscriptions are payable in advance and all rates include postage. Journals are sent by air to the USA, Canada, Mexico, India, Japan and Australasia. Subscriptions are entered on an annual basis, i.e. January to December. Payment may be made by sterling cheque, dollar cheque, euro cheque, international money order, National Giro or credit cards (Amex, Visa and Mastercard).

Survival (USPS 013095) is published bimonthly (in Feb, Apr, Jun, Aug, Oct and Dec) by Routledge Journals, Taylor & Francis, 4 Park Square, Milton Park, Abingdon, OX14 4RN, United Kingdom.

The US annual subscription price is $842. Airfreight and mailing in the USA by agent named WN Shipping USA, 156-15, 146th Avenue, 2nd Floor, Jamaica, NY 11434, USA. Periodicals postage paid at Jamaica NY 11431.

US Postmaster: Send address changes to Survival, C/O Air Business Ltd / 156-15 146th Avenue, Jamaica, New York, NY11434.

Subscription records are maintained at Taylor & Francis Group, 4 Park Square, Milton Park, Abingdon, OX14 4RN, United Kingdom.

ORDERING INFORMATION

Please contact your local Customer Service Department to take out a subscription to the Journal: **USA, Canada:** Taylor & Francis, Inc., 530 Walnut Street, Suite 850, Philadelphia, PA 19106, USA. Tel: +1 800 354 1420; Fax: +1 215 207 0050. **UK/ Europe/Rest of World:** T&F Customer Services, Informa UK Ltd, Sheepen Place, Colchester, Essex, CO3 3LP, United Kingdom. Tel: +44 (0) 20 7017 5544; Fax: +44 (0) 20 7017 5198; Email: subscriptions@tandf.co.uk.

Back issues: Taylor & Francis retains a two-year back issue stock of journals. Older volumes are held by our official stockists: Periodicals Service Company, 351 Fairview Ave., Suite 300, Hudson, New York 12534, USA to whom all orders and enquiries should be addressed. *Tel* +1 518 537 4700 *Fax* +1 518 537 5899 *e-mail* psc@periodicals.com *web* http://www.periodicals.com/tandf.html.

The International Institute for Strategic Studies (IISS) and our publisher Taylor & Francis make every effort to ensure the accuracy of all the information (the "Content") contained in our publications. However, the IISS and our publisher Taylor & Francis, our agents, and our licensors make no representations or warranties whatsoever as to the accuracy, completeness, or suitability for any purpose of the Content. Any opinions and views expressed in this publication are the opinions and views of the authors, and are not the views of or endorsed by the IISS and our publisher Taylor & Francis. The accuracy of the Content should not be relied upon and should be independently verified with primary sources of information. The IISS and our publisher Taylor & Francis shall not be liable for any losses, actions, claims, proceedings, demands, costs, expenses, damages, and other liabilities whatsoever or howsoever caused arising directly or indirectly in connection with, in relation to or arising out of the use of the Content. Terms & Conditions of access and use can be found at http://www.tandfonline.com/page/terms-and-conditions.

The issue date is August–September 2019.

The print edition of this journal is printed on ANSI-conforming acid-free paper.

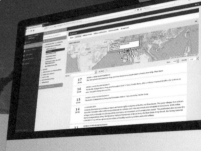

Populism in Europe: What Scholarship Tells Us

Erik Jones

European politics is going through a period of profound transformation. This can be seen in the structures of representation: traditional political parties are losing support; new parties are emerging; and national parliaments are splintering into larger numbers of smaller groups. It can also be seen in the balance between representative democracy and direct democracy: referendums are increasing in frequency and importance; political parties are developing new instruments for harnessing popular input; and non-majoritarian institutions, such as 'politically independent' central banks, and supranational organisations, such as the European Union, are facing challenges to their legitimacy, as well as calls for more comprehensive political oversight. Finally, it can be seen in the style of politics: the old rules of comity, collegiality and discourse are weakening; identity politics, both positive ('us') and negative ('them'), is gaining prominence; and polarisation is replacing consensus as the norm.

Analysts and commentators have tried to capture the many dimensions of this transformation with the word 'populism'. They often use modifiers to signal some larger ideological orientation, such as 'nationalist', 'authoritarian', 'separatist', 'right-wing' or 'left-wing'. Unfortunately, as the published literature on this topic has rapidly increased, a gap has opened between the scholarly use of the term 'populism' and its meaning (or use)

Erik Jones is Professor of European Studies and Director of European and Eurasian Studies at the Paul H. Nitze School of Advanced International Studies (SAIS), Johns Hopkins University; Senior Research Associate at the Istituto per gli Studi di Politica Internazionale in Milan; and a contributing editor to *Survival*.

Survival | vol. 61 no. 4 | August–September 2019 | pp. 7–30   DOI 10.1080/00396338.2019.1637125

in conventional speech. This gap creates ambiguity in the interpretation of the term that distorts or limits the insights that analysts can garner from scholarly research and argument. This distortion is particularly important whenever scholarly definitions are used as the basis for data coding in statistical analysis: analysts using a conventional-speech interpretation of the term run the risk of drawing inferences from statistical models without understanding precisely what the data means.

Policing the use of language in popular commentary on Europe's political transformation is an impossible task. Hence, even in the best-case scenario, the gap between academic and non-academic use of 'populism' as a concept will remain significant. If anything, variations in the academic usage of the term – and in the application of modifiers by scholars to add nuance to what they are studying – is likely to increase. The only solution for ensuring that academic work remains accessible to analysts outside academia is to place such work in a wider intellectual context, sketching the broad contours of academic debates on the transformation of European politics and exposing the role of populism, in its various guises, within those dynamics.

The purpose of this review is to map four dimensions of the scholarly literature: what scholars are seeing, how they explain it, what the implications are and how they manifest differently from one country to the next.[1] In doing so, this review relies more heavily on books than on journal articles. It also incorporates a significant number of works that fall more clearly in the 'public intellectual' category than in the narrower contemporary definition of 'academic scholarship'. That choice reflects an ambition to bridge the gap between conventional-speech discussion of Europe's political transformation and the wider scholarly literature. The literature on populism in Europe is expanding at a frenetic pace, particularly in journals. Book-length treatments tend to provide a first attempt at synthesis. This review is an attempt at further distillation.

What are we seeing?

When scholars point to the rise of populism, they have a very specific notion of it in mind. That notion is important methodologically. Conceptually, however, there has been some confusion as both scholars and other analysts have tried to describe or characterise the many transformations under way in European politics. As a result, any narrow discussion of populism rapidly broadens to encompass the decline of traditional political parties, the rise of nationalism and identity politics, and the turn away from democratic institutions toward more authoritarian structures.

The most popular academic definition of populism comes from a 2004 essay by Cas Mudde called 'The Populist Zeitgeist'. In that essay, Mudde defines populism as 'an ideology that considers society to be ultimately separated into two homogenous and antagonistic groups, "the pure people" versus "the corrupt elite", and which argues that politics should be an expression of the *volonté générale* (general will) of the people'. Mudde goes on to explain that populism is only 'a thin centered ideology' that 'can be easily combined with … other ideologies, including communism, ecologism, nationalism or socialism'.[2] In this way, Mudde is able to make connections between the protest movements of the late 1960s and early 1970s on the political left, and the more nationalistic or xenophobic movements that emerged on the political right in the 1980s and 1990s. This definition is popular because it feeds into a 'manifesto' approach to identifying populist groups and distinguishing them from other political movements that relies on coding the language used in political speeches or documents – or on expert assessments as to how that language should be coded – to determine how well different groups fit the definition. Any group that pits a pure people against a corrupt elite is populist; any group that fails to make that distinction is not.

There are reasons to be sceptical that this definition captures the full extent of the political challenges facing European democracies. When popular commentators refer to the 'populist threat to democracy', they are usually speaking about something bigger and more complicated than the rhetorical turns deployed by specific political parties as they claim to represent the people and criticise the elite. Moreover, scholars of populism have never claimed that the phenomenon they study is comprehensive. On the contrary, they usually push in the opposite direction in the hopes of bringing greater precision to the analysis of political parties. This strategy is very successful in ring-fencing a conversation about how specific political parties – or the competition between political parties – have changed over time.

It is not difficult to find prominent authors who mirror the language used in Mudde's definition, even if they do not cite his work. Hence, *The Populist Explosion* by John Judis starts off insisting that it is 'a mistake' to try to define populism 'like entropy or photosynthesis', and yet later concedes that it is important to highlight the distinction between 'the ordinary people' and 'their elite opponents', if only to acknowledge that these concepts have different interpretations on the left and right. For Judis, the important point is that 'the exact referents of "the people" and "the elite" don't define populism; what defines it is the conflictual relationship between the two'.[3] In the same vein, Jan-Werner Müller makes it clear in *What Is Populism?* that 'it is a necessary but not sufficient condition to be critical of elites in order to count as a populist'. He explains that, 'in addition to being anti-elitist, populists are always anti-pluralist. Populists claim that they, and they alone, represent the people.'[4] A third illustration comes from Pippa Norris and Ronald Inglehart. In *Cultural Backlash*, they assert that 'populism is understood … minimally as a style of rhetoric reflecting first-order principles about who should rule, claiming that legitimate power rests with "the people" not the elites'.[5] These notions are all subtly different. Mudde talks about an ideology, Judis focuses on a pattern of conflict, Müller emphasises rhetoric, and Norris and Inglehart highlight implicit claims to legitimacy. The point to note is that these notions converge on language as the primary indicator, coding populists based on what they say in their political speeches and documents.

This coding strategy is widespread and makes it possible for scholars to map the growth in support for populist parties across different countries using a common definition. Norris and Inglehart provide a good illustration of this kind of coding strategy, both in terms of the narrow focus on populism – which they juxtapose with pluralism – and across an array of other political dimensions (captured primarily through expert surveys) that provide the underlying structure for party competition.[6] In this way, they can show that support for populist parties has increased since the 1940s from just over 5% of the electorate across 32 Western countries to just over 12%

by the 2010s.[7] The technique is far from perfect, however. For example, it is never clear how Norris and Inglehart can use contemporary expert surveys to code political parties that competed in the 1950s and 1960s. Presumably the coding of those earlier contests relied more heavily on analysis derived from the comparative party-manifesto project.

What is even less clear is how to interpret this increase. The big jump comes between the 1970s, at 5.8% support for populist parties, and the 1980s, with 10.9%. Moreover, the data gives no reason to believe that there is anything new about populism in Western democracies, but only that support for populist parties has increased. Since one party's gain is another party's loss, it may be more relevant to ask what happened to the political forces that used to keep the populists at bay. The declining impor- *Support for* tance of mainstream or traditional political parties *populist parties* is another development that has captured consid- erable scholarly attention. Peter Mair's *Ruling the* *has increased* *Void* is a good illustration.[8] Virtually every standard work on the rise of populism, however, treats the decline of mainstream political parties as a secondary phenomenon.

The rise of nationalism or nationalist sentiments is another trend that has drawn the interest of scholars. Most take pains to distinguish between nation- alism and populism, often using one term to modify the other, as in 'national populism' or 'populist nationalism'. Roger Eatwell and Matthew Goodwin explain in *National Populism* that 'national populists prioritize the culture and interests of the nation and promise to give voice to a people who feel that they have been neglected, even held in contempt, by distant and often corrupt elites'.[9] Meanwhile, Sergio Fabbrini argues that 'nationalist popu- lism' is anti-technocratic and anti-European, while 'populist nationalism' is more obviously anti-immigration; his point is that while the two different tendencies may work together, they remain distinct. The key to unpack- ing this distinction is to see 'nationalist populism' as an attempt to save the nation from the rule of experts, both at home and abroad. By contrast, popu- list nationalism is focused more clearly on traditional values and cultures, which need to be rescued from both immigration and cosmopolitanism.[10]

This distinction is challenging to make cleanly in abstract terms, and yet it is important to unlock the Italian case (discussed in more detail below).

What is worth noting, however, is that this distinction between nationalism and populism is historically inaccurate – at least given the definition of populism embraced by most scholars. Nationalism developed in late-eighteenth-century Germany to liberate the German people (and their culture) from a corrupt, Francophile elite. This romantic nationalism worked to establish 'the people' as a coherent group and to tie political legitimacy to the service of that group. In doing so, romantic nationalism created a positive form of identity politics while at the same time encouraging negative forms of identity politics, such as xenophobia.[11] Francis Fukuyama picks up on this theme in *Identity* by sketching two different dynamics, one through which efforts to represent repressed or disadvantaged identities lead to the splintering of the political community into ever smaller groups, and another through which identities asserted on one side of the political spectrum encourage political actors on the other side to respond with their own form of identity politics, often using the same arguments and rhetoric.[12] Thus, the rise of nationalism and nationalist sentiments is part of the wider turn to identity politics, all of which wraps around the notion of populism.

A fourth indicator of change is the turn to more authoritarian political institutions. Here the conceptual link rests on two foundations: the corruption of the ruling elite, which will presumably use any means to retain its control; and the homogeneity of the people, which means that they do not need to divide into groups, and that the populists hold a monopoly on legitimate representation as the only true voice of the people. When populists come to power, they seek to close off the political process in order to root out traditional elites from key institutions and then prevent their return to power. They are able to legitimate this closure by pointing to the strong mandate they have received from the 'true people' they claim to represent. Hence, scholars such as Jan Zielonka look at efforts to shift from representative to plebiscitary democracy, principally through the use of referendums but also via periodic assessments of what the people 'want' through 'listening tours', rallies and online voting. They also look at efforts to engage in constitutional reforms intended to restrict political competition, tighten political control over the media or upset the constitutional balance of power.[13] These things are not essentially 'populist' given the definition used in coding exercises, but they are linked to the notion of populism by affinity and implication. Moreover, one can see these efforts both in the European context – where the current governments of Hungary and Poland are the clearest examples – and in other countries.

The same can be said about the growing disillusionment with multilateral institutions, such as the EU or the World Trade Organization, and the increasing assault on non-majoritarian institutions such as central banks. These are institutional arrangements that politicians across Europe have used to remove contentious issues from democratic politics. In doing so, however, those same politicians created the impression that these institutions were beyond democratic accountability.[14] Now a growing chorus of voices is calling for such institutions to be subject to greater political oversight. The Leave campaign's emphasis on 'taking back control' during the British referendum campaign on membership in the EU was an extreme form of this argument, as was the complaint made by supporters of this campaign (both inside and outside the Conservative government) that the Bank of England had somehow tried to interfere in the democratic process by publishing estimates of the high costs in terms of output and income of leaving the EU.[15]

How did Europe come to where it is today?

One question scholars are asking about this broad array of changes is why they are all happening at once. The temptation is to look for broad causal mechanisms, such as industrialisation, globalisation, the economic and financial crisis, or migration. Industrialisation brought a rise in prosperity that changed social values and so unmoored the electorate from more traditional political parties; it also created and then transformed the working class in ways that strengthened and then fractured the left of the political spectrum. Along the way, globalisation created winners and losers without ensuring that those who lost out were remembered by political elites. The economic and financial crisis confronted policymakers with problems for which they lacked solutions, further reducing trust in traditional political parties while at the same time widening economic and social inequalities. Finally, the migration crisis that started shortly after the Arab Spring triggered a deep sense of insecurity among voters even as it made them more susceptible to the lure of identity politics.[16]

The story of industrialisation is one with deep roots in the literature on comparative politics going back to the 'end of ideology' debates in the late 1950s and extending through the debate about value change and political dealignment up to more current conversations about the impact of modernisation and post-modernism. The basic idea is that modern politics, and hence modern political parties, emerged alongside the traditional division between labour and capital to form a stable competition between left and right – stable so long as competition between these two groups was predominant. As industrialisation raised standards of living, however, competition between labour and capital became less important. The ideological hold of traditional political parties over their voters became less powerful as a consequence.[17]

The impact of this weakening of traditional political ideologies was not immediately obvious. To be sure, the 1960s and 1970s were a turbulent period. Nevertheless, the record of electoral data does not support the idea that voters suddenly liberated themselves from established parties and hence became available for populist political mobilisation in those years. Indeed, the most important statistical work done in the 1980s suggested that European party systems had stabilised despite the tumult in the streets. This supported the paradoxical notion that a weakening of the salience of ideological competition might coincide with the stabilisation of political identities rather than with their dissolution.[18]

That paradoxical conclusion proved to be premature, probably because the change in political behaviour had not yet made its way into the voting data. Here it is useful to recall from Norris and Inglehart that the big jump in the support for populist parties across Europe took place between the 1970s and the 1980s[19] – a period which falls at the end of the long-term statistical analysis done by Stefano Bartolini and Peter Mair in their classic work, *Identity, Competition and Electoral Availability*.[20] That transformation was, however, captured in public-opinion polling. In previous work, Inglehart

demonstrated that the spread of industrial development and associated relative economic prosperity had a transformative impact, both over time and
across countries, on the underlying structure of political and social values,
undermining the authority of traditional political institutions and nurturing new patterns of political involvement within the electorate.[21] Bartolini
and Mair amended their analysis of the development of European politics to show how European voters lost their traditional political identities
and party affiliations in ever greater numbers over time. In doing so, they
allowed for the possibility that new political movements would emerge to
challenge the predominance of the mainstream political parties.[22]

The globalisation argument, which runs
alongside the industrialisation argument, has
grown in prominence with the rise of China
in the 1990s and 2000s, and with the rapid
growth of migration from the Islamic world
into Europe prior to the global economic and
financial crisis. These issues – industrialisation,
trade, migration – are interconnected in complex ways. Barry Eichengreen
offers perhaps the most comprehensive account in *The Populist Temptation*,
in which he argues that any shift from relative economic autonomy to
a more complex division of labour – whether from self-sufficient towns
to larger national markets, or from self-sufficient countries to a global
economy – causes economic hardship and hence resentment. Such shifts
also tend to coincide with changes in communication technology that
make it easier for new voices to participate in political life. Thus, major
economic transformations tend to correlate with major challenges to the
existing political order. That we would see a rise in populist political
parties alongside a major acceleration in the globalisation of economic
activity is part of a larger pattern in that sense.[23]

European voters lost their traditional political identities

The changes seen at the outset of the twenty-first century are different
both in terms of scale and of intensity. The integration of the global economy
fostered a huge movement of people, which is where the scale of this process
becomes important. The challenge for Europe as an early beneficiary of the
globalisation process has been to accommodate large inflows of migrants

from less developed parts of the globe. These new immigrants often came from very different cultural backgrounds, and many had difficulty assimilating European cultural norms. This resulted, by the late 1990s and early 2000s, in a strong backlash from those Europeans who perceived a threat to their local or national cultures. Often, these were the same Europeans who had experienced the greatest hardship from changes in their country's own economic patterns. Such hardship may or may not have been directly connected to the inflow of new migrants – that link is the subject of active controversy among economists and political scientists. What matters in political terms is that the two situations – migration and economic dislocation – have been connected both by prominent analysts and by political challengers – such as Jörg Haider in Austria and Pim Fortuyn in the Netherlands[24] – who have sought to pull support from the mainstream political parties.[25]

The intensification of trade and migration within Europe has been another important source of economic and political adjustment both within individual countries and across the continent.[26] The (re)integration of post-communist Europe into the wider European economy has resulted in a significant shift in the location of economic activity from West to East and from rural to urban areas. Urban centres have largely benefited across the continent; smaller communities and rural areas have lost out. This large–small, urban–rural division has disrupted the geographic pattern of political competition within European countries. Whereas European politics used to be defined by 'frozen' cleavages, among which the urban–rural divide played a role in reinforcing party identification, divergence in conditions across urban and rural electors worked to undermine voter identification with traditional parties. This happened first as voters in rural areas and smaller communities felt ignored and so pulled away from the mainstream political parties (which seemed largely ignorant of, or indifferent to, the problems these voters faced), and then as new challenger parties arose that promised to address local concerns and protect local political identities.[27] The remarkable success of the UK Independence Party in traditional Labour heartlands in the north of England is a good illustration; the success of Italy's Five Star Movement (M5S) in the traditionally Christian Democratic strongholds of the Italian south is another.

The onset of the global financial crisis added a new dimension to the problems facing mainstream European political parties by reinforcing the perception that many of Europe's frontbench politicians are incompetent, indifferent or corrupt. The charge of incompetence stems from the handling of the crisis. This is a big and complex argument that is difficult to summarise, but Adam Tooze makes a worthy attempt in his book *Crashed*, in which he argues that no one benefited from the way European policymakers have responded to the global economic and financial crisis, and so everyone can find grievances in how the crisis was managed. 'The loss of credibility is flagrant, and it is comprehensive', he writes.[28] He identifies the mainstream political parties as the biggest losers:

> Since 2007 the scale of the financial crisis has placed [the] relationship between democratic politics and the demands of capitalist governance under immense strain. Above all, that strain has manifested itself not in a crisis of popular participation, or the ultimate control of policy by elected leaders, but in a crisis in the political parties that have historically mediated the two.[29]

The charge of indifference stems from the delegation of authority to non-majoritarian institutions, both domestically and at the international level. Wolfgang Streeck is the most compelling advocate of this position.[30] The essence of Streeck's argument in *How Will Capitalism End?* is that if a liberal market economy can only be managed if key policy positions are held outside the democratic process, then capitalism may have to surrender to the need for political accountability. The problem is not that these institutions are necessarily ineffective; it is that they are perceived to be irresponsive. That irresponsiveness, in turn, has tended to undermine their legitimacy. Here it is worth noting that even high-level policymakers such as Paul Tucker, the former deputy governor of the Bank of England, have accepted the logic behind the argument.[31]

The charge of corruption stems from the close relationship between central banks and financial institutions. This problem runs deeper than the political independence that central banks possess as monetary policymakers, touching on the crucial role they play in stabilising the financial system. The problem is that too many banks, both in Europe and in the United States, were either too big to fail or too connected to fail. Moreover, politicians sought to escape responsibility for the fragility of the financial system (which is primarily a function of financial regulation) and for the inevitable bailout of key financial institutions. This created the widespread impression that banks enjoyed an exorbitant privilege during the recent economic and financial crisis that ordinary households and taxpayers did not.[32]

Finally, the European migration crisis created a new dynamic that tended to favour both the political right and more authoritarian forms of government. The impact of migration on local voting patterns has already been noted.[33] This was only reinforced by the surge of migration from across the Mediterranean following the political transformation of the Arab world in 2011. In *After Europe*, Ivan Krastev argues that the sudden wave of migrants and refugees both undermined the prospects for European solidarity (or any vision of European unity) and reinforced national identities, particularly to the benefit of more extremist parties. The result has been to transform European 'democracy from an instrument for inclusion to an instrument of exclusion'.[34]

All this suggests that the rise of populism and the decline of mainstream political parties have many different and reinforcing origins. By implication, these are not trends that will be easily reversed, either in terms of the structure of European politics or its style.[35] Still, most analysts are unwilling to predict the collapse of liberal democracy altogether. Even those books with the most dramatic titles conclude on relatively optimistic notes. Steven Levitsky and Daniel Ziblatt argue in *How Democracies Die*, for instance, that a potential solution to contemporary political problems would be to build a more just society, particularly in terms of the distribution of income; while David Runciman, author of *How Democracy Ends*, seems to conclude that the solution is to lower expectations of democratic performance.[36] Neither book urges complacency, and both argue that democracy is the best way to promote human dignity. If they are right, then in keeping with Eichengreen's historical analysis, this may be just another phase in European political development.[37]

What are the implications of this transformation?

Many analysts have focused on the question of what the implications of this historical period will be for the functioning of existing political institutions. Their arguments point in many different directions, ranging from changes in underlying norms and conventions to identity policies, political discourse and constitutional arrangements. Scholars also look at popular attitudes toward the role of science in policymaking, at support for multilateralism beyond the nation-state and at the possibility of some kind of fundamental change in the way the EU is structured. While these implications fall short of an existential threat to democracy, they are important nonetheless.

At a very basic level, the rise of populist political parties will usher in a higher level of tension and conflict. As Runciman explains: 'democracy is civil war without the fighting. Failure comes when proxy battles turn into real ones.'[38] Yet for democracy to work, participants must trust in democratic institutions to handle conflicts in a just and equitable manner, a requirement that is at odds with the populist notion of democracy as the expression of the unified will of the one true people. Indeed, populist political challengers tend to be deeply intolerant of pluralism. As a result, they also tend to be intolerant of political norms that reinforce comity and collegiality. Such norms are important because they underpin constitutional arrangements. Levitsky and Ziblatt make the argument that no written constitution can be complete, and that constitutional arrangements cannot function properly if there is no desire among political actors that they do so. By undermining basic norms, therefore, populist political challengers lower the effectiveness of existing constitutional arrangements. In turn, both political conflict and institutional ineffectiveness tend to undermine confidence in democratic institutions.[39]

The weakening of democratic norms coincides with the strengthening of political identities, both positive and negative. Supporters of populist parties identify themselves ever more forcefully as the 'true people' and characterise opponents as either corrupt elites or dangerous outsiders. For their part, opponents of populist parties characterise their adherents as insular and retrograde. This emphasis on identity politics tends to lead not only to conflict but to polarisation, fear and exclusion.[40] These identities are imposed as often as they are chosen. As Kwame Anthony Appiah explains in *The Lies That Bind*: 'not only does your identity give you reasons to do things, it can give others reasons to do things to you … [A]mong the most significant things people do with identities is use them as the basis of hierarchies of states and respect and of structures of power.'[41]

Democratic societies are able to overcome such dynamics, but only with considerable effort and understanding. Critics of multiculturalism argue that the problems in evidence today are a consequence of the excessively liberal policies of the past rather than the politics of the present.[42] Whatever its origins, European populism may leave a lasting impression on social relationships. It has already changed political discourse in ways that allow greater scope for exclusionary language.

This shift in language is not limited to identity politics. Populist political challengers also have a distinctive relationship with 'truth'. This is the argument that Catherine Fieschi makes in *Populocracy*. Drawing on a long and detailed analysis of the French National Front (now called National Rally), Fieschi shows how the party's political leaders have openly spread falsehoods, both to challenge conventional speech norms and to provoke conflict, with little impact on their own credibility. Fieschi argues that credibility has less to do with 'truth' and more to do with 'authenticity'. Supporters do not have to believe everything that the leadership says – they just have to trust that the leadership will remain true to itself.[43] As Krastev explains: 'what populists promise their voters is not competence but intimacy'.[44]

Yet any political discourse that undermines truth will also challenge the status of expertise.[45] Hence another implication of the rise of populism is the declining use of science in policymaking. This is the central claim made by Tom Nichols in *The Death of Expertise*. Nichols's concern is not only that politicians will degrade the status of experts, but also that the result will be less effective policymaking, resulting in a kind of 'death spiral that presents an immediate danger of decay either into rule by the mob or toward elitist technocracy'.[46] Alternatively, public policy will be captured by 'thought leaders' in the pay of powerful, monied interests. In this version of the argument, the rise of populism runs alongside the failures of the 'marketplace of ideas' insofar as populists tend to misunderstand the world of ideas and overestimate the possibility of living without ideas or expertise. Ironically, therefore, populists make it easier for monied interests to dominate 'thought leadership'.[47]

A further implication of the rise of populism is the weakening of political institutions. Populist governments can weaken existing institutions in two different ways. Firstly, they can staff public institutions with people who are either incompetent or uninterested in actual policy. Reflecting on the Trump administration in his book *The Fifth Risk*, Michael Lewis describes this as 'people risk'.[48] Alternatively, populist political movements can attempt to change their country's constitutional arrangements to make them less pluralistic. As Krastev explains: 'populist and radical parties aren't just parties; they are constitutional movements. They promise voters what liberal democracy cannot: a sense of victory where majorities – not just political majorities, but ethnic and religious majorities – can do what they please.'[49] These possibilities are manifest not only in countries such as Hungary and Poland, where the governments have a clear constitutional agenda, but also in countries such as Austria and Italy, where populist political movements have the power to impose their personnel on public institutions with relatively few constitutional checks and balances. The point to note is that this problem runs alongside the natural inclination of populist parties to seek to remove traditional elites from power and to emphasise the mandate they hold from the 'true people' they claim to represent.

Populists tend to misunderstand the world of ideas

The implications of the rise of populism for the European project are perhaps even more important. Mair has noted that there is a close connection between popular attitudes toward domestic political elites and popular attitudes toward European institutions.[50] The strength of that connection derives from the long history of European integration as an elite project. Moreover, the link continues to show up in public-opinion polling, even at the local level.[51] The constitutional structure of the EU further strengthens this connection by confusing lines of accountability and areas of competence. Both Fabbrini and Zielonka make this point in different ways. Fabbrini leans toward the claim that the failure of Europe is fostering populism within EU member states, while Zielonka leans toward the view that the popular revolt against domestic elites is weakening support for European integration. The two dynamics could operate simultaneously.[52] There is no obvious way to resolve the inevitable tension.

A new wave of scholarship is attempting to theorise the possibility of European disintegration. Hans Vollaard, in his recent book *European Disintegration*, shows how the transformation of domestic politics and the progressive dysfunction of European institutions are closely interconnected.[53] It would be a stretch to say that all of Europe's problems derive from the rise of populist political movements; the point is simply that the transformation of European integration is closely connected to the drivers of populism.

Three illustrations of developments under way

There is a danger that any discussion of populism can become too open-ended. Populism is not the sole challenge facing European democracies, even as it exerts a powerful influence on democratic performance. Therefore, it is useful to try to ground the discussion in concrete examples of cases where populism has had an influence. The most obvious illustrations can be found in the United Kingdom and Italy. The situation in Poland and Hungary is more confusing: the governments of both countries are engaged in constitutional efforts that display significant authoritarian tendencies, and yet it is difficult to see the political leadership of either country as somehow outside the political establishment. They may have been 'populist' at one time, but they now constitute the political mainstream. This may be a preview of the longer-term implications of the rise of European populism.

The British case is interesting because it shows the influence of populist political movements operating outside the government. The events leading up to the UK's EU referendum have been ably detailed by journalists and insiders.[54] That story demonstrates just how easily populist political pressure can shift the policy agenda; it also shows how challenging it is for mainstream politicians to push back against disinformation by relying on 'expertise'. In *Brexit and British Politics*, Geoffrey Evans and Anand Menon explain why the referendum result went against the government, and what it means for British politics. In the process, they do an excellent job of revealing the underlying social and political trends. British politics has changed fundamentally in the sense that society is now deeply polarised and the electorate more volatile, and the 'socially liberal, pro-market consensus that dominated UK politics for the last four decades' has ended.[55] The United Kingdom is now a very different country than it was before the referendum took place.

Italy has also changed. What distinguishes the Italian case, however, is that the country's politics is dominated by the two varieties of populism embodied by M5S and Lega. Here it is useful to recall Fabbrini's distinction between populist nationalism and nationalist populism. M5S represents a revolt of urban youth against a system they believe to be corrupt and unmeritocratic.[56] Lega is a right-wing political movement that blends appeals to traditional family values with a promise to uphold the economic interests of the entrepreneurial class.[57] Lega also has deep ties to Italy's fascist traditions, ties that have become even stronger as Lega leader Matteo Salvini has worked to transform the northern separatist movement into a true national party by absorbing the older support base of the National Alliance (which sprung from the Italian Social Movement) and the more anti-communist elements of Silvio Berlusconi's party. Originally, most Italians believed that the M5S and Lega would be incompatible, given that they have very different constituencies, both demographically and geographically. In the March 2018 parliamentary elections, M5S drew votes nationally but concentrated its support in the south, while Lega drew votes primarily from the north. It was not at all clear how these different strains of populism would interact, or whether a coalition of these forces would prove to be stable.[58]

The constitutional changes brought about by the governments of Hungary and Poland constitute a third interesting case, of which one distinguishing feature is the degree to which the governments of both countries have sought to concentrate power and eliminate checks and balances. This emphasis on challenging existing constitutional arrangements is consistent with the arguments made by Krastev, and is a recurrent theme in Mudde's political commentary.[59] The challenge is to assess how much of this transformation is anti-democratic or anti-pluralist, and how much is a function of a long-running struggle against the institutional and political legacies of communism.[60] What is interesting to note, however, is how differently the two countries have been treated by politicians elsewhere in Europe. R. Daniel Kelemen argues that the Hungarian government has benefited from the political shelter provided by the European People's Party, while the Polish government has had fewer powerful allies. In this way, these two countries reveal the complicated relationship between European politics and national politics. The EU has proven to be less of a staunch advocate of democratic liberalism than many analysts might presume.[61]

Lessons to be learned and avenues for further study

There is no easy conclusion to draw from these three vignettes. It would be tempting to foresee the end of Europe as Krastev does, or the end of democracy as Levitsky and Ziblatt do, but a close reading of their books (and others like them) does not point to that conclusion – nor does it suggest a readiness on the part of the authors to embrace the full implications of their titles.[62] Europe is undergoing a transformation and populism is playing a significant role in that process, but it is unclear where that transformation is headed.

Eichengreen may be right that what we are seeing – the increasing polarisation of politics, the fragmentation of representative assemblies and so on – is just another stage in Europe's political development. If he is right, then European democracies can be expected to survive the challenges they are facing.[63] The only question is how much institutional damage, in the form of poor policymaking and misguided institutional reforms, they will experience in the meantime. Lasting social divisions could be a problem as well. These symptoms will play out differently from one country to the next, but their impact on the European project will affect all European democracies.

A question that needs more careful study is how long the current phase of electoral volatility and parliamentary fragmentation can persist. Most European constitutional arrangements are ill-suited to support minority governments or weak executives. At the same time, constitutions are hard to change without supermajorities. Hence the danger is not that Europe will succumb to populism but rather that European political institutions will decline into ineffectiveness – until a group that is strong enough to command a supermajority finds a way to change them.

It is useful when considering the weakening of national political institutions over time to distinguish between popular attitudes toward national democracy and popular attitudes toward the EU. Europeans learned from the EU's constitutional debate in the early 2000s that it is not enough to express support for European integration in general; Europeans must support the same conception of Europe for the project to flourish.[64] Where national interpretations of the European project differ – and where national political dynamics complicate efforts to accommodate differences from one country to the next – the EU tends to falter.

The current tension in the Franco-German relationship is a good illustration of this dynamic at work; the role played by the Netherlands as spoiler in the debate about European macroeconomic governance reform is an even better one. The French government has pushed hard for the EU to provide some form of common fiscal resources either to backstop national unemployment insurance or to engage in a more ambitious form of macroeconomic stabilisation for countries that move outside the European business cycle. By contrast, the German government has resisted any new fiscal-transfer mechanism and has even begun to row back on commitments to complete the European banking union with common resolution financing or deposit insurance. The French want a Europe of solidarity; the Germans are more eager to see a Europe of national responsibility. Within this division, the Dutch have staked out a position that is even less generous and more self-reliant than the German one – and it has gathered a number of smaller member states in a new Hanseatic League to add weight to its determination to resist any efforts to use European institutions to move money from one member state to the next. Hence a third question that requires further research is whether the evolution of national politics in Europe is placing ever tighter constraints on what European integration can accomplish.

A final topic that warrants research attention is the impact of the rise of populism on the transatlantic relationship and on the conduct of US foreign policy. Given that populist parties differ in their ideological commitments, it is tempting to ask whether some parties will prove more amenable to a strong transatlantic partnership than others. This is one area where the narrow definition of populism is helpful. A common theme running through the literature is the importance of 'the people', a feature that has implications for attitudes toward national sovereignty. In countries where populist parties pose a credible threat to traditional elites, we should expect those elites to make more strenuous efforts to demonstrate that they are defending the national interest.[65] Where populist parties are in government, this defence of the national interest becomes even more vigorous and idiosyncratic. Here the best illustrations centre on the implausible alliance that appears to be developing between the governments of Italy, Hungary and Poland.

Such developments pose an array of challenges for the conduct of US foreign policy because they call into question the durability of multilateral institutions and the credibility of bilateral commitments. The full extent of this change requires deeper exploration. The point to note, however, is that the difficulties created by populist political dynamics in Europe are not limited to the ideological commitments of any given political party. Should the Greens come to power in Germany, for example, we should expect them to push their conception of the national interest and not to sacrifice their view of what is right for the Germans on the altar of some greater project. They may be pro-European, but they have a very specific understanding of what the EU is meant to accomplish, and they are not supportive of other interpretations. The surprisingly vigorous politicisation of the Transatlantic Trade and Investment Partnership illustrates the constraints that this type of populism can place on international cooperation. The bottom line is that European politics is becoming more difficult for US policymakers to navigate. More research is required to map the obstacles.

Notes

1   This survey is at least partly the result of my work as a contributing editor to *Survival*. In that role, I have the privilege of reviewing ten books each year, five on Europe and another five on political economy. As a result, I have had the opportunity to review many of the books that are cited in this essay. Those books are indicated by an asterisk (*) after their authors' names

the first time they appear in the notes.

2   Cas Mudde, 'The Populist Zeitgeist', *Government & Opposition*, vol. 39, no. 4, Autumn 2004, pp. 543–4.

3   John B. Judis, *The Populist Explosion: How the Great Recession Transformed American and European Politics* (New York: Columbia Global Reports, 2016), pp. 13–15.

4   Jan-Werner Müller, *What Is Populism?* (Philadelphia, PA: University of Pennsylvania Press, 2016), pp. 2–3.

5   Pippa Norris and Ronald Inglehart, *Cultural Backlash: Trump, Brexit, and Authoritarian Populism* (Cambridge: Cambridge University Press, 2019), p. 4.

6   *Ibid.*, chapter seven.

7   *Ibid.*, p. 8.

8   Peter Mair, *Ruling the Void: The Hollowing Out of Western Democracy* (London: Verso, 2013).

9   Roger Eatwell and Matthew Goodwin, *National Populism: The Revolt Against Liberal Democracy* (London: Pelican, 2018), p. ix.

10 Sergio Fabbrini*, *Europe's Future: Decoupling and Reforming* (Cambridge: Cambridge University Press, 2019), p. 66.

11 Pankaj Mishra, *Age of Anger: A History of the Present* (London: Penguin, 2018), chapter five.

12 Francis Fukuyama, *Identity: Contemporary Identity Politics and the Struggle for Recognition* (New York: Farrar, Straus and Giroux, 2018), chapter eleven.

13 Jan Zielonka, *Counter-Revolution: Liberal Europe in Retreat* (Oxford: Oxford University Press, 2018), chapter three.

14 Mair, *Ruling the Void*, chapter four.

15 These were not isolated incidents. See Paul Tucker*, *Unelected Power: The Quest for Legitimacy in Central Banking and the Regulatory State* (Princeton, NJ: Princeton University Press, 2018).

16 For a survey of these developments, see Edward Luce*, *The Retreat of Western Liberalism* (New York: Atlantic Monthly Press, 2017). For an extended review of Luce's book, see Erik Jones, 'From the End of History to the Retreat of Liberalism', *Survival*, vol. 59, no. 6, December 2017–January 2018, pp. 165–74.

17 Seymour Martin Lipset, *Political Man: The Social Bases of Politics* (New York: Doubleday & Company, 1960), chapter thirteen.

18 Stefano Bartolini and Peter Mair, *Identity, Competition and Electoral Availability: The Stabilization of European Electorates, 1885–1985* (Cambridge: Cambridge University Press, 1990), chapter eleven.

19 Norris and Inglehart, *Cultural Backlash*, p. 9.

20 Bartolini and Mair, *Identity, Competition and Electoral Availability*.

21 Ronald Inglehart, *Modernization and Postmodernization: Cultural, Economic, and Political Change in 43 Societies* (Princeton, NJ: Princeton University Press, 1997), chapter ten.

22 See Stefano Bartolini, *Restructuring Europe: Centre Formation, System Building, and Political Structuring Between the Nation State and the European Union* (Oxford: Oxford University Press, 2005); and Mair, *Ruling the Void*.

23 Barry Eichengreen, *The Populist Temptation: Economic Grievance and Political Reaction in the Modern Era*

(Oxford: Oxford University Press, 2018).

24 Erik Jones, 'Populism in Europe', *SAIS Review*, vol. 27, no. 1, Winter–Spring 2007, pp. 37–47.

25 See, for example, Christopher Caldwell, *Reflections on the Revolution in Europe: Immigration, Islam, and the West* (New York: Doubleday, 2009); and David Goodhart*, *The British Dream: Successes and Failures of Postwar Immigration* (London: Atlantic Books, 2013).

26 Philipp Ther*, *Europe Since 1989: A History* (Princeton, NJ: Princeton University Press, 2016).

27 See Jennifer Fitzgerald*, *Close to Home: Local Ties and Voting Radical Right in Europe* (Cambridge: Cambridge University Press, 2018).

28 Adam Tooze, *Crashed: How a Decade of Financial Crises Changed the World* (London: Allen Lane, 2018), p. 22.

29 *Ibid.*, p. 614.

30 Wolfgang Streeck, *How Will Capitalism End? Essays on a Failing System* (London: Verso, 2016), chapter two.

31 Tucker, *Unelected Power*. See also Erik Jones and Matthias Matthijs, 'Beyond Central Bank Independence: Rethinking Technocratic Legitimacy in Monetary Affairs', *Journal of Democracy*, vol. 30, no. 2, April 2019, pp. 127–41.

32 See Lawrence R. Jacobs and Desmond King*, *Fed Power: How Finance Wins* (New York: Oxford University Press, 2016).

33 Fitzgerald, *Close to Home*.

34 Ivan Krastev, *After Europe* (Philadelphia, PA: University of Pennsylvania Press, 2017), p. 73. For an extended review of Krastev's book, see Erik Jones, 'Fragile Europe',

International Spectator, vol. 53, no. 1, March 2018, pp. 168–71.

35 Benjamin Moffitt, *The Global Rise of Populism: Performance, Political Style, and Representation* (Stanford, CA: Stanford University Press, 2016), chapter nine.

36 Steven Levitsky and Daniel Ziblatt*, *How Democracies Die* (New York: Crown, 2018); and David Runciman, *How Democracy Ends* (New York: Basic Books, 2018). For an extended review, of Levitsky and Ziblatt see Erik Jones, 'Democracies Don't Die, They Are Killed', *Survival*, vol. 60, no. 2, April–May 2018, pp. 201–10.

37 Eichengreen, *The Populist Temptation*.

38 Runciman, *How Democracy Ends*, p. 14.

39 Levitsky and Ziblatt's book, *How Democracies Die*; see also Erik Jones and Matthias Matthijs, 'Democracy Without Solidarity – Political Dysfunction in Hard Times', *Government and Opposition*, vol. 52, no. 2, 2017, pp. 185–210.

40 See Fukuyama, *Identity*; and Martha C. Nussbaum, *The Monarchy of Fear: A Philosopher Looks at Our Political Crisis* (New York: Simon & Schuster, 2018), chapter four.

41 Kwame Anthony Appiah, *The Lies that Bind: Rethinking Identity* (New York: Liveright Publishing Corporation, 2018), p. 10.

42 See Caldwell, *Reflections on the Revolution in Europe*; and Goodhart, *The British Dream*.

43 Catherine Fieschi, *Populocracy: European Populism and the Politics of Authenticity* (London: Agenda, 2019).

44 Krastev, *After Europe*, p. 91.

45 See Jennifer Kavanagh and Michael D. Rich, *Truth Decay: An Initial Exploration of the Diminishing Role of*

Facts and Analysis in American Public Life (Santa Monica, CA: RAND Corporation, 2018).

46 Tom Nichols, *The Death of Expertise: The Campaign Against Established Knowledge and Why It Matters* (Oxford: Oxford University Press, 2017), p. 216.

47 See Daniel W. Drezner, *The Ideas Industry* (Oxford: Oxford University Press, 2017).

48 Michael Lewis, *The Fifth Risk* (New York: W. W. Norton & Company, 2018), chapter two.

49 Krastev, *After Europe*, p. 75.

50 Mair, *Ruling the Void*.

51 See Fitzgerald, *Close to Home*.

52 Fabbrini, *Europe's Future*; Zielonka, *Counter-Revolution*.

53 Hans Vollaard, *European Disintegration: A Search for Explanations* (London: Palgrave Macmillan, 2018). Vollaard's argument draws on many of the references cited here and relies heavily on Bartolini, *Restructuring Europe*.

54 See, for example, Tim Shipman, *All Out War: The Full Story of Brexit, Revised and Updated* (London: William Collins, 2017); and Craig Oliver*, Unleashing Demons: The Inside Story of Brexit* (London: Hodder & Stoughton, 2016).

55 Geoffrey Evans and Anand Menon, *Brexit and British Politics* (Cambridge: Polity Press, 2017), p. 122.

56 See Fabbrini, *Europe's Future*. For a discussion of M5S, see Piergiorgio Corbetta and Elisabetta Gulamini (eds), *Il Partito di Grillo* (Bologna: Il Mulino, 2013).

57 See Gianluca Passarelli and Dario Tuorto, *La Lega di Salvini: Estema Destra di Governo* (Bologna: Il Mulino, 2018).

58 See Paolo Graziano, *Neopopulismi* (Bologna: Il Mulino, 2018); and Ilvo Diamanti and Marc Lazar, *Popolacrazia: La metamorfosi delle nostre democrazie* (Rome: Gius. Laterza & Figli, 2018).

59 Krastev, *After Europe*; Cas Mudde*, On Extremism and Democracy in Europe* (London: Routledge, 2016).

60 William Drozdiak highlights the importance of anti-communism in the Polish case in *Fractured Continent: Europe's Crises and the Fate of the West* (New York: W. W. Norton & Company, 2017), chapter seven. Grigore Pop-Elches and Joshua A. Tucker* make the more general case in *Communism's Shadow: Historical Legacies and Contemporary Political Attitudes* (Princeton, NJ: Princeton University Press, 2017).

61 See R. Daniel Kelemen, 'Europe's Other Democratic Deficit', *Government & Opposition*, vol. 52, no. 2, April 2017, pp. 211–38.

62 Krastev, *After Europe*; Levitsky and Ziblatt, *How Democracies Die*.

63 Eichengreen, *The Populist Temptation*.

64 Erik Jones, 'European Crisis, European Solidarity', *Journal of Common Market Studies: Annual Review*, no. 50, August 2012, pp. 53–67.

65 The current Dutch government's obstructionist position in European reform debates is a good illustration, as is the current German government's reluctance to acknowledge its NATO spending commitments.

Subversion, Statecraft and Liberal Democracy

Henrik Breitenbauch and Niels Byrjalsen

As the post-Cold War era expires, great-power competition is returning. Conflictual relations below the threshold of war increasingly affect international affairs. The United States, China, Russia and other states are seeking influence across different conflict domains. In this context, subversion is re-emerging as a powerful tool of statecraft – and as a difficult challenge for liberal democracies.

Subversion is best understood as a state's purposive destabilisation and undermining of the authority and functioning of other states in order to achieve significant political gains. It involves a number of different instruments below the threshold of war but above the level of diplomacy, employed by state actors to advance political objectives. These instruments include cyber attacks, election meddling, assassinations, espionage, disinformation campaigns, seizure of foreign territory without using traditional means of warfare, strategic investments abroad, and external sponsorship and support of repressive autocrats. Political objectives, in turn, may include creating confusion and sowing discord, gradually eroding the legitimacy of a political system, nourishing counter-elites, facilitating regime change, and exerting far-reaching control over the foreign-policy decisions of other states. The high end of this spectrum, in particular, appears to be critically unaddressed by Western states, possibly due to excessive confidence

Henrik Breitenbauch heads the Centre for Military Studies in the Department of Political Science at the University of Copenhagen. **Niels Byrjalsen** is a PhD fellow in the Department of Political Science at the University of Copenhagen.

Survival | vol. 61 no. 4 | August–September 2019 | pp. 31–41   DOI 10.1080/00396338.2019.1637118

in Western dominance and the stability of US hegemony following what American journalist Charles Krauthammer called 'the unipolar moment'.[1]

As noted by Hal Brands, currently 'the differences between liberal and illiberal forms of government have profound implications for the strategic fitness and competence of the great powers'.[2] For liberal democracies and thus for Western states, the rise of subversion brings uncomfortable questions. At home, counter-subversion efforts of liberal democracies are necessarily limited by the relative openness of their politics, society and economy. Abroad, Western states have less freedom of action than their autocratic adversaries because subversion clashes with key liberal principles such as non-interference. In addition, Western states seem to be caught in a kind of ideological crossfire that weakens their collective resolve. On the one hand, they cling to the comfortable but simplistic post-Cold War vision of global, UN-based cooperation, liberated from zero-sum logic and international risk management. On the other hand, they are plagued by self-doubt and internal disagreements after nearly two decades of failed military efforts in the greater Middle East, financial crises, paralysis over climate change and autocratic backlash, as well as divisive political polarisation in the United States, the United Kingdom and elsewhere in Europe.

Yet the new situation also holds opportunities for Western states. Liberal democracy still enjoys robust legitimacy as a political system at home and abroad, and correspondingly open societies are relatively agile and flexible in crafting effective policy responses to strategic challenges. Existing power structures in global politics and the West's customary role as sponsor and guarantor of the rules-based international order, moreover, afford such democracies both a head start in the new kind of global competition and an aspirational ideal for states and populations across the globe. To exploit these opportunities and fashion a comprehensive response to subversion, liberal-democratic leaders need to think harder about the increasing significance of subversion as a geopolitical instrument and its ramifications.

Subversion during the Cold War

Subversion played a major part in the Cold War, as both the Soviet Union and Western states became heavily involved in subversive and counter-subversive operations. For the Soviet Union, they were part of a long Russian tradition of conceptualising international relations as 'protracted conflict' and using 'active measures' in this conflict.[3] For Western states, subversion and counter-subversion were framed and justified as necessary elements of what was considered an existential global struggle.[4] Like the Soviet Union, the United States and its allies actively sought to destabilise and undermine – that is, to subvert – the political status quo in countries on the other side of the ideological confrontation between liberal democracy and communism, including, to specify a few, Chile, Cuba, the Democratic Republic of the Congo, Guatemala, Indonesia, Iran and several Eastern European states.[5] As for counter-subversion, the United States and its Western European allies pursued widespread anti-communist campaigns at home and supported similar efforts around the world in both allied and non-aligned countries.[6] A prominent example of Western counter-subversion was the long-term support for the shah of Iran.[7] Western measures included extensive covert surveillance, spreading propaganda, imposing legal frameworks and arming local political-resistance groups.

The Cold War experience with subversion and counter-subversion yields important insights for today's challenges.[8] While some are merely practical, others reveal unpleasant dilemmas that the re-emergence of the subversive logic creates for liberal democracies. Executing foreign policy in the grey area between war and diplomacy entails a risk of backlash if the activities are exposed and assessed to be proof of double standards – or simply constitute unwarranted interference in the affairs of others. The reaction to American subversive efforts in Cuba in the 1950s and 1960s illustrates this risk. Moreover, by virtue of being neither war nor diplomacy, subversion obscures the question of agency, as demonstrated by the complicated interplay among political, bureaucratic and intelligence organisations in the United States during the Cold War.[9]

While the historical record provides a useful baseline for reintroducing subversion into the national-security debate in liberal democracies, the international politics of subversion are unfolding under different circumstances than those that prevailed during the Cold War. The advent of the cyber domain, new transnational issues (including globalisation, human rights and migration), and growing ideological divides worldwide (including market vs state capitalism, liberalism vs illiberalism and globalism vs nationalism) all make managing and resisting subversion unprecedentedly complex for state actors, especially liberal democracies.

Counter-subversion in an open society

Two main challenges face open societies rediscovering the problem of counter-subversion. Firstly, since open societies limit state control, counter-subversive efforts in the domestic sphere are subject to restrictions. This problem has been especially salient since 2001, with the introduction of far-reaching counter-terrorism laws after the 9/11 attacks. Recently, outside interference in the political processes of liberal democracies by state actors – including Russia and China – has made it clear that its scope extends well beyond fighting terrorism.[10] In liberal democracies, legal frameworks typically constrain internal-intelligence services more than external-intelligence services. As a result, the state ironically risks having less information about its own society and citizens than it does about foreign societies and citizens. Furthermore, liberal democracies are disinclined to respond to subversive efforts to spread disinformation, cultivate covert networks, and gain political and economic leverage through foreign investments with measures such as censorship, bans on certain groups and limits on market access because such measures undermine liberty, including freedom of association and the free market. Favouring ideologically kindred (hence more trusted) states and non-state actors may be an effective option. Recent examples include Denmark's decision to have the Swedish company Ericsson roll out the 5G network instead of the Chinese company Huawei, and Poland's decision to rely on gas from Norway rather than Russia. Yet such dispensations risk impeding the aim of globalisation to make markets more open and inclusive.

Secondly, counter-subversion is a challenge to the governance of liberal democracies. Counter-subversive activities are more cumbersome in a democracy than in an autocracy because the state is obliged to act on behalf of its citizens and to protect their civil liberties. It is supposed to observe due process of law even when doing so inhibits effective counter-subversion. At the same time, the fact that subversion almost always calls for a discretionary and inferential interpretation of intent makes those in charge of monitoring and oversight, as well as direct counter-subversion, vulnerable to accusations of partisanship. Americans' divided reactions to Russian meddling in the 2016 US presidential election is a case in point. Subversion also challenges customary bureaucratic lines of authority. In national-security matters, the defence ministry or department traditionally handles armed conflict, while the foreign-affairs ministry or department manages diplomacy, with the intelligence, law-enforcement, legal and economic-regulatory bureaucracies informing and advising both primary agencies. Which government organisation should take the lead on subversion or counter-subversion, however, is unclear.

More broadly, the institutions and people governing Western states are not used to thinking in terms of counter-subversion. At the same time, they must comprehensively understand those terms in order for counter-subversion to be effective. This means that the US and other governments will need to implement 'whole-of-government' and 'whole-of-society' approaches to counter-subversion. This requirement poses a stiff challenge to the political culture of liberal democracies. Politicians, bureaucrats, journalists, business executives, union leaders and others taking part in policymaking processes will need to recalibrate their understanding of international politics and recognise subversion as part of the process. This is a far more formidable task than simply drawing new lines on an organisational diagram.

Handling subversion internationally

At the international level, four interrelated challenges loom large for liberal democracies. They concern perception and response, the struggle for political influence, legitimacy, and the balance between conflict and cooperation.

In the subversion business, perceptions matter. Activities with subversive intent can be misperceived as normal politics, and vice versa. If subversion is misapprehended as an escalation towards war, there is a risk of responding in a way that reinforces the escalatory dynamic. Particularly in light of ongoing confusion about the real aims of Russia's 'hybrid warfare', it is important that Western states take care to respond prudently to subversive

Russian activities.[11] Conversely, there is a risk of misperceiving subversion as counter-subversion and opting for insufficient responses. Exemplifying this kind of misplaced complacency is the proposition that Russian activities in the post-Soviet sphere have no subversive aspect and are legitimate attempts to thwart Western subversion that has taken the form of support for so-called 'colour revolutions'.[12] In addition, unlike war and diplomacy, subversion and counter-subversion are not subject to well-established rules of the game. It is unclear what constitutes a proportionate response to subversive activities; this problem is particularly acute in the cyber domain.[13] Navigating the risks of an inappropriate or counterproductive response is even trickier if subversive efforts are directed at an ally or partner, as when Western states feel compelled to counter Russian meddling in the Balkans or the Baltics, or to answer Chinese assertiveness in the South China Sea.

With the return of great-power competition, a global struggle for influence is already on. It is especially fierce in places where high-end subversion – aimed at fostering counter-elites, facilitating regime change and ultimately making other states switch sides – is a concrete possibility. For Western states, therefore, counter-subversion in coordination with and sometimes on behalf of allies and partners is becoming part of the foreign-policy agenda. Running counter-subversion programmes in friendly territory while keeping bilateral relations stable is by no means an easy proposition, as shown by the turbulence that has afflicted American and Western European diplomacy towards Egypt, Hungary, the Philippines and Turkey in recent years. Moreover, in regions where states and political authorities are weak, counter-subversion must proceed alongside development, stabilisation and counter-terrorism efforts. In such situations, Western states may not be able to offer a palpably more attractive package than their autocratic competitors. In this connection, China's increasing influence in Africa as a result of assistance unburdened by governance conditionalities sheds light on the quandaries facing liberal democracies.

Another challenge for liberal democracies concerns reconciling the legitimacy of subversion with liberal principles and, if it enjoys qualified legitimacy, knowing when and when not to engage in it. Knowledge of subversion is needed, of course, to effectively counter it. The tough threshold question is whether undertaking a subversive course of action is ever legitimate for liberal states.

Even if liberal democracies generally disfavour subversion, as they ought to do, they should still consider whether and when some kinds of subversive efforts are justified in the service of international justice or international order. If there is just war, perhaps there is also just subversion. As in all conflictual dynamics, however, a risk arises of perpetuating a chain of subversive and counter-subversive actions that is ultimately destabilising. Liberal democracies contemplating subversion should therefore bear in mind that their overriding objective is to preserve and nourish a rules-based international order centred on cooperation and diplomacy, and assess the propriety of any prospective subversive activities substantially on the basis of whether they are likely to impede or advance that objective.

Closely related to this vexing inquiry is the delicate task of finding the right balance between the conflictual logic of subversion and the cooperative logic of diplomacy. It would be irresponsible to make counter-subversion the only or even the primary order of business in foreign affairs. But it would also be imprudent to discount the emerging global trend of subversion and the necessity of rethinking statecraft in light of this trend. Liberal democracies need to reconcile their self-images with this new reality, and craft policies that carefully embrace it.

*   *   *

Liberal democracies must do whatever they can to minimise their vulnerability to subversion. Protective measures include closing loopholes, increasing resilience, fortifying critical infrastructure, countering disinformation and regulating foreign-investment authorisations. But liberal democracies must also acknowledge the increasing salience and effectiveness of subversion in international affairs, and recognise that it may sometimes be efficacious, if not necessary, to fight fire with fire, albeit selectively. There appear to be five key guidelines.

Firstly, subversion should be included among the specified threats and responses studied in international affairs and national-security curricula in liberal democracies. That is, subversion needs to enter the national-security vocabulary as part of strategic statecraft, alongside war and diplomacy. This is essential to defend against subversion, but also to better assess the different ways it can be governed and controlled.

Secondly, the silo mentality that tends to prevail in foreign-policy apparatuses needs to be overhauled in favour of more horizontal, interactive and coordinated governance and oversight structures that are better suited for the complex enterprises of subversion and counter-subversion. This implies new responsibilities not only for operational government agencies but also for legislatures and other oversight authorities.

Thirdly, given the centrality of the information sphere to the contemporary conduct of international affairs, a more stable and transparent partnership among states, big tech companies and media organisations is required. Now at least feasible at the domestic level, such partnerships will be more difficult to establish at the international level.

Fourthly, since subversion as a geopolitical tool crucially involves inducing tenuously aligned parties to switch sides, Western states should pay more careful attention to countries on the peripheries of their security communities and diplomatic circles. Counter-subversion with an eye to preserving a given alignment may be vital in such cases, but it cannot stand alone. Rather, it should be coupled with diplomatic means that ensure that marginal countries will not be pushed farther away. The currently tense relationship between the European Union and Hungary shows the importance and difficulty of calibrating statecraft to strike this balance.

Finally, great-power competition fuelled by subversion and counter-subversion is likely to be a defining feature of the international landscape for many years to come. As they did during the Cold War, liberal democracies need to prepare to re-immerse themselves in these often uncomfortable issues and activities over the long haul.

Notes

[1] See Charles Krauthammer, 'The Unipolar Moment', *Foreign Affairs*, vol. 70, no. 1, 1990–91, pp. 23–33.

[2] Hal Brands, 'Democracy vs Authoritarianism: How Ideology Shapes Great-power Conflict',

Survival, vol. 60, no. 5, October–November 2018, pp. 61–114.

3   See Steve Abrams, 'Beyond Propaganda: Soviet Active Measures in Putin's Russia', *Connections: The Quarterly Journal*, vol. 15, no. 1, January 2016, pp. 5–31; and Robert Strausz-Hupé et al., *Protracted Conflict: A Challenging Study of Communist Strategy* (New York: Harper Colophon Books, 1963).

4   For an illustrative analysis of such justifications in the Central American context, see Doug Stokes, 'Countering the Soviet Threat? An Analysis of the Justifications for US Military Assistance to El Salvador, 1979–92', *Cold War History*, vol. 3, no. 3, April 2003, pp. 79–102.

5   See Kenneth Roberts, 'Bullying and Bargaining: The United States, Nicaragua, and Conflict Resolution in Central America', *International Security*, vol. 15, no. 2, Fall 1990, pp. 67–102; Audrey R. Kahin and George McT. Kahin, *Subversion as Foreign Policy: The Secret Eisenhower and Dulles Debacle in Indonesia* (New York: New Press, 1995); and John P.C. Matthews, 'The West's Secret Marshall Plan for the Mind', *International Journal of Intelligence and CounterIntelligence*, vol. 16, no. 3, July 2003, pp. 409–27.

6   See Thomas J. Maguire, 'Counter-subversion in Early Cold War Britain: The Official Committee on Communism (Home), the Information Research Department, and "State–Private Networks"', *Intelligence and National Security*, vol. 30, no. 5, 2015, pp. 637–66; Paul M. McGarr, 'The Information Research Department, British Covert Propaganda and the Sino-Indian War of 1962: Combating Communism and Courting Failure?', *International History Review*, vol. 41, no. 1, 2019, pp. 130–56; 'Control of Communist Activities', *Stanford Law Review*, vol. 1, no. 1, November 1948, pp. 85–107; and William Rosenau, *US Internal Security Assistance to South Vietnam: Insurgency, Subversion and Public Order* (Abingdon: Routledge, 2005).

7   See Roham Alvandi, *Nixon, Kissinger, and the Shah: The United States and Iran in the Cold War* (Oxford: Oxford University Press, 2014); and Darioush Bayandor, *Iran and the CIA: The Fall of Mossadeq Revisited* (Basingstoke: Palgrave Macmillan, 2010). For another interesting example of Western counter-subversion in practice, see Stephen Blackwell, 'Saving the King: Anglo-American Strategy and British Counter-subversion Operations in Libya, 1953–59', *Middle Eastern Studies*, vol. 39, no. 1, January 2003, pp. 1–18.

8   Since the end of the Cold War, subversion has mainly been discussed in the narrower context of counter-insurgency, regime change and counter-terrorism, particularly as related to the so-called 'global war on terror' after 2001. See, for example, David J. Kilcullen, 'Countering Global Insurgency', *Journal of Strategic Studies*, vol. 28, no. 4, August 2005, pp. 597–617.

9   See Paul W. Blackstock, *The Strategy of Subversion: Manipulating the Politics of Other Nations* (Chicago, IL: Quadrangle Books, 1964).

10 See Mikael Wigell, 'Hybrid Interference as a Wedge Strategy: A Theory of

External Interference in Liberal Democracy', *International Affairs*, vol. 95, no. 2, March 2019, pp. 255–75.

[11] Lawrence Freedman, 'Ukraine and the Art of Limited War', *Survival*, vol. 56, no. 6, December 2014–January 2015, pp. 7–38.

[12] For an example of this line of reasoning, see John J. Mearsheimer, 'Why the Ukraine Crisis Is the West's Fault', *Foreign Affairs*, vol. 93, no. 5, September/October 2014, pp. 77–89.

[13] Alex Grigsby, 'The End of Cyber Norms', *Survival*, vol. 59, no. 6, December 2017–January 2018, pp. 109–22.

Noteworthy

36
Percentage of the world's electricity provided by zero-carbon sources in 1998

36
Percentage in 2018[1]

IISS Shangri-La Dialogue

'We're not going to ignore Chinese behaviour and I think in the past people have kind of tiptoed around that.'
Patrick Shanahan, acting US secretary of defense, comments on potential threats to the security of the Asia-Pacific region at the IISS Shangri-La Dialogue on 1 June 2019.[2]

'Faced with daunting and complex security challenges, the PLA [People's Liberation Army] vows not to yield a single inch of the country's sacred land, but it will not seize anything from others either. The PLA has no intention of causing anybody trouble, but it is not afraid to face up to troubles. Should anyone risk crossing the bottom line, the PLA will resolutely take action and defeat all enemies … As for the recent trade friction started by the US, if the US wants to talk, we will keep the door open. If they want a fight, we will fight till the end. As the general public of China says these days, "A talk? Welcome. A fight? We are ready. Bully us? No way."'
Chinese Minister of National Defence General Wei Fenghe speaks during a session on China and international security cooperation at the IISS Shangri-La Dialogue on 2 June 2019.[3]

Damocletian compromise?

'The Chief Executive apologizes to Hong Kong citizens … and promises that she will take on criticisms in the most sincere and humble way, striving to improve and serve the general public.'
Carrie Lam, chief executive of Hong Kong, responds on 16 June 2019 to large-scale protests triggered by proposed legislation to allow residents to be extradited to mainland China.[4]

'Suspending the law but not cancelling it is like holding a knife over someone's head and saying, "I'm not going to kill you now", but you could do it any time.'
A protester named Betty expresses concern that the legislation had been suspended but not withdrawn.[5]

Honey flap

'After yesterday's video, I have to honestly say, enough is enough.'
Austrian chancellor Sebastian Kurz calls a snap election after viewing a secretly filmed video of vice-chancellor Heinz-Christian Strache promising government contracts to a woman who claimed to be the niece of a Russian oligarch.[6]

'I behaved boastfully like a teenager.'
Strache resigns as vice-chancellor and leader of the Freedom Party.[7]

'Far-right parties all over Europe have become a sort of fifth column for Russia. In Austria, that fifth column has been in government.'
Peter Pilz, an independent Austrian lawmaker, comments on the presence of Strache's far-right Freedom Party in Austria's ruling coalition.[8]

   DOI 10.1080/00396338.2019.1637121

Blinkmanship

'If Iran wants to fight, that will be the official end of Iran. Never threaten the United States again!'

US President Donald Trump tweets on 19 May 2019 after a rocket fell near the US Embassy in Baghdad.[9]

'@realdonaldTrump hopes to achieve what Alexander, Genghis & other aggressors failed to do. Iranians have stood tall for millennia while aggressors all gone. #EconomicTerrorism & genocidal taunts won't "end Iran".'

Javad Zarif, Iran's foreign minister, tweets at Trump on 20 May.[10]

'We do not believe at all that the U.S. is seeking genuine negotiations with Iran; because genuine negotiations would never come from a person like Trump. Genuineness is very rare among U.S. officials.'

Iranian Supreme Leader Ayatollah Sayyid Ali Khamenei rejects the possibility of talks with the US via Twitter on 13 June.[11]

'I thought about it for a second and I said, you know what, they shot down an unmanned drone, plane, whatever you want to call it. And here we are sitting with 150 dead people that would have taken place probably within half an hour after I said go ahead. And I didn't like it.'

Trump comments during an interview with NBC on 21 June on his decision to cancel military strikes on Iran after a US drone was shot down on 20 June.[12]

'The last 48 hours have reminded us that [Trump] doesn't want to get the U.S. sucked into another Middle Eastern war.'

An unnamed senior European diplomat involved in negotiations with Iran speaks to the New York Times *on 23 June.[13]*

2.7
Average number of refugees per 1,000 national population hosted by high-income countries

5.8
Average hosted by middle- and low-income countries per 1,000 national population[14]

What – me worry?

'In terms of violating Security Council resolutions, there is no doubt about that.'

John Bolton, national security advisor to US President Donald Trump, characterises missile tests carried out by North Korea in May 2019 as violations of UN Security Council resolutions.[15]

'North Korea fired off some small weapons, which disturbed some of my people, and others, but not me. I have confidence that Chairman Kim will keep his promise to me.'

Trump tweets on 26 May 2019.[16]

Flight risks

'These suspects are seen to have played an important role in the death of 298 innocent civilians. Although they did not push the button themselves, we suspect them of close co-operation to get the [missile launcher] where it was, with the aim to shoot down an aeroplane.'

Dutch Chief Prosecutor Fred Westerbeke comments on the issuance of international arrest warrants for four suspects charged with shooting down the Malaysia Airlines flight MH17 over Ukraine in July 2014.[17]

Sources

1 Ed Crooks, 'Western Countries Urged to Maintain Nuclear Power Plants', *Financial Times*, 28 May 2019, https://www.ft.com/content/c141fdf4-80a8-11e9-b592-5fe435b5 7a3b?emailId=5cecb5266f45530004b759f0&segmentId=22011ee7-896a-8c4c-22a0-7603348b7f22.

2 Patrick M. Shanahan, 'The US Vision for Indo-Pacific Security: Question & Answer Session', IISS Shangri-La Dialogue, Singapore, 1 June 2019, p. 2, https://www.iiss.org/-/media/files/shangri-la-dialogue/2019/speeches/plenary-1-qa.ashx.

3 General Wei Fenghe, 'China and International Security Cooperation', IISS Shangri-La Dialogue, Singapore, 2 June 2019, pp. 4–5, https://www.iiss.org/-/media/files/shangri-la-dialogue/2019/speeches/plenary-4---general-wei-fenghe-minister-of-national-defence-china-transcript.ashx.

4 'Huge Turnout by Protesters Keeps Heat on Hong Kong's Leader', *New York Times*, 16 June 2019, https://www.nytimes.com/2019/06/16/world/asia/hong-kong-protests.html?action=click&module=Top%20Stories&pgtype=Homepage.

5 Emma Graham-Harrison and Verna Yu, '"They're Kids, Not Rioters": New Generation of Protesters Bring Hong Kong to Standstill', *New York Times*, 16 June 2019, https://www.theguardian.com/world/2019/jun/16/hong-kong-protests-carrie-lam-china.

6 Katrin Bennhold and Christopher F. Schuetze, 'Austrian Leader Calls for Snap Election After Far-Right Chancellor Resigns', *New York Times*, 18 May 2019, https://www.nytimes.com/2019/05/18/world/europe/austria-strache-resigns-video.html?action=click&module=Top%20Stories&pgtype=Homepage.

7 *Ibid.*

8 *Ibid.*

9 Donald J. Trump (@realDonaldTrump), tweet, 19 May 2019, https://twitter.com/realDonaldTrump/status/1130207891049332737.

10 Javad Zarif (@JZarif), tweet, 20 May 2019, https://twitter.com/JZarif/status/1130419673756049410.

11 Sayyid Ali Khamenei (@Khamenei_ir), tweet, 13 June 2019, https://twitter.com/khamenei_ir/status/1139104230285946881.

12 Daniella Silva, 'Trump Says He Doesn't Want War with Iran, but There Will Be "Obliteration" if It Comes', NBC, 21 June 2019, https://www.nbcnews.com/politics/politics-news/trump-says-he-did-not-given-final-approval-iran-strikes-n1020386.

13 Patrick Kingsley, 'Trump's Iran Reversal Raises Allies' Doubts over His Tactics, and U.S. Power', *New York Times*, 23 June 2019, https://www.nytimes.com/2019/06/23/world/europe/trump-iran-usa.html.

14 UNHCR, 'Global Trends: Forced Displacement in 2018', https://www.unhcr.org/globaltrends2018/.

15 Motoko Rich, 'John Bolton Says North Korean Missile Tests Violated U.N. Resolutions', *New York Times*, 24 May 2019, https://www.nytimes.com/2019/05/24/world/asia/john-bolton-north-korea.html?module=inline.

16 Donald J. Trump (@realDonaldTrump), tweet, 26 May 2019, https://twitter.com/realDonaldTrump/status/1132459370816708608.

17 'MH17: Four Charged with Shooting Down Plane over Ukraine', BBC, 19 June 2019, https://www.bbc.co.uk/news/world-europe-48691488.

Cyber War and Nuclear Peace

David C. Gompert and Martin Libicki

As bellicose as human beings can be, it is notable that they have not used the most destructive weapons ever invented since dropping them on Hiroshima and Nagasaki three-quarters of a century ago. Upon witnessing the first atomic explosion at Alamogordo, New Mexico, in July 1945, J. Robert Oppenheimer, scientific director of the Manhattan Project, said, 'It worked.' More famously, he also remarked, 'I am become death, the destroyer of worlds.'[1] Over the objections of fellow Los Alamos scientists, Oppenheimer supported dropping the bomb on Japan because he believed that nothing less would so shock humans that they would not use such weapons again. This stratagem too seems to have worked. Despite super-power confrontation punctuated by crises, bloated nuclear arsenals, and the spread of nuclear weapons to nine states and counting, Oppenheimer's wish that nuclear weapons would not be used again has been fulfilled – so far. Can nuclear peace last?

The main reason for nuclear peace these 70-plus years is not human goodness but human dread. Mutual deterrence rooted in fear of retaliation has kept the nuclear monster in the closet. Neither the United States nor Russia has had the assured ability to conduct a disarming first strike or to defend itself against a devastating second strike. Each is determined to have

David C. Gompert is Distinguished Visiting Professor at the US Naval Academy and was US Principal Deputy Director of National Intelligence from 2009 to 2010. **Martin Libicki** is the Maryellen and Richard L. Keyser Distinguished Visiting Professor in Cyber Security Studies at the US Naval Academy.

Survival | vol. 61 no. 4 | August–September 2019 | pp. 45–62   DOI 10.1080/00396338.2019.1637122

more than sufficient second-strike capability to convince the other that a first strike would be tantamount to suicide. Agreements to limit and reduce strategic nuclear weapons, from the Strategic Arms Limitation Treaty (SALT) I to the New Strategic Arms Reduction Treaty (START), though commendable, have been less important in maintaining this stability than the large arsenals they codified. Meanwhile, China has built a credible, if smaller, nuclear force that allows it to deter attack by either the United States or Russia. The United States, Russia and China are in a triangular strategic equilibrium – idiomatically, mutual assured destruction (MAD).

While MAD has worked, efforts by the original nuclear states to prevent the proliferation of nuclear weapons have been less successful: of the four more recent nuclear states, India and Pakistan are locked in a cold war of their own, Israel has foes that desire its extinction as a state and North Korea is run by a megalomaniac. Yet none of these states has used nuclear weapons – again, not because they are peace-loving, but because they are afraid of what would follow.

Neither massive arsenals nor the spread of nuclear weapons so far has shattered Oppenheimer's wish that Japan would be their last target. But what if a nuclear first strike or even non-nuclear strikes to wipe out nuclear-deterrent forces were to become feasible, or to be feared as feasible even if not? What if a lesser but rasher nuclear state discounted the threat of retaliation or thought it was doomed anyway? Geopolitical crises – say, NATO–Russia confrontation or conflict in Korea – could cause such dangers to spike. But our chief concern is that nuclear stability could be threatened by new technology, which would make crises more dangerous.

Since the dawn of the nuclear age, and arguably the industrial age, the technologies that have affected human endeavours more than any others are those that have revolutionised the gathering, storing, processing, sharing and use of information. For better or worse, the progress of these technologies is transformative, destabilising and unstoppable. Moreover, because they work best when networked and accessible, they have become susceptible to interference – that is, to cyber war. The implications of these technologies for nuclear peace warrant a close look. Three questions in particular arise. Firstly, could progress in digital systems and networking affect the dependability of nuclear command, control and communications (NC3) systems? Secondly, could improvements in intelligence, surveillance and reconnaissance (ISR) affect the survivability of nuclear-deterrent forces? Thirdly, could cyber war interfere with the reliability, control and use of nuclear forces?

NC3 in the digital age

In the beginning, before digital networks, were computers and, quite separately, telephones. Certain technological breakthroughs, notably in microprocessing, fibre-optic and satellite transmission, packet-switching and cellular telephony, led to data networking (or distributed processing). Deregulation of telecommunications and the break-up of the Bell System in 1984 enabled, rewarded and propelled integration and competition in computer communications. The resulting innovations profoundly changed the everyday world: email, the internet, the World Wide Web, global digital infrastructure, and the network-based restructuring of organisations from banks to airlines to utility companies to government agencies. All were US-led. Now, artificial intelligence and quantum computing herald another burst in information technology, with consequences that are barely understood.

The US military was a prime mover of the digital revolution, though its acquisition red tape and industrial inertia held it back from the accelerating progress of these technologies in the economy at large. Nonetheless, by 1990, as first on display in the Gulf War, the US military was leading a 'revolution in military affairs', centred on non-nuclear forces. The resolution and coverage of sensors were rapidly improving; data networks fused their voluminous products; munitions gained pinpoint accuracy at any range; global-positioning systems gave ships, planes and weapons near-perfect navigation regardless of location; off-board guidance and microelectronics brought per-weapon costs down and lethality up; and networking facilitated integrated joint command and control and operations. US forces had a near-monopoly in applying digital technologies, which were mostly driven by vast commercial markets and resources in which the United States has also led. Until recently – with China's technological and military rise – this boost to military superiority enabled the United States to dispatch forces worldwide to win lopsided wars with few casualties. (Protracted post-9/11 wars in Iraq and Afghanistan, of course, have shown that US technological capability to project decisive force does not assure military success under all conditions.)

While the digital revolution's impact on conventional military affairs has been revolutionary, its impact on strategic nuclear capabilities, strategy and stability has been muted. Warning systems, missile guidance, infrastructure for command, control and communications, and computerised weapon-testing have all been modernised, and nuclear weapons themselves have been updated. But core strategic hardware – bombers, bombs, ballistic missiles and missile-bearing submarines – has endured. Moreover, the need for humans to manage nuclear operations, from interpreting enemy moves to choosing targets to releasing a nuclear strike, has inhibited a comparable information-technology-driven revolution in nuclear affairs.

Even as the United States achieved superiority in conventional military capabilities, it did not seek to parlay its technological lead into strategic-nuclear superiority. It was content with mutual deterrence – rough quantitative strategic-nuclear equivalence with Russia and survivable US nuclear forces qualitatively second to none. Even with the latest digital technology, large arsenals of offensive strategic weapons cannot be entirely destroyed with a first strike, so stability has held up. Although the United States has applied information technology to ballistic-missile defence (BMD), it has directed BMD at the likes of North Korea – not Russia or China, their suspicions notwithstanding.

Digital technologies could even enhance strategic stability by improving warning and testing, and thus confidence. Improvement in the coverage and fidelity of sensors has permitted accurate and timely evaluation of nuclear tests and launches, making mistakes less likely. With the right simulation and supercomputer technology, nuclear devices no longer need to be detonated to assess their reliability and effects, which is surely a good thing. Thanks to packet-switching, satellite communications and ubiquitous wireless, the ability to utilise innumerable transmission pathways can make NC3 more resilient.

Even with advances in digital technology and expansion of network infrastructure, security dictates that most critical NC3 networks remain closed – dedicated and partitioned (air-gapped), with strictly controlled access. At the same time, exploiting the heterogeneity and ubiquity of open, public telecommunications can make it harder for an adversary to cripple NC3 by physical – that is, nuclear or conventional – attack. The key is to know how to exploit public networks without becoming reliant on them.

It is widely believed that a likely cause of a nuclear war would be mis-perception or miscalculation under conditions of urgency and fractured or ambiguous information. Advances in warning and NC3 can reduce pres-sure to launch retaliatory strikes hastily and afford decision-makers more time to assess threats, consider targets and weigh consequences before deciding whether and how to retaliate. In sum, improved NC3 using digital technologies can add to nuclear stability by bolstering confidence during decision-making. So far, so good.

ISR and nuclear peace

Digital technologies might also contribute to nuclear peace indirectly insofar as high-precision ISR and conventional strike capabilities obviate the need to use nuclear weapons for certain missions, such as destroy-ing hard or buried targets. But this is a double-edged sword: digital technologies can also potentially improve means of targeting and destroy-ing nuclear-deterrent forces by a conventional first strike, without using nuclear weapons. Apart from intercontinental ballistic missiles in hard-ened silos, land-based nuclear weapons and infrastructure are becoming easier to destroy with non-nuclear weapons enabled by the latest ISR. While nuclear-armed submarines remain hard to target because of per-sistent difficulties in anti-submarine-warfare technology, it may not take nuclear weapons to effectively attack them once they are detected, much less if they are still in port.

Hunting for land-based nuclear weapons, launchers, bombers and other infrastructure exploits the technologies of cyberspace: sensors (optical, infrared, radar, acoustic) to collect information; networks to amalgam-ate it; and data-mining and machine-learning to analyse it.[2] Once targets' locations and tracks are known, precision-guided weapons, many aided by global positioning, can take advantage of this information. In addition, advances in navigation, guidance and remote sensing have propelled the development of autonomous vehicles (drones), which in turn is pushing the technology of flight for tiny objects. The more that software can replace people in controlling vehicles, the more tasks can be transferred from manned to unmanned aircraft. The more drones that are produced, the more economical and numerous they will be (a phenomenon previously seen with precision-guided munitions). Likewise, though the cost of launching satellites into orbit is declining more slowly, the ability to cram more sensing and processing power into ever smaller satellites could lead to a profusion in their numbers and coverage.

The US has a decided edge

Some nuclear powers, including Russia and China, depend on mobile missile launchers to reduce vulnerability. But technological advances in ISR and precision strike mean that 'mobile systems are not nearly as survivable as was believed a decade ago', as Paul Bracken assessed in 2016.[3] As one Chinese observer points out, 'the launch units of mobile missiles are composed of a large number of service trucks, which makes the weapon more visible to detection by foreign intelligence assets'.[4] Well-placed attacks on road or rail networks would impede the movement of mobile missiles, thereby increasing their vulnerability and limiting their firing ranges – all without necessitating the use of nuclear weapons.

In a war involving the United States and Russia or China, a conventional counter-nuclear campaign could have several elements. A range of ISR systems could reveal the exact location of submarines in or near port, missile launchers on the move or parked aircraft. Such systems could include satellites, drones or offshore aircraft with side-looking sensors for gleaning images, emissions and signals intelligence, as well as cyber espionage. Long-range precision strikes could then destroy second-strike nuclear forces.[5]

Because of its technological prowess, the United States has a decided edge over China and Russia in hunting for hidden or mobile nuclear weapons.

(China has more formidable capabilities than Russia for shrinking that US lead.) One US advantage comes from the versatility of its well-funded and steadily improving stand-off conventional-warfare capabilities, which could be used in an attrition campaign against enemy nuclear forces. Another US advantage is geographic: it can keep hostile hunters thousands of miles from its shores. China, by contrast, does not have to look far to see US allies, bases and fleets near its territory; ditto for Russia. A third US advantage, for now at least, is its abundance of air-launched, sea-launched and submarine-launched long-range weapons, especially accurate cruise missiles.

Sure enough, the Chinese and Russians have made known their concern about the implication for their nuclear deterrents of superior American ISR and conventional precision-strike capabilities. The Russians became especially concerned with the advent in the 2000s of US Conventional Prompt Global Strike (CPGS), described by a senior Russian official in 2007 as a 'means of seeking to dominate the world politically and strategically … when combined with global [sic] missile defense'.[6] CPGS, as the Russians see it, constitutes a putative non-nuclear first-strike capability: it could decimate their nuclear-deterrent force, leaving their surviving missiles to be intercepted by American BMD.

The notion that the United States would try to wipe out the nuclear-deterrent forces of Russia or China with non-nuclear attacks so that it could then launch a nuclear attack is practically unimaginable, if only because it could not be confident of destroying them all. Still, there could be other reasons to attack Russian or Chinese nuclear forces, especially in a spiralling crisis. One would be simply to diminish the enemy's ability to mount a nuclear threat. But attacking on that basis could be attractive only if differences in the sizes of extant nuclear arsenals could affect who would blink first in such a crisis.[7] Even if such considerations are exaggerated, there is also a damage-limitation rationale to consider: simply put, the fewer nuclear weapons an enemy has, the less damage it can do if nuclear war should erupt. Systematically thinning down the enemy's nuclear arsenal to the point that what is left can be taken out with a nuclear first strike may persuade that enemy to seek peace and thereby preserve its deterrent capability and its survival.

Even without such intent, there is the danger that non-nuclear-armed missile strikes could be misinterpreted as a nuclear first strike, perhaps triggering retaliation. Although intercontinental trajectories are distinct, submarine-launched cruise missiles could easily be mistaken for strategic weapons. Bombers using gravity bombs or long-range missiles could be used for conventional or nuclear strikes. Generally speaking, any large-scale and high-intensity non-nuclear attack on a nuclear power could seem to jittery decision-makers to be the 'real thing', and if they believe they might lose their deterrent, they could adopt a use-it-or-lose-it rationale with respect to their country's nuclear weapons.

Accordingly, there is a genuine risk that non-nuclear attacks on an enemy's nuclear deterrent could cause a general nuclear war. As early as 2006, Russian President Vladimir Putin warned that a conventional missile launch 'could spark ... full-scale [nuclear] retaliation strikes'.[8] Also, according to one high-ranking Chinese officer, China would likely make a 'nuclear-counterattack of some sort' if the United States were to use conventional weapons to strike an important nuclear command-and-control node for China's nuclear forces, or, presumably, those forces themselves.[9]

A military campaign to reduce enemy nuclear forces using non-nuclear weapons could take time. The enemy may satisfy itself that enough of its nuclear weapons can survive to deter nuclear attack, thus restraining it from launching nuclear weapons even in the face of non-nuclear strikes on its deterrent forces. Yet such rationality is not assured, for humans cannot be trusted always to use inputs from information technology wisely, no matter how high the stakes. The history of bad judgement in matters of war and peace is long and chilling.[10]

In the context of non-nuclear warfare against nuclear forces, once it begins, both sides will be engaged in a contest involving rapid measure–countermeasure cycles and pressure-cooker decisions. Insofar as hunting and hiding deterrent forces still depend on human choices, advantages in the contest could hinge on learning, objectivity and discipline. When the course of conflict can be bent by finding and exploiting vulnerabilities, there may be sudden swings in success and failure, particularly when faults in hiding or finding one class of systems apply to all systems of that class.[11]

This is especially true for software in which every one of a class of targets or sensors runs off the same code and particular security vulnerabilities may affect all of them.

How great, then, is the danger to nuclear peace posed by ISR and long-range precision-strike conventional weapons? If neither side believes the other would use them against nuclear-deterrent forces, the danger is obviously slight. But if one side did believe that the other would use conventional weapons for that purpose, it could try to pre-empt that possibility, and the danger could be great. Although it might not be rational to conduct a nuclear response in the face of a counter-nuclear attack so long as enough retaliatory forces survive to deter a nuclear attack, there is too much scope for human misjudgement and emotion or technical error to bank on sound reasoning. And if the side being attacked interprets a conventional counter-nuclear attack as a prelude to a nuclear one, launching nuclear forces would not be altogether irrational. So much for Oppenheimer's hope.

Cyber war and nuclear deterrence

ISR-enabled conventional strikes against nuclear-deterrent forces could be all the more deleterious to nuclear peace if combined with cyber-war attacks on NC3. How serious is the threat of such attacks?

Warfare against computer networks, not unlike nuclear warfare, tends to be 'offence-dominant' in that the efforts, resources and time it takes to defend or restore networks generally surpass what it takes to corrupt or crash them. After all, networks are generally meant to be accessible to facilitate the sharing of information and collaborative work. The growing importance of computer networks, both civilian and military, has given rise to sophisticated efforts to hack into them. Given the pay-offs, cyber-war capabilities are rapidly being developed, diffused and used. This does not necessarily portend a threat to NC3 networks, which are singularly hard to penetrate. Yet the consequences of infected NC3 are dire enough to warrant concern.

At the behest of those who sponsor them, hackers can upset stability by working to induce, prevent or delay the launch of nuclear weapons.[12] Directly inducing nuclear launch is extremely difficult and improbable, mainly because launch orders go through human authorities. Moreover, it would take a character from *Dr. Strangelove* to see the advantage of launching a nuclear weapon without authority.[13] Somewhat less difficult and improbable is to create false information that persuades authorities to launch weapons, particularly in the heat of a crisis. We know that indications-and-warning assets, such as satellites and over-the-horizon radar, have mistaken test alerts for real ones.[14]

Preventing launch or detonation could obviously have huge advantages for the side on which those weapons would otherwise fall. This is somewhat more likely than inducing launch, but still very difficult because cyber attacks generally cannot disable weapons by issuing bad instructions unless the weapons are already capable of disabling themselves based on bad instructions. Delaying nuclear launch may be the least unlikely outcome: early-warning systems could be compromised or launch operations delayed by confusion; commands necessary to launch weapons could be tampered with; and false messages could be inserted to override true messages or persuade operators to distrust true messages. Delaying enemy missile-launch could expose retaliatory forces to destruction or cause the enemy to consider a truce.

While a wide variety of non-state actors engage in cyber war, states remain the most proficient actors. Few of them would have the ability to interfere with NC3 in the ways just described. However, the world's three leading cyber powers are, not coincidentally, the same as the leading nuclear powers. Cyber war is being used for a variety of geopolitical purposes by Russia, and it is being integrated into warfare capabilities and operations by the United States and China. (All three powers engage in cyber espionage, but that's a different matter.) This state of affairs presses us to ask whether the mutual deterrence that underpins strategic-nuclear stability among the Big Three could be weakened by the offensive cyber-war potential of those same powers.

Again, nuclear stability depends on fear of retaliation devastating enough to overwhelm any justification for a first strike. Of interest here is whether cyber warfare directed against an enemy's NC3 could allay that fear by reducing the certainty or efficacy of retaliation. The answer to that question depends on which of the big nuclear powers one considers. Because it has the most survivable retaliatory forces, and because neither Russia nor China has BMD or the equivalent of global conventional strike, the United States has the least reason to worry about the strength of its strategic deterrent.

Nevertheless, any cyber attack on its NC3 would be cause for grave concern. The diversity of the US deterrent elements mitigates the risks of Russian or Chinese cyber attack on US NC3. At the same time, because it functions as the central nervous system of the US nuclear infrastructure, loss of NC3 could undermine US deterrence. Consequently, the United States would react strongly to any trace of Russian or Chinese interference with its ability to control and operate its nuclear systems. In fact, the US 2018 Nuclear Posture Review indicates that attacks on its NC3 systems could result in nuclear retaliation.[15]

Russians have dismissed American assurances

A US cyber threat to Russia's NC3 could be an even greater danger to nuclear peace. Context matters in this regard. Even in the absence of such a threat, the Russians worry more than the United States does – even more than they should – about the survivability and credibility of their strategic nuclear deterrent. Since the early 2000s, when the United States withdrew from the 1972 Anti-Ballistic Missile Treaty, the Russians have dismissed American assurances, however valid, that US BMD is aimed at the likes of North Korea and Iran. US technical briefings and political pledges have not mollified the concerns of Russians consumed by the belief that BMD would expand and improve to the point that a large percentage of Russia's retaliatory force could be intercepted. When combined with their fear that a highly accurate US nuclear first strike could destroy much of Russia's predominantly land-based deterrent force on the ground, including missiles in silos, the Russians have long seen American BMD as a threat to strategic equilibrium.

Moreover, as noted, the Russians are fearful of US capabilities to decimate their nuclear deterrent with non-nuclear strike forces. Lastly, US anti-satellite capabilities could potentially take out Russian warning systems and space-based communications. Russia's lack of such capabilities, as well as effective BMD and global precision-strike, has compounded its fears – not so much that the United States would launch a disarming first strike as that it could use this advantage as leverage in a crisis or even peacetime.

The Russians' view of US anti-deterrent capabilities and intentions may be exaggerated. But it is a strongly held one, as evidenced by Russia's modernisation programmes for strategic-offensive forces. Despite a struggling economy, declining state revenues and competing demands on the defence budget, Russia is investing in at least two strategic-nuclear delivery systems that are expressly intended to penetrate US BMD: a transoceanic nuclear torpedo aimed at US coastal cities; and a hypersonic, manoeuvrable 'glide' vehicle. The alarm that these have caused in some US circles overlooks the fact that they are inherently second-strike weapons developed in response to US BMD.

In addition to deploying new second-strike systems, however, Russia could resort to nuclear launch-on-warning. This doctrine, inherited from Soviet days, calls for launch of a retaliatory attack when an incoming strike is observed by warning sensors. It is unclear whether launch-on-warning is stabilising or destabilising: it could be the former if it makes a surprise disarming first strike virtually impossible; it could be the latter insofar as it compresses decision time to a few minutes. In any case, US interference with Russia's NC3 could be interpreted in Moscow as a precursor to nuclear or non-nuclear attack on its deterrent, augmented by BMD and anti-satellite operations. In this context, cyber war could disturb strategic equilibrium and even threaten nuclear peace.

China has been satisfied that its comparatively small deterrent force – numbering hundreds, not thousands, of weapons – will suffice to deter a nuclear strike by the United States or Russia. Why waste resources, the Chinese ask themselves, on an outsized offensive nuclear arsenal just because the two larger nuclear powers do? Consistent with this logic, China has pledged not to use nuclear weapons first. However, because of their 'minimal deterrence' posture, the Chinese are highly sensitive to indicators that the United States might assemble first-strike capabilities, combining accurate nuclear weapons, conventional precision-strike capabilities enabled by advanced ISR, BMD and anti-satellite capabilities. Adding a US counter-NC3 cyber-war option to this suite of potential first-strike capabilities would further alarm the Chinese. They are already moving towards placing their retaliatory forces on higher alert than they have been, and a looming US cyber threat could impel them to rely on launch-on-warning.[16]

All three big nuclear powers are sensitive to the danger of counter-NC3 cyber war. As a result, any interference with these systems could trigger fear of nuclear or non-nuclear attack, which could in turn threaten nuclear peace. Assigning a probability to such a contingency is foolhardy. The consequences could be catastrophic, but the risks can be mitigated. As far as is publicly known, the United States has been extremely selective in its offensive cyber-war operations – not to be confused with cyber-intelligence operations – and presumably has not tampered with either Russia's or China's NC3. It is imperative to maintain this policy. Also, the United States could propose agreements that cyber war will not be used against NC3 (unless nuclear war occurs, in which case all bets are off).

In sum, if the United States, Russia and China treat NC3 as off-limits for cyber war, if their retaliatory forces remain survivable against nuclear or non-nuclear attack, and if BMD does not progress beyond what known technology offers, the probability of nuclear war among them should remain low. But nerves could be more on edge, which is bad for stability.

Cyber war and counter-proliferation

It is possible that a newer, smaller nuclear state will be tempted to use nuclear weapons if it thinks its survival is threatened. North Korea, Iran and Pakistan all face hostile nuclear powers with enough conventional military capabilities to conquer them. In this light, using nuclear weapons and running the risk of retaliation might not be entirely mad (no pun intended). Moreover, it is conceivable that one of them would contemplate using nuclear weapons against a non-nuclear state – maybe North Korea against South Korea or Japan – in the belief that it would not suffer nuclear retaliation (that is, that the US would not act on its extended-deterrence pledge of defending them). Lastly, a proliferation domino effect cannot be ignored.

For instance, Iran's development of a nuclear-weapons capability could be followed by Saudi Arabia's or Turkey's. For these reasons, nuclear peace is more likely to end because of proliferation than because of crisis instability among the large nuclear powers. Even if such scenarios seem far-fetched, they would be so consequential that we ought to reduce their likelihood as far as possible.

The proliferation problem presents the United States with a different calculus concerning cyber war and nuclear peace than it does Russia and China. The objectives of counter-proliferation are quite simple: prevent the acquisition of deliverable nuclear weapons; failing that, prevent their use. It has been reported that the United States has conducted cyber operations twice to impede the acquisition of deliverable nuclear weapons: once by crashing centrifuges used by Iran to enrich uranium; once to spoil a North Korean missile test.[17]

Generalising from these reported examples, US cyber operations could curb or at least slow nuclear proliferation by impeding efforts to obtain and deploy nuclear weapons; interfering with technological and industrial programmes to produce and weaponise nuclear material; reducing confidence in weapon-system reliability; disrupting launch preparations; and degrading sensors. Moreover, although attempting to disrupt Russian or Chinese NC3 could be extremely perilous given their ability to retaliate, doing so against a nuclear rogue state could be indicated in certain circumstances. These cyber-war measures would complement other efforts to prevent acquisition and use, such as economic sanctions, supply-chain interruption, nuclear deterrence, conventional deterrence and, if it came to war, conventional strike and missile defence.

Cyber measures to slow nuclear proliferation must be applied carefully and on a case-by-case basis for several reasons. Firstly, the United States, on account of its own vulnerabilities, should be wary of normalising cyber war. Secondly, it is possible that conducting cyber war against a nuclear rogue could make it even more determined to acquire nuclear weapons. Thirdly, a cyber attack on any nuclear state's NC3 could trigger the use of a nuclear weapon if interpreted as a precursor to an attempt to disarm it by conventional or nuclear strike. This said, countering the spread of nuclear weapons is a matter of critical importance to the United States and to international peace that would justify offensive cyber operations.

*   *   *

Revolutionary digital technologies will not necessarily endanger nuclear peace. Thus far, networking options have arguably enhanced stability by making NC3 more resilient. Advances in ISR that enable US global conventional-strike capabilities do not in and of themselves endanger Russian or Chinese deterrent forces unless used against those forces or otherwise used in a conflict in a manner that might be misinterpreted as a strategic threat. Although capabilities can be driven by technological forces, using them is still up to humans.

Conducting cyber operations against the NC3 of a major nuclear state, particularly one already concerned about a disarming nuclear or non-nuclear first strike, might cause it to adopt a hair-trigger launch policy, and could lead to nuclear war. The United States should propose understandings with Russia and China that NC3 is categorically off-limits for cyber operations against one another. On this point, the House Armed Services Committee's focus on cyber and other new technologies is salutary. As of June, the draft National Defense Authorization Act for FY2020 required the Pentagon to develop a plan for ensuring NC3 resiliency that includes options for negotiating a ban on cyber and other attacks against NC3 networks with US rivals. More broadly, the bill would task the 'Secretary of Defense to establish a senior working group to engage in military-to-military dialogue with Russia, China, and North Korea, to reduce the risk of miscalculation, unintended consequences, or accidents that could precipitate a nuclear war'.[18] At the same time, US cyber operations could inhibit nuclear proliferation to rogue states.

Whether technological change could endanger nuclear peace depends on the human stewards of these weapons. These stewards are mainly Americans, given the US strengths in NC3, ISR, conventional strike, BMD, cyber warfare and information technology generally. Thus, for now, the perpetuation of nuclear peace in the digital age is largely up to the United

States. But China and Russia, among others, are advancing their own capabilities and trying intently to close the gap with the US. In this light, it is all the more incumbent on the United States to take the lead in reconfiguring nuclear deterrence to withstand cyber war, and soon.

Notes

1   See, for example, Richard Rhodes, *The Making of the Atomic Bomb* (New York: Simon & Schuster, 1986).

2   See, for instance, Keir A. Lieber and Daryl G. Press, 'The New Era of Counterforce: Technological Change and the Future of Nuclear Deterrence', *International Security*, vol. 41, no. 4, Spring 2017, pp. 9–49.

3   Paul Bracken, 'The Cyber Threat to Nuclear Stability', *Orbis*, vol. 60, no. 2, Summer 2016, pp. 188–203.

4   Wu Riqiang, 'Certainty of Uncertainty: Nuclear Strategy with Chinese Characteristics', *Journal of Strategic Studies*, vol. 36, no. 4, May 2013, p. 587.

5   See Keir A. Lieber and Daryl G. Press, 'The End of MAD?', *International Security*, vol. 30, no. 4, Spring 2006, pp. 7–44.

6   Quoted in James M. Acton, 'Russia and Strategic Conventional Weapons: Concerns and Responses', *Nonproliferation Review*, vol. 22, no. 2, 2015, pp. 141–54, https:// carnegieendowment.org/2016/02/03/ russia-and-strategic-conventional- weapons-pub-62676. The official was Anatoly Antonov – then director of the Security and Disarmament Department at the Russian Ministry of Foreign Affairs and now Russia's ambassador to the United States.

7   See Matthew Kroenig, *The Logic of American Nuclear Strategy: Why Strategic Superiority Matters* (Oxford: Oxford University Press, 2018).

8   Quoted in Pavel Podvig, 'Russia and the Prompt Global Strike Plan', PONARS Policy Memo No. 417, December 2006, http://russianforces. org/podvig/2006/12/russia_and_the_ prompt_global_s.shtml.

9   Quoted in Thomas J. Christensen, 'The Meaning of the Nuclear Evolution: China's Strategic Modernization and US–China Security Relations', *Journal of Strategic Studies*, vol. 35, no. 4, August 2012, pp. 447–87.

10 See, for example, David C. Gompert, Hans Binnendijk and Bonny Lin, *Blinders, Blunders, and Wars: What America and China Can Learn* (Santa Monica, CA: RAND Corporation, 2014), which presents numerous cases of flawed strategic decision-making despite abundant, accurate informa- tion. Causes include leaders' egos, intuitions, excessive self-confidence, aversion to information that contra- dicts beliefs and the reluctance of advisers to 'speak truth to power'.

11 Just as, for instance, a vulnerability in Windows 10 potentially per- mits exploiting every Windows 10 machine. See, for example, Bruce Schneier, 'Class Breaks', Schneier on Security, 3 January 2017, https://www. schneier.com/blog/archives/2017/01/ class_breaks.html.

12 In theory, they can also misdirect launches, but a great deal of targeting is virtually hardwired in advance.

13 We have in mind General Jack D. Ripper, of course.

14 Russian examples include Moscow's initial misreading of NATO's *Able Archer* war-gaming exercise in 1983 and its initial misinterpretation of a Norwegian research-rocket launch in 1995. See Dylan Matthews, '35 Years Ago Today, One Man Saved Us from World-ending Nuclear War', *Vox*, 26 September 2018, https://www.vox.com/2018/9/26/17905796/nuclear-war-1983-stanislav-petrov-soviet-union; and Dylan Matthews, '24 Years Ago Today, the World Came Disturbingly Close to Ending', *Vox*, 25 January 2019, https://www.vox.com/future-perfect/2019/1/25/18196416/nuclear-war-boris-yeltsin-1995-norway-rocket. See also Gordon Barass, '*Able Archer 83*: What Were the Soviets Thinking?', *Survival*, vol. 58, no. 6, December 2016–January 2017, pp. 7–30. There are also US examples, but none brought the world nearly as close to the brink of nuclear war. See Andrew Futter, *Hacking the Bomb: Cyber Threats and Nuclear Weapons* (Washington DC: Georgetown University Press, 2018), especially chapter two.

15 US Department of Defense, 'Nuclear Posture Review', February 2018, https://media.defense.gov/2018/Feb/02/2001872886/-1/-1/1/2018-NUCLEAR-POSTURE-REVIEW-FINAL-REPORT.PDF.

16 See, for instance, Gregory Kulacki, 'China's Military Calls for Putting Its Nuclear Forces on Alert', Union of Concerned Scientists, January 2016, https://www.ucsusa.org/sites/default/files/attach/2016/02/China-Hair-Trigger-full-report.pdf.

17 The first operation, apparently undertaken in collaboration with Israel, involved the introduction of the 'Stuxnet' worm into Iranian computer systems. See Kim Zetter, *Countdown to Zero Day* (New York: Crown, 2014). On the possible use of cyberspace operations to interfere with North Korean rocket production, see David Sanger and William Broad, 'Trump Inherits a Secret Cyberwar Against North Korean Missiles', *New York Times*, 4 March 2017, https://www.nytimes.com/2017/03/04/world/asia/north-korea-missile-program-sabotage.html.

18 Theresa Hitchens, 'HASC Adds NC3 Funds; Wants Talks With Russia and China', *Breaking Defense*, 10 June 2019, https://breakingdefense.com/2019/06/hasc-adds-nc3-funds-wants-talks-with-russia-china/.

Argentina's Defence Deficit

Juan Battaleme and Francisco de Santibañes

The tragic loss of the Argentine submarine ARA *San Juan* and its 44 crew members in November 2017, during a training exercise near the Argentine coast, was not an isolated event. It was just the most notable of a series of operational accidents.[1] These mark the decline of the once-powerful Argentine armed forces, which during the late twentieth century were considered among the most capable in the southern hemisphere.[2]

Despite its volatile politics and recurrent economic crises, Argentina is not an unimportant state. With an area of 2,780,400 square kilometres, it is the eighth-largest country in the world. Its economy is the third-largest in Latin America and one of the 30 largest worldwide. Its population is relatively well educated, having produced three Nobel Prize winners in the sciences – more than any other Latin American country. Argentina is a member of the G20 and, with Brazil, the most frequent Latin American member of the United Nations Security Council. Argentina also leads Latin America in numerous strategic technologies, including nuclear power and satellites, while having among the largest shale-oil and -gas reserves in the world. Indeed, the latent strength of Argentina is one of the factors that makes the decline of its military so incongruous and significant. Next to its

Juan Battaleme is head of the Defense Master's Degree programme at Argentina's National Defense University, associate professor at Buenos Aires University and head of the academic department of the Argentine Council for International Relations (CARI). **Francisco de Santibañes** is a Global Fellow at the Woodrow Wilson International Center for Scholars, a member of CARI's executive committee and author of *When Nations Revolt: The Crisis of Liberalism and the Rise of Popular Conservatism* (Del Dragon, 2019).

Survival | vol. 61 no. 4 | August–September 2019 | pp. 63–78   DOI 10.1080/00396338.2019.1637123

substantial political and economic power, Argentina's lack of operationally effective armed forces makes it an anomaly in the international system.

In 1982, the Argentine armed forces had 180,500 personnel in a country with a total population of 28 million.[3] The annual defence budget approached $10 billion in current dollars.[4] Today, Argentina's military personnel number 74,200, while its population has grown to almost 50m. The combined budget of the military and security forces of Argentina in 2018 was around $4.23bn.[5] Total expenditure for defence represents less than 1% of GDP. Moreover, up to 90% of the defence budget covers wages for military personnel and civilian workers. Only 4–6% is for equipment, and a similar portion for maintenance and operations. As a result, Argentina's combat and transport aircraft, armoured vehicles and artillery units are in a dilapidated state, constituting little more than a military museum. Naval vessels have, on average, more than 35 years of service, and maintenance is poor.[6] Accidents involving naval surface vessels have increased.[7] French *Mirage* combat aircraft have been decommissioned.[8] Argentina is no longer a capable military power.[9] Its military decline was taking place while its two biggest neighbours, Chile and Brazil, were implementing a series of plans to modernise their armed forces and increasing their defence budgets at a faster rate than Argentina. Argentina now has what might be called a 'token' defence system. It is unlikely that its armed forces could respond effectively to a direct military threat to its security or vital interests.[10]

A dubious policy evolution

The decline started with the government of the Radical Civic Union's leader Raúl Alfonsín, who became president after the fall of the military junta in 1983 and ruled until 1989, and has continued since then. Some have argued that low defence spending is an unavoidable consequence of Argentina's economic requirements and priorities – that the country's poor economic performance, marked by weak and inconsistent growth cycles, has both heightened social-welfare exigencies and constrained public spending, making it practically impossible to sustain major military programmes. Certainly, the economic pressures Argentina has faced have been, and remain, formidable. But there is also a more positive argument: that

Argentina need not invest in defence because South America is effectively a 'peace zone' in which countries do not face existential military threats and are best cast as mere elements of a larger collective and regional security scheme, such as the Council of South American Defense and the South Atlantic Peace and Cooperation Zone.

Although the latter rationale has been raised constructively to divert public spending to other areas of government, it has also compromised the international position of the country. Argentina needs a capable military because the regional and international strategic environments have become more uncertain. Ten years ago, for example, few would have predicted that the situation in oil-rich Venezuela would degenerate into an international political and humanitarian crisis that could produce military conflict and burgeoning regional instability. Now this scenario is a reality. Catastrophic environmental phenomena, such as climate change, could also give rise to large-scale humanitarian and engineering needs that a robust Argentine military could help meet. Climate change could also affect military conflict. Given the transnationalisation of extremist threats – jihadist and now right-wing – a strong and flexible military could be required for counter-terrorism or even counter-insurgency operations. Furthermore, especially in light of its traditional role as South America's most extroverted country, Argentina has a diplomatic interest in contributing actively to the preservation of international peace and stability, as it did in joining the US-led military coalition in the Gulf War in 1990–91. Substantially as a result of its participation, the US named Argentina a major non-NATO ally in 1998; it has remained the only such ally in Latin America, although US President Donald Trump indicated earlier this year that he intended to grant Brazil that status.

To meet prospective challenges, Argentine officials must first understand how the political marginalisation of the military establishment after Argentina's defeat in the Malvinas (Falklands) War in 1982 played out. The military ruled the country intermittently between 1955 and 1983. Like most Latin American countries, Argentina had faced internal guerrilla movements, economic disruptions and attempted coups, and its security apparatus had committed massive violations of human rights – notably in the 'Dirty War' from 1974 to 1983. Unlike any other Latin American government, however,

Argentina's military junta decided to fight an international war against a NATO member in a Cold War context. Although some components of the armed forces, such as the air force, performed well, Argentina was not prepared militarily, diplomatically, politically or economically to fight a war against the United Kingdom. Suddenly, a dictatorship that had been an ally of the Reagan administration and a purchaser of UK military hardware was flirting with the Soviet Union and Libya as sources of such equipment.[11]

The loss of the war, together with the junta's mismanagement of the economy, altered the balance of power between the political and military sectors of the government. Now ascendant, the political leadership used its recently gained legitimacy to limit the role of the military, because in the leadership's view the military represented – at least until the 1990s – a clear threat to both the political system and the democratic process. The end of the military's involvement in politics in favour of democracy and the functional exclusion of the military from internal-security matters were, to be sure, estimable achievements of Argentine reformism and consensus-building. One of the strategies chosen to acclimatise the Argentine military to the new dispensation was to send the soldiers abroad to participate in peacekeeping operations, working and training with professionalised militaries and learning how military institutions should work in democracies.

In 1995, the army's leaders recognised the role the force played in the violation of human rights during the 1970s, asked for forgiveness, and cited the necessity of creating a new kind of relationship between the civilian and the military authorities. At this point, the military officers who prosecuted the Dirty War had retired, died or been arrested, though amnesty laws passed in 1986 and 1987 on the dubious rationale of advancing national reconciliation shielded them from prosecution. Evidence that a more enlightened mentality had taken hold became manifest in 2001, when, during the worst economic and political crisis in Argentina's recent history, the government refrained from employing the armed forces to regain control of the streets from demonstrators. In 2003, Argentina's National Congress voted overwhelmingly to repeal the amnesty laws and, in 2005, the Argentine Supreme Court conclusively overturned them. By 2008, several former senior members of the military junta had been tried, found guilty and imprisoned.[12] While there remains some tension within the armed forces between liberal and nationalistic attitudes – unsurprisingly, the latter are particularly strong in the army – civilian control has been firmly institutionalised.

Doctrinal reform, however, appears to have gone too far. In 2006, president Néstor Kirchner, a Peronist populist, decreed that national defence contemplated only an armed attack from a state on the national territory. This did embrace the possibility of a prospective state threat to Argentina's territorial integrity or vital interests, but few politicians or academics considered such a threat salient. Accordingly, Kirchner's disposition did not practically allow for a comprehensive military doctrine or the thorough exploration of conflict scenarios on which to base capability requirements, and gave rise to systematic defence-budget cuts. Not only did these cuts reinforce Argentina's hidebound conception of national security, they also eroded even those defence capabilities that the country had deemed necessary for national defence. Combat aircraft, for example, were taken out of service without being replaced. Argentina's Joint Training Center for Peace Operations, which had been the first institution of its kind in the region and attracted military personnel from around the world for peacekeeping training, was defunded and effectively supplanted by other peace-operations centres elsewhere in South America.

Doctrinal reform has gone too far

Although this restrictive approach to national defence might have been useful during the democratic transition, it did not accommodate new threats – in particular, those of transnational terrorism and asymmetric warfare. From 2003 to 2015, the period spanning Kirchner's administration and that of his wife Cristina, who succeeded him, the political–military discourse focused on ideas such as 'confluence scenarios', 'Latin American defence integration' and 'soft power'. These were valid ideas, but Argentina's situation left little space for developing them there. The military junta had violated Samuel Huntington's 'objective control' model of civil–military relations, which dictated that civilians determine the political objectives of military activity and the military their practical realisation on the battlefield. During the Kirchners' tenure, civilian officials severely curtailed military officers' operational authority. By thus skewing the Huntingtonian balance in the other direction, they exacerbated the shortcomings of the defence policies inherited from the administrations of their predecessors.[13]

At the same time, politically beleaguered civilian officials opportunistically inveigled the military into insinuating itself into political disputes. For example, General César Milani, who was in charge of the army, declared that the military supported the Kirchners' political project.[14] Some factions of the military were even involved in illegal espionage.[15] The government also used the military's assertiveness to support a foreign policy of confrontation against some Western countries, including the United States and the United Kingdom, with an eye to gaining populist approval from domestic audiences – especially the left wing of the Peronist party. The Kirchners, for instance, restarted the dispute over the Malvinas (Falklands) Islands, increasing pressure in international forums, decreeing a 'distant blockade' to isolate the islands and seeking the assistance of fellow members of the Union of South American Nations to enforce the restrictions.[16] The policy was unsustainable. Within six months, Chile, traditionally friendly with the UK, began to assist British efforts to replenish the islands and to reprovision their own ships.[17] Soon, most countries in the region followed the Chilean example, training with the Royal Navy and allowing its vessels to visit their ports.

In response, the British reimposed sanctions on Argentina in 2012, establishing an embargo on weapons and military equipment. Items with degraded British components stopped functioning.[18] The sanctions remained in place until 2018, and the affected equipment was never replaced. To underline its anti-Western orientation at the time, the government decided to purchase from China trucks and 8x8 vehicles, and from Russia helicopters and four second-hand multipurpose polar vessels, christening the latter with names commemorating the Malvinas War. In an apparent attempt to leaven these moves with an exercise of soft power, Argentina dispatched the ARA *Fragata Libertad*, a flagship and training vessel, to several West African ports in hopes of opening up markets with southern countries with kindred histories of colonial oppression. In the event, a US hedge fund that had sued Argentina for its 2001 default on sovereign debt prevailed on a judge in the port of Tema, Ghana, to order the ship detained for three months in connection with the lawsuit.[19] This development abruptly cut short the ARA *Fragata Libertad*'s mission of defence diplomacy; the ship would not venture beyond Latin American waters again until 2016.

In addition to manipulating the military for primarily domestic political purposes, the Kirchners derogated the military's educational traditions and promotion system. They started this process by using the professional military academic curriculum to deconstruct the military ethos. Many of the changes were salutary. Wary of any residue of fascistic repressiveness from the Dirty War era, civilian officials undertook to broaden the mindset of military officers by way of courses about gender, multiple types of laws, sociology, political science and Latin American history.[20] But this came at the cost of military strategy, tactics and history. Even the code of military justice, an instrument used by armed forces around the world to preserve discipline, was eliminated in favour of civil justice. Civilians at the Ministry of Defense even handled decisions regarding military promotions and billets. Those in disagreement with this new dispensation were encouraged to retire and seek more appropriate opportunities in the private sector. That, in addition to lower salaries, was how the military lost well-trained pilots, soldiers and sailors, communications specialists, engineers and logistics officers.

Halting progress

The election of Mauricio Macri of the centre-right Republican Proposal party as president in 2015 augured guardedly well for the positive reorientation of the Argentine military. But the new administration did not give defence priority. There were valid reasons for this. The Macri administration inherited an economically exhausted country, one that was politically divided and facing intense social and economic pressures. The administration made it clear that it did not immediately have the time or the interest to address major military overhaul and reform.[21] And the Argentine population understandably remained sensitive to any heightened role for the military in domestic affairs. As part of the political-coalition agreements, the president decided to confer leadership of the Ministry of Defense on the Radical Civic Union, which has customarily elevated social-justice issues well above national defence. Its stewardship, marked by the sinking of the ARA *San Juan*, generally has been desultory.[22]

One notable exception has been the ministry's establishment of the position of national security adviser. The adviser's office has instituted several new programmes that have benefited the armed forces. Argentina has decided to acquire from France four *Adroit*-class oceanic-patrol vessels, while naval aviation has received funding for the purchase of five *Super Etendard Modernisé* strike fighters. The air force was authorised to purchase 12 *Texan* II trainer aircraft, a life-extension programme for transport aviation. In September 2018, the Argentine manufacturer Fábrica Argentina de Aviones completed the production of three new IA-63 *Pampa* advanced training jets. The manufacturer has also started to provide maintenance service for commercial planes as a way to finance military programmes. The army received some funding for resuming tank modernisation. The military has also begun to develop new capacities in the area of cyber defence after years of neglect.

In the realm of scenario and force planning, there is also some modestly good news. Last year, Macri effectively revoked the decree limiting the military to responding only to external state aggression, according it a broader but still limited role in internal security.[23] Centre-left politicians and human-rights groups vigorously criticised the move, and its practical effect is likely to be highly circumscribed.[24] But it does indicate that now military officers can at least think, talk and teach about new types of conflict without facing civilian reprimand. A new National Defense Policy Directive also recognised broader risks to the country's sovereignty, more in line with global threat perceptions.[25] In addition, the G20 summit held in Buenos Aires in 2018 helped to raise the national consciousness about the importance of developing an integrated security and defence outlook and capability. Argentina's economic weakness, however, hinders any serious reconstruction of its military capabilities. Large-scale personnel increases, for instance, are not expected. Defence is still a low budgetary priority, and is likely to remain so in the medium term.

While implementing major reforms might be expensive, planning for the future is not. Yet no vibrant academic debate appears to be under way about

Argentina's defence system. There are few defence specialists in political parties or academic institutions discussing possible strategic scenarios and the risks and opportunities they might present to Argentina. Meanwhile, key technocratic questions remain unanswered. Should Argentina develop a major military industry or purchase weapons from foreign powers? If the latter, which providers should it prefer? Should it perhaps follow Brazil's example and form joint ventures to produce foreign equipment at home? How should Argentina educate the members of the armed forces and resituate its military bases to accommodate new challenges? How can Argentina's ailing security sector gain strength from its quite successful IT sector? Unless these questions are effectively addressed and acted on, Argentina could become, in the worst case, a Gulliver-like version of Costa Rica – that is, a country without a functional military.

A warning from Buenos Aires

All states need functional armed forces. The reason is clear: leaders can never be certain about what the future might bring. Circumstances change, and today's friends might become enemies tomorrow. While the Argentine military has an admittedly dark past, as long as its civilian overseers and the Argentine electorate are satisfied that it has been purged and reformed, it is self-defeating for the country to field a dysfunctional military. Given the rising uncertainty in the international system, the increasing salience of non-state transnational threats and the inescapable reality that most states harbour offensive capabilities, even a state at peace, with no current enemies, has little choice but to develop and maintain modern armed forces of its own to dissuade or confront potential adversaries. States that do not accept this reality are likely at some point to face insecurity, including the possibility of military invasion and the loss of sovereign control.[26] Armed forces are useful for other reasons too. They can serve, for example, as effective instruments of foreign policy. When they are used in a judicious manner, they can prevent political conflicts and resolve disputes in ways that advance important state interests. Forming a functional military takes not years but generations, in no small part because developing a professional military culture is arduous, long-term work.

In this light, Argentina is out of step. While it has preserved a decent share of regional economic and political power, it has forsaken commensurately functional armed forces without the backstop of a strong and reliable military alliance. Despite being a major non-NATO ally for 20 years, Argentina has reaped few special benefits from this status. While it did acquire some US military equipment on a preferential basis under linked US Foreign Military Sales and Excess Defense Articles programmes for a brief period, under the Kirchner administrations Argentina requested no US military equipment except for the M113 armoured personnel carrier. Indeed, Peronists and other left-of-centre politicians seemed almost embarrassed about being a major non-NATO ally of the United States.[27] Consciously or unconsciously, Argentine leaders appear to have predicted or assumed that the country will not face any major threat for the foreseeable future. In the highly dynamic contemporary global-security environment, this kind of thinking is risky and irresponsible. The distribution of economic and military power is moving eastward, towards China in particular, while numerous countries – including, in Latin America, Venezuela and Brazil – are facing profound political and ideological challenges at home. Technological changes, notably the emergence of cyber warfare, are posing new risks to all states' national security.

The ongoing and potentially intensifying strategic confrontation between the United States and China may one day reach Latin America, as the rivalry between the US and the Soviet Union did during the Cold War. Indeed, with China's expansion of its Belt and Road Initiative to Latin America, there are early signs that this is already happening.[28] China has invested about $18bn in Argentina over the past decade, mainly in infrastructure, and is looking to continue.[29] Cristina Kirchner's administration allowed the Chinese government to construct a space-observatory base in the Argentine province of Neuquén, which contains most of Argentina's shale-oil and -gas reserves. This station is administered by the Chinese People's Liberation Army, utilises technology that can be used both for civilian and military purposes, and is shrouded in secrecy.[30] Moreover, during the G20 summit in Buenos Aires, while Chinese President Xi Jinping was on a state visit to Argentina, Trump implicated the country directly in the United States' trade dispute with Beijing by bruiting Argentina's rejection of China's 'predatory economic practices'. Consternated Argentine officials were compelled to walk back Trump's representation.[31] Thus, tensions between great powers already seem to have reached and affected Argentina. The relatively benign and remote geopolitical status the country has enjoyed since the end of the Malvinas War may be coming to an end.

There are no clear signs that the political and intellectual classes in Argentina are reconsidering the state of the defence system. Admittedly, there are practical impediments, including national economic dysfunction and scarce financial resources for funding modern armed forces. Nevertheless, many other nations have confronted these circumstances and limitations without neglecting defence to the extent that Argentina has done. While it is true that the Argentine military as an institution bears the historical stigmas of both the Dirty War and the defeat by the UK in 1982, other South American states with comparable baggage – including Brazil, Chile and Peru – have kept their militaries in better shape. In any case, the Argentine military has been substantially purged of the vestiges of its sordid past. There are residual fears of potential martial repression, and some Argentines believe that the reckoning for past military abuses has been insufficient.[32] But polls indicate that the Argentine military is increasingly trusted and respected, and that 62% of Argentines favour increased military spending.[33] Accordingly, there appears to be no insuperable political obstacle to reinvigorating the military.

*   *   *

Argentina's military debility is tied to the country's general malaise. In just a couple of generations, Argentina went from being one of the richest countries in the world to one racked by recurrent economic crises. As a result, no technocratic elite has emerged to preserve the country's long-term interests, which include a healthy military and a coherent defence policy. Instead, politics in Argentina has resembled an open-ended scramble among interest groups that perceive an unstable, zero-sum competition for scarce and diminishing resources, and are intent only on securing short-term gains.[34]

The players are politicians, union officials and business leaders, but after the defeat in the Malvinas, the military lost its place at the table. Under these circumstances, developing a common vision of Argentina's national security has become a remarkably difficult task.

The Argentine experience should serve as a warning to Western societies in which populist or other iconoclastic movements are challenging the work, and even the existence, of their countries' establishments on a wholesale basis. On the pretext that liberal, cosmopolitan elites have distanced themselves from the interests and values of the communities they are supposed to represent, such movements often weaken national institutions without offering viable alternatives. In Latin America, one extreme consequence has been Venezuela's implosion. Another result, less dramatic but still highly deleterious, is a state of affairs like Argentina's, in which insidiously malign neglect rather than overtly reckless demagoguery has made national security quietly but unmistakably vulnerable.

Notes

1   See Tomas Aurelio, 'El mal estado del equipamiento militar causó 30 muertos en los últimos 15 años', *Perfil*, 26 November 2017, https://www.perfil.com/noticias/politica/el-mal-estado-del-equipamiento-militar-causo-30-muertos-en-los-ultimos-15-anos.phtml.

2   See, for example, Robert L. Scheina, 'Latin American Navies', *Proceedings*, vol. 107, no. 3, March 1981, https://www.usni.org/magazines/proceedings/1981-03.

3   IISS, *The Military Balance 1982–1983* (London: IISS, 1983), p. 99.

4   Juan Battaleme, 'El futuro de la defensa nacional después de la tragedia del ARA San Juan', Grupo de Inserción de Argentina en el Mundo, Consejo Argentino para las Relaciones Internacionales, June 2018, http://www.cari.org.ar/pdf/ara_sanjuan_

battaleme.pdf. Past Argentine defence expenditures are difficult to assess due to high inflation and volatile exchange rates. Some estimates were lower. For 1981, *The Military Balance 1982–1983* (p. 99) estimated Argentina's defence spending to be 44,400 billion pesos, then roughly equal to $10.08bn, and today to $29.2bn.

5   IISS, *The Military Balance 2019* (Abingdon: Routledge for the IISS, 2019), p. 380.

6   IISS, *The Military Balance 2017* (Abingdon: Routledge for the IISS, 2017), pp. 423–8.

7   See Mariano De Vedia, 'Combatió en las Malvinas y hoy se hunde por abandono', *La Nación*, 22 January 2013, https://www.lanacion.com.ar/1547909-combatio-en-las-malvinas-y-hoy-se-hunde-en-el-abandono; and

Mariano De Vedia, 'Por otra deuda, la Corbeta Espora sigue retenida en Sudafrica', *La Nación*, 16 November 2012, https://www.lanacion.com. ar/1527123-por-otra-deuda-la-corbeta-espora-sigue-retenida-en-sudafrica.

8   See 'La Fuerza Aérea se despide de los aviones Mirage después de 43 años de servicio', Infobae, 27 November 2015, https://www.infobae. com/2015/11/27/1772810-la-fuerza-aerea-se-despide-los-aviones-mirage-luego-43-anos-servicio/; and Guido Braslavsky, 'Con el último vuelo de los Mirage, no quedan aviones supersónicos', *Clarín*, 1 December 2015, https://www.clarin.com/politica/ mirage-fuerza_aerea_0_ryVgJsytwmx. html. See also Robert Beckhusen, 'Argentina Has Just Three Years to Invade the Falklands', *National Interest*, 6 January 2017, https:// nationalinterest.org/blog/the-buzz/ argentina-has-just-3-years-invade-the-falklands-18964.

9   See George Allison, 'Argentina Has Now Ceased to Be a Capable Military Power', *UK Defence Journal*, 16 May 2018, https://ukdefencejournal.org. uk/argentina-has-now-ceased-to-be-a-capable-military-power/; and Benjamin Gedan and Kathy Lui, 'As It Reengages with the World, Will Argentina Rebuild Its Military to Resume Its Historic Global Role?', Wilson Center, Argentina Project, 14 May 2019, https://www.wilsoncenter. org/article/it-reengages-the-world-will-argentina-rebuild-its-military-to-resume-its-historic-global.

10   See Carlos Escude, '¿Somos un protectorado de Chile y Brasil?', *La Nación*, 24 January 2013, https://www. lanacion.com.ar/1548409-somos-un-protectorado-de-chile-y-brasil.

11   Israel played an important part in the supply of aircraft to Argentina´s air force during the conflict and thereafter. Its motivation, incentives and consequences are well documented in Hernan Dobry, *Operación Israel: El Rearme Argentino Durante la Dictadura (1976–1983)* (Buenos Aires: Editorial Lumiere, 2013).

12   See Christine A.E. Bakker, 'A Full Stop to Amnesty in Argentina: The *Simón* Case', *Journal of International Criminal Justice*, vol. 3, no. 5, November 2005, pp. 1,106–20; Terence Roehrig, 'Executive Leadership and the Continuing Quest for Justice in Argentina', *Human Rights Quarterly*, vol. 31, no. 3, August 2009, pp. 721–47; and Alexandra Starr, 'Cleaning Up a Dirty War', *Foreign Policy*, 27 February 2013, https:// foreignpolicy.com/2013/02/27/ cleaning-up-a-dirty-war/.

13   See Samuel P. Huntington, *The Soldier and the State: The Theory and Politics of Civil–Military Relations* (Cambridge, MA: Harvard University Press, 1981). See also Francisco de Santibañes, 'The Efficiency of the Military Governments During War: The Case of Argentina in Malvinas', *Armed Forces and Society*, vol. 33, no. 4, April 2007, pp. 612–37.

14   See Mariano De Vedia, 'Inquieta a oficiales el alineamiento de Milani con Cristina', *La Nación*, 23 December 2013, https://www.lanacion.com. ar/1650196-inquieta-a-oficiales-el-alineamiento-de-milani-con-cristina; and Rut Diamint, 'Contar con los militares como apoyo del poder

político no es conducción democrática de las FF.AA.', *La Nación*, 19 January 2014, https://www.lanacion.com.ar/1656427-rut-diamint-contar-con-los-militares-como-apoyo-del-poder-politico-no-es-conduccion-democrat.

15 See Claudio Savoia, *Espiados: Cómo Controla el Gobierno a Todos los Argentinos* (Barcelona: Planeta, 2015), pp. 205–26.

16 See 'Argentina Wins Wider Falklands Blockade', Space Daily, 29 November 2010, http://www.spacedaily.com/reports/Argentina_wins_wider_Falklands_blockade_999.html; and Alexander Harriet, 'British Cruise Ship Tests Argentine Blockade in Falklands', *Daily Telegraph*, 21 February 2010, https://www.telegraph.co.uk/news/worldnews/southamerica/argentina/7279507/British-cruise-ship-tests-Argentine-blockade-in-Falklands.html.

17 See 'After Five Months Patrolling the Falklands, HMS York Returns to Portsmouth', MercoPress, 16 June 2011, http://en.mercopress.com/2011/06/16/after-5-months-patrolling-the-falklands-hms-york-returns-to-portsmouth-july.

18 See, for instance, Tim Sculthorpe, 'Defence Secretary Rejects Claims Britain Is Unable to Defend Falklands', *Independent*, 2 April 2012, https://www.independent.co.uk/news/uk/home-news/defence-secretary-rejects-claims-britain-is-unable-to-defend-falklands-7608483.html.

19 See Sam Jones and Jude Weber, 'Argentine Navy Ship Seized in Assets Fight', *Financial Times*, 3 October 2012, https://www.ft.com/content/edb12a4e-0d92-11e2-97a1-00144feabdc0.

20 See Sabrina Frederic, 'La formación de los militares argentinos en democracia: panorama y desafíos futuros', *Voces en el Fenix*, no. 48, 23 November 2015, http://www.vocesenelfenix.com/content/la-formación-de-los-militares-argentinos-en-democracia-panorama-y-desaf%C3%ADos-futuros.

21 See, for example, William Ostrove and Shaun McDougall, 'No, Argentina Will Not Be Spending $2 Billion on Military Equipment', Defense & Security Monitor, 12 April 2017, https://dsm.forecastinternational.com/wordpress/2017/04/12/no-argentina-will-not-be-spending-2-billion-on-military-equipment/.

22 See, for instance, Cassandra Garrison and Rosalba O'Brien, 'No Hike in Argentina Defense Spending Despite Sub Tragedy: Senator', Reuters, 1 September 2017, https://www.reuters.com/article/us-argentina-politics-bullrich/no-hike-in-argentine-defense-spending-despite-sub-tragedy-senator-idUSKBN1DV5SF.

23 Defensa Nacional, Decreto 683/2018, http://servicios.infoleg.gob.ar/infolegInternet/anexos/310000-314999/312581/norma.htm.

24 See, for example, 'Argentine Military Will Be Involved in Domestic Security Issues, Announces Macri', MercoPress, 24 July 2018, https://en.mercopress.com/2018/07/24/argentine-military-will-be-involved-in-domestic-security-issues-announces-macri; and Livia Peres Milani, 'Remilitarizing Argentina', NACLA, 3 January 2019, https://nacla.org/news/2019/01/03/remilitarizing-argentina.

25 Ministerio de Defensa, Directiva de Politica de Defensa Nacional-Aprobacion Decreto 703/2018, 30 July 2018, https://www.argentina.gob.ar/sites/default/files/decto-2018-703-apn-pte_-_directiva_de_politica_de_defensa_nacional._aprobacion.pdf.

26 See John Mearsheimer, *The Tragedy of Great Power Politics* (New York: W. W. Norton, 2001); and Kenneth N. Waltz, *Theory of International Politics* (Reading, MA: Addison-Wesley, 1979).

27 See, for example, Larry Rohter, 'Powell Visits Argentina and Finds It Wary on Foreign Policy', *New York Times*, 11 June 2003, https://www.nytimes.com/2003/06/11/world/powell-visits-argentina-and-finds-it-wary-on-foreign-policy.html.

28 See, for instance, IISS, 'China's Belt and Road Initiative in Latin America and the Caribbean', *Strategic Comments*, vol. 24, no. 40, December 2018, https://www.iiss.org/publications/strategic-comments/2018/chinas-bri-in-latin-america.

29 See Cassandra Garrison and Matt Spetalnick, 'China, Vying with U.S. in Latin America, Eyes Argentina Nuclear Deal', Reuters, 28 November 2018, https://www.reuters.com/article/us-argentina-china-insight/china-vying-with-u-s-in-latin-america-eyes-argentina-nuclear-deal-idUSKCN1NX0FE.

30 See Cassandra Garrison, 'China's Military-run Space Station in Argentina Is a "Black Box"', Reuters, 31 January 2019, https://www.reuters.com/article/us-space-argentina-china-insight/chinas-military-run-space-station-in-argentina-is-a-black-box-idUSKCN1PP0I2. See also Laura Seligman, 'U.S. Military Warns of Threat from Chinese-run Space Station in Argentina', *Foreign Policy*, 8 February 2019, https://foreignpolicy.com/2019/02/08/us-military-warns-of-threat-from-chinese-run-space-station-in-argentina/.

31 See Jesus Rodriguez, 'White House Statement Drags Argentina into U.S.–China Brawl', Politico, 30 November 2018, https://www.politico.com/story/2018/11/30/us-china-argentina-g20-1036939.

32 See, for example, Sebastián Vargas, 'The Grim Legacy of Dictatorship', *Development and Cooperation*, 3 October 2018, https://www.dandc.eu/en/article/end-military-dictatorship-argentinas-governments-have-found-it-difficult-deal-armed-forces.

33 See Demian Bio, 'Poll Reveals What Institution Argentines Distrust the Most', Bubble, 26 September 2017, https://www.thebubble.com/poll-reveals-what-institution-argentines-distrust-the-most/; and 'Should Argentina Increase or Decrease Military Spending?', iSideWith, ongoing online survey begun 5 December 2015, https://argentina.isidewith.com/en/poll/1549397788.

34 See generally Andres Schipani, 'Opinion: G20 and the Painful Price of Argentina's Tumultuous Past', *Financial Times*, 29 November 2018, https://www.ft.com/content/4a511e32-deb4-11e8-b173-ebef6ab1374a.

Building Franco-German Consensus on Arms Exports

Lucie Béraud-Sudreau

The consolidation of European defence industries is a key element of more capable European defence. But industry needs markets, the fragmented domestic European markets are insufficient, and European arms companies quickly run into the problem of different export policies and cultures among European Union member states. Differences between French and German policies are singularly vexing, in part because they are far less political in France than they are in Germany. A better-coordinated Franco-German approach to arms exports would facilitate the development of future weapons programmes and strengthen European defence.

The differences are not new. In 1971, the Stockholm International Peace Research Institute (SIPRI) characterised France as an 'industrial exporter', preoccupied mainly by maintaining its defence industry, which meant arms were supplied 'indiscriminately to any recipient which can afford to pay for them'. In contrast, West Germany was 'restrictive' towards countries at war.[1] Twenty years later, Keith Krause, distinguishing between the French and Japanese models of second-tier arms suppliers, indicated that these predispositions had continued. The United Kingdom, Italy and Spain followed the permissive French model; Canada, Sweden, Switzerland and West Germany the more restrictive Japanese one.[2]

Lucie Béraud-Sudreau is Research Fellow for Defence Economics and Procurement at the IISS, responsible for the collection and assessment of data on defence budgets and the defence industry for *The Military Balance* and Military Balance+.

Survival | vol. 61 no. 4 | August–September 2019 | pp. 79–98   DOI 10.1080/00396338.2019.1637124

The biases have continued, and are especially consequential in cases involving exports from jointly developed armaments programmes or components produced in one country that are integrated into export-able weapons systems of another.[3] In 2012, German authorities prevented exports to Saudi Arabia by Nexter, France's main land-weapons manu-facturer.[4] In 2014 and 2015, French media also accused Germany of vetoing MBDA Systems contracts with Qatar and Airbus contracts with Uzbekistan.[5] Since 2015, when Saudi-led military operations in Yemen in support of the Yemeni government began, and even more emphatically since the murder of *Washington Post* journalist Jamal Khashoggi in October 2018, Berlin has reportedly blocked exports to Saudi Arabia related to a number of joint programmes with France and other countries, such as the Eurofighter *Typhoon, Meteor* missiles, A330 tanker aircraft, the H145 heli-copter and the CASA C295 transport aircraft.[6] According to the French ambassador in Berlin, Germany has also denied export licences for prod-ucts to India and Niger.[7]

The existing bilateral agreement on arms exports – known as the Schmidt–Debré letter and signed by German defence minister Helmut Schmidt in 1971 and French defence minister Michel Debré in 1972 – is now considered obsolete because of Germany's position on arms deals involv-ing joint programmes with third countries and its slow-rolling of licences for supplying German sub-components for French programmes. Under Article 2 of the letter, neither of the two governments can prevent the other from exporting to third countries military equipment that results from joint projects. Each country also committed to allowing delivery of components for jointly produced armaments to the other except in 'exceptional' circum-stances.[8] Some French defence companies have begun replacing German sub-components such as gearboxes or engines to circumvent Germany's more restrictive export policy.[9] While this position is at odds with the pro-European approach of French President Emmanuel Macron's admin-istration, the fact remains that France's long-standing apolitical approach to arms exports has become an obstacle to deepened defence cooperation with its main European partner and is impeding France's goal of building a European defence-industrial base.

Given industrial consolidation across Europe – for instance, the corporate affiliation of Krauss-Maffei Wegmann (KMW) and Nexter under a single holding company and the joint venture between Naval Group and Fincantieri – the number of joint armaments projects in Europe is set to increase. France and Germany are also launching new weapons projects, notably a Future Combat Air System with Spain and a new Main Ground Combat System. The recently established European Defence Fund and Permanent Structured Cooperation are designed to encourage intergovernmental defence collaboration and cooperation in armaments programmes. If they are to succeed, greater mutual trust and reliability with respect to arms-export controls will become even more crucial.

Bureaucratic and industrial similarities

In a number of legal, procedural and industrial respects, France and Germany are similar. In theory at least, this should be conducive to mutual trust on arms-export issues.[10] Both countries have undertaken similar international commitments. At the EU level, the most important framework is the Common Position 2008/944/CFSP, which originated from a Code of Conduct on Arms Exports adopted in 1998. The Common Position lists eight criteria that member states should apply when assessing arms-export licences, ranging from the human-rights situation in the country of destination to risks of the diversion of the arms in question. Its implementation entails consultation among member states within the Working Party on Conventional Arms Exports. If an EU member state aims to export a product to a country to which such a product was denied earlier by another member state, it should justify its position.

At the multilateral level, a 1998 Letter of Intent, incorporated as a treaty by the Farnborough Framework Agreement in 2000, created a forum in which the six parties (France, Germany, Italy, Spain, Sweden and the UK) could discuss technical and political aspects of arms exports. The primary objective was to reduce barriers to the establishment of intra-European defence groups that were then emerging. For exports of products of joint programmes, the six countries agreed on lists of recipients 'by consensus'.[11] Countries could be removed from the agreed lists in the event of 'significant changes' in the recipient country's internal situation, including a 'serious deterioration of the human rights situation'. The Farnborough Framework Agreement also contemplated harmonising and simplifying licencing procedures for exports between the parties. At the international level, France and Germany ratified the Arms Trade Treaty, adopted by the UN General Assembly in 2013. The treaty lists criteria, largely tracking the European regulations, for assessing industry export-licencing requests. Other notable agreements include the Missile Technology Control Regime, the Wassenaar Arrangement, the Australia Group, the Nuclear Suppliers Group, the Anti-Personnel Mine Ban Convention, the Convention on Cluster Munitions and the Convention on Certain Conventional Weapons.

France and Germany follow similar procedures

Domestically, France and Germany follow very similar export-control procedures. At the administrative level, the process is inter-ministerial in both countries, and for the most sensitive and controversial cases, decisions are made at the highest political level.

In France, there is an elaborate process for approving an arms-export sale known, in French, as the 'Commission interministérielle pour l'étude des exportations de matériels de guerre' (in English, inter-ministerial commission for the study of the export of war materials), or CIEEMG. Defence companies apply for export licences to the Ministry of the Armed Forces' Directorate General of Armaments (DGA). Within the ministry, the strategic directorate and the defence staff provide their own assessments, primarily as to the defence relationship with the customer and the safety of French armed forces in operations. The licence is also circulated to the Ministry of Foreign Affairs, which assesses it from a diplomatic point of view. The Ministry for the Economy and Finance examines the request in light of the recipient country's economic capacity and debt levels, particularly if France plans to extend a loan to facilitate the sale. While routine decisions are made through an electronic procedure, the Secretariat-General for National Defence and Security (SGDSN), the inter-ministerial agency responsible for defence and security matters, convenes a formal monthly CIEEMG meeting of senior officials to address the more sensitive and contentious cases. When the participants cannot agree, or in cases of extraordinary economic importance or diplomatic sensitivity, the prime minister's office makes the decision. This is where it becomes acutely political. After each CIEEMG meeting, the prime minister convenes a post-CIEEMG meeting gathering the political staffs of the Ministry of the Armed Forces and the Ministry of Foreign Affairs, and the directors of the DGA's international directorate, the Directorate General for International Relations and Strategy and the SGDSN. If they too cannot agree, and the prime minister is compelled to decide himself, he endeavours to reach agreement with the French president.

In Germany as well, the administrative handling of licences is interministerial. While the Ministry for Economic Affairs and Energy (BMWi) oversees the licencing process for both categories of defence product, it elicits input from the ministries of defence, foreign affairs, finance and interior.[12] The specific bureaucratic route that licence applications follow depends on whether the products to be exported are 'war weapons' (*Kriegswaffen*) or 'other military equipment' (*sonstige Rüstungsgüter*). War weapons are in the first instance presumed to be prohibited and non-exportable, while items in the category of other military equipment are considered free-trade goods and initially presumed to be exportable. If the BMWi grants a licence for the export of war weapons, further authorisation is required from the Office for Economic Affairs and Export Control (BAFA), though it is usually pro forma. For 'other military equipment', BAFA first assesses whether the potential export requires a licence or not. If that agency rules that a licence is needed, the BMWi, in consultation with the Ministry of Foreign Affairs and sometimes the Ministry of Defence, decides whether to grant the licence. In case of disagreements within or between the BMWi and BAFA, licence requests are sent up to the state secretaries, the second-highest-ranking ministerial officials. As in France, if the case is especially sensitive or complex and they cannot agree, the Federal Security Council, composed of the respective ministers, is asked to decide the matter, with the chancellor presiding. If the ministers cannot agree, the chancellor makes the decision.

The French and German arms-export policy regimes are also comparable in terms of the economic importance of exports to their

Figure 1: **French, German and trans-European companies' defence-related revenue (2017)**

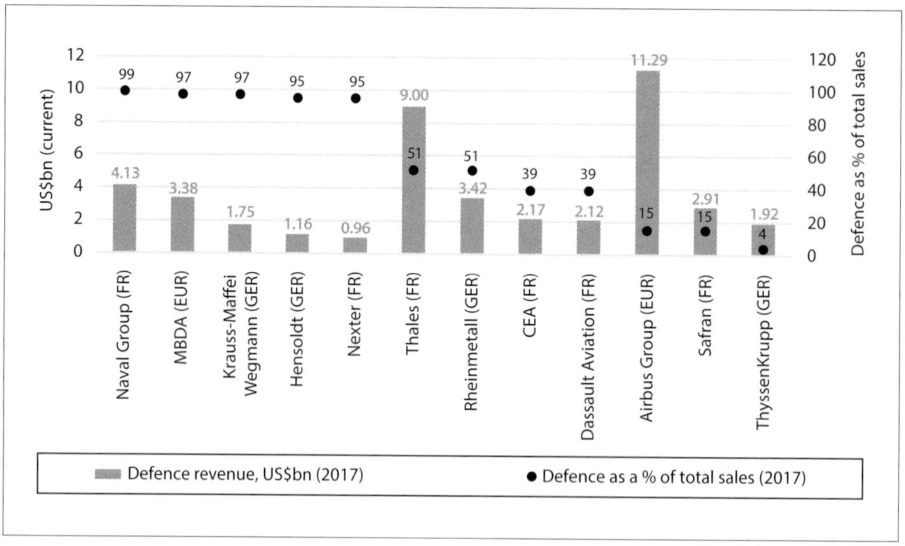

Source: SIPRI Top 100 database, accessed May 2019

respective arms industries. Both countries are home to some of the largest defence companies in the world, as shown in SIPRI's annual Top 100 ranking of arms-producing and military services.[13] Companies such as Naval Group, KMW, Hensoldt and Nexter are almost entirely defence-focused, with 95% or more of their annual turnover reliant on defence (see Figure 1). To compare French and German companies' reliance on exports, I used arms orders and deliveries of major conventional weapons, for both domestic and foreign procurements, available on the Military Balance+ database. The database allows us to determine the share of exports in total orders per company by the number of orders (see Table 1). Based on the existing sample, French and German defence companies appear similarly

Table 1: **Proportion of domestic and foreign orders for French and German defence companies**

	France		Germany	
	Prime contractors	Subcontractors	Prime contractors	Subcontractors
Total orders	76	106	56	120
Domestic orders	17	12	18	10
Foreign orders	59	94	38	110
% Exports	78	89	68	92

Source: IISS Military Balance + database, accessed May 2019[14]

dependent on arms exports, with a particularly high level of dependence when positioned as subcontractors. For Airbus, a group in which the French, German and Spanish governments are key stakeholders, out of the 76 orders listed by the group or its subsidiaries in the database, 60, or 79%, were outside these three markets.

Political differences

As they did throughout the de Gaulle era, the main political parties in France broadly support arms exports, which are seen as a means of financing national strategic autonomy. During the 2017 presidential campaign, Amnesty International France asked the candidates to sign a list of ten human-rights commitments. One was to 'conform French exports of arms, security and related equipment to the Arms Trade Treaty'. Marine Le Pen, president of the right-wing National Front, and former centre-right prime minister François Fillon simply did not respond. La République En Marche!'s Macron, the eventual winner, signed the commitment with no comment, and did not adopt any explicit public position on arms exports apart from mentioning 'export successes' in an interview.[15] Leaked emails revealed that his team preferred continuity with the traditional arms-export policy.[16] The Socialist Party candidate Benoît Hamon not only signed but also specified that 'I want France to be exemplary on abiding by the treaty on this topic. France should not, through this means [arms sales], facilitate the violation of human rights and international law.'[17] Yet Hamon did not publicly insist on limiting arms sales during the campaign, and his manifesto advocated observing environmental norms in arms manufacturing to make them 'more autonomous and therefore more attractive for exports'.[18] While the Green Party and Communist Party traditionally adopt more restrictive stances on arms exports, they have little power and in any event have not dwelled on the subject. Since taking office, prominent figures in the Macron administration have generally dismissed changing the course of France's arms-sales policy.[19]

In Germany, the issue features more prominently in electoral campaigns. While neither the centrist Christian Democratic Union (CDU) nor the right-wing Alternative for Germany (AfD) brought up the arms trade in the 2017 election season, the left-wing populist Die Linke party claimed its goal was 'to prohibit armament exports and stop all arms production' in the country, and the Green Party promised to 'stop arms exports in crisis areas and in states with a highly problematic human-rights situation'.[20] In 2007, the Social Democratic Party (SPD) committed to 'a strict arms-export policy'.[21] Its restrictive stance became part of the CDU/CSU–SPD coalition agreements. In 2013, the two main parties agreed that there should be 'restraint' in armament exports and promised increased transparency.[22] The SPD's 2017 manifesto defended recently enacted arms-export-control reforms; supported the 'containment' of arms exports; noted that the SPD had implemented 'the most transparent and restrictive arms-export policy that has ever existed in the history of the Federal Republic'; pledged to introduce a ban on small-arms exports to non-EU or non-NATO countries; and advocated a more harmonised and restrictive arms-export policy in Europe.[23] The coalition agreement adopted in February 2018 stated that under the new government, Germany would not licence any more arms sales to states involved in the war in Yemen, and would tighten its political guidelines on arms exports.[24]

French and German newspapers also do not frame the issue in the same way.[25] Previous academic research has looked at French and German newspaper coverage of arms transactions with Saudi Arabia between 2007 and 2012 across a broad political spectrum, examining Germany's sale of 200 *Leopard-2* main battle tanks in 2011 and France's contract to overhaul four *Al-Medinah* frigates and two *Boradia* oil-supply ships in 2013.[26] In France, the contract was mentioned in only three articles. None discussed human-rights aspects of the deal, looking instead at its economic and industrial dimensions. In Germany, by contrast, the sale of the tanks sparked strong media coverage and public debate. Some 40 articles were published regarding the sale, 36 of them discussing human-rights issues and existing export-control rules. Prompted by intense campaigning by non-governmental organisations (NGOs) and investigative journalism regarding the war in Yemen, however, the French media have recently intensified their coverage of arms-export issues, incorporating an approach more sensitive to human rights.[27]

France's Assemblée Nationale has no substantial involvement in the arms-export-control process. It receives relevant substantive information only after the government has granted the licences, in an annual report on arms exports. That report is the only tool available to legislators for influencing the government's arms-export policy decisions, and they have made little use of it.[28] But Florence Parly, minister of the armed forces since 2017, has personally presented the report to the Assembly and Senate defence committees. This has prompted legislators to ask a number of questions related to human rights and French foreign-policy choices.[29] Left-of-centre parties are becoming increasingly vocal on the issue, demanding more transparency.[30]

The German Bundestag is not directly involved in the export-control process. But its members have been vastly more proactive than France's on the issue. MPs posed 28 parliamentary questions on the process in 2017, and 48 in 2016.[31] Most, to be sure, came from Die Linke and the Green Party. But activist legislators

Leftist parties are becoming more vocal

have leveraged their modest powers of oversight by using the judicial process. In 2011, three Green Party representatives petitioned the Federal Constitutional Court to require the Federal Security Council to provide MPs with more information on licencing decisions. In 2014, the court ruled that once licences had been approved, although the Federal Security Council did not have to justify its decision, it was obliged to provide the legislators with details on request.[32] The government then decided to inform the Bundestag on licencing decisions not only if MPs requested it, but on its own initiative after each licencing session. It has also published all licencing decisions on arms exports since 2002.[33] As a result, although the French government provides data for the value of all its arms deliveries and the German government only for war weapons, the Bundestag is generally much better informed about political decision-making on arms exports than the Assemblée Nationale (see Table 2 and Figure 2). However, in April 2018, French MP Sébastien Nadot, then affiliated with Macron's La République En Marche! and now an independent, called for a parliamentary inquiry into French arms sales related to the war in Yemen.[34] La République En

Table 2: **Substantive aspects of information on arms exports, France and Germany**

	France	Germany
Level of reporting	Country of destination	Country of destination
Types of licences reported	Individual & global	Individual & global
Information on end users	No info	No info
Information on refused licences	Aggregated by geographical area and country	Yes
Value of actual arms exports	Country of destination	Export war weapons and surplus defence materials
Additional substantive information	• Gifts by defence ministry by country of destination and value • Approved re-export per country of end use, military list (EU) and number of applications • Export small arms and light weapons by country of destination, description of the product and number	Export small arms and light weapons to non-EU and non-NATO countries
Categorisation of goods	Military list (EU)	National

Figure 2: **Transparency and parliamentary involvement in arms-export control in Europe**

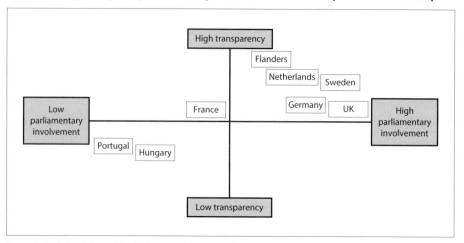

Source for Table 2 and Figure 2: Diederik Cops, Nils Duquet and Gregory Gourdin, 'Scrutinizing Arms Exports in Europe: Reciprocal Relationship Between Transparency and Parliamentary Control', *Sicherheit und Frieden*, vol. 35, no. 2, January 2019, pp. 79–84

Marche!'s majority inhibited this effort, downgrading it to a less powerful *'mission d'information'*.[35] Overall, the French assembly is slowly moving towards a more activist oversight role.[36]

Transparency is also greater in Germany due to the promulgation of the political norms that the government applies when assessing export-licence applications, which allows export decisions to be challenged on the basis of confirmed official information. In France, by contrast, the political criteria for licencing decisions are not revealed. Such criteria are released exclusively in classified internal CIEEMG documents known as 'high-level government directives', and have been disclosed only once, in a 2000 parliamentary report.[37] Like other EU member states, France committed to use the EU 2008 Common Position criteria in its licencing process. In practice, however, the French government has so far refused, over NGOs' and some MPs' objections, to incorporate those criteria into its domestic legislation.[38]

For its part, Germany published political criteria in 1982, updating them in 2000. They are applied differently to EU and NATO members, and to NATO-equivalent countries such as Australia, New Zealand, Japan and Switzerland, on the one hand, and 'other countries' on the other.[39] The former enjoy a presumption of approval of the licence, while the latter face a presumption of denial. Accordingly, for arms exports to non-EU, NATO or NATO-equivalent countries, a licence must be justified by 'special foreign policy or security policy interests' of Germany. The guidelines also stress the 'special interest' in developing armaments programmes in cooperation with EU and NATO states.[40] Germany's political principles incorporate the Common Position, but appear to be more restrictive. Whereas the EU rule is to not grant a licence when there is a 'clear risk' that the exported products would be used in human-rights violations, the German framework requires disapproval merely on the basis of 'sufficient suspicion'. The German guidelines also state that Germany 'will raise objections' to joint-programme exports using German products to countries involved in armed conflict; where an outbreak of armed conflict is imminent; where exports may stir up, perpetuate or exacerbate latent tensions and conflicts; or where there are reasonable grounds for suspecting they may be used for internal repression or abuse of human rights.

On balance, while the German contention that France does not have serious export-control processes is an exaggeration, France does lag behind Germany in the degree of political and ethical scrutiny it applies to licencing decisions. In France, however, the war in Yemen has precipitated heightened parliamentary concern, media coverage and NGO activism that have produced a marginal increase in government scrutiny. Accordingly, there appears to be some momentum behind convergence between the French and German positions on arms exports.

Building consensus

For convergence to progress, Germany would need political reassurances from France on how it deals with export controls, while France would require greater predictability on Germany's part. With the Schmidt–Debré letter effectively dead, a new arrangement should logically be tied to the bilateral Aachen/Aix-la-Chapelle Treaty of January 2019. The treaty indicates that 'the two states will formulate a common approach on arms exports for joint projects'.[41] Although this remains a vague objective, a 'binding agreement', as an appendix to the treaty, is reportedly under discussion, with the French hoping that Germany does not insist on an overly restrictive approach to future common programmes.[42] According to media reports on a leaked version of the document, each government has agreed to inform the other in advance of export opportunities, and will oppose exports to third countries only if they would affect its direct interests or national security. In that event, the two countries would undertake high-level consultations to identify solutions. In cases involving the integration of sub-components from one state to the other's weapons programmes, a threshold rule would apply. The supplying country could deny the licence only if it produces more than a certain portion – reportedly 20% – of the total system. France and Germany also agreed to establish a permanent bilateral framework for consultations on arms-export policy issues.[43]

Germany has long favoured greater European harmonisation on export controls, reiterating this preference in its 2016 Defence White Paper.[44] France has regarded supranational political responsibility for arms exports as an impingement on its national sovereignty, as well as a potential detriment to its defence industry. Yet a more Europeanised policy could also hold advantages for France and other European countries. In the early 2000s, the creation of transnational defence companies gave impetus to a more consolidated and integrated European defence market. There is now increased tension between transnational consolidation and national policy considerations, substantially due to the Franco-German spat and also Germany's opposition to UK export of Eurofighter *Typhoon* aircraft.[45] Yet France itself has long been calling for a 'Europe of defence'. Such a position clearly requires Paris to accept more compromises and interdependence on arms-export controls. This, of course, is hardly unprecedented. EU arms embargoes have targeted specific countries. These include the 1989 political statement that underpinned national embargoes against China following the Tiananmen Square massacre,[46] and the 2014 embargo against Russia after its illegal annexation of Crimea and initiation of armed conflict in eastern Ukraine.

As a precondition to developing joint armaments programmes and facilitating the Europeanisation of defence supply chains, EU member states could strengthen their common export-policy rules. For industry, this would reduce uncertainty, decrease compliance costs and eliminate current variations among national export-control policies. For states, it would preclude the dislocations of 'licence shopping' on the part of industry. The European Parliament has put forward some ideas for the further development of the 2008 Common Position, inspired by SIPRI recommendations. Suggestions include establishing a peer-review process for licencing decisions and procedures, similar to existing practices for dual-use goods; improving the EU common report as well as national reports; enhancing the exchange of information; and generating a comprehensive review of the Common Position criteria and the User's Guide.[47] Additional measures could include 'white lists' of recipient countries agreed by partners on joint armaments projects – as contemplated by the Farnborough Framework Agreement, for instance – or the institutionalisation of licencing procedures by EU entities such as the European Defence Agency.

*   *   *

With an eye to energising movement in this direction, Paris might consider softening its stance. The strongest signal it could send to Germany and other EU member states would be to unilaterally renounce Saudi Arabia and the United Arab Emirates as markets for its defence products – that is, to impose a temporary embargo, as Germany has already done. This would make it politically easier for German authorities to defend broad arms-export cooperation with France down the road. But Saudi

Arabia was France's second-largest market for arms orders between 2009 and 2018. In 2017, Saudi Arabia accounted for 10% of French arms orders, and 20% of its deliveries.[48] Accordingly, this step would be a difficult one for the French government to take – all the more so in that it would contradict France's customary position that it does not sell weapons with conditions attached.

A more modest option would be to increase the Assemblée Nationale's involvement in arms-export-control processes. Several models could inspire French reforms. In the United States, Congress is notified of an export sale prior to its final authorisation if the amount of the sale is above a designated threshold, and is allowed to block or modify the sale up to the point of delivery.[49] In Sweden, the independent agency in charge of processing licences can elicit non-binding advice on sensitive licences from a parliamentary committee.[50] This example might inspire the French government to allow MPs to attend the CIEEMG meeting. And, in the UK, the Committee on Arms Export Controls assembles MPs from four select committees (defence, foreign affairs, international development and international trade) to assess the government's arms-export policy. Although its scrutiny is retrospective, it can inform future legislation.

More quietly still, the French government could simply increase the transparency of existing decision-making processes, aligning its practices with those of Germany. For instance, France could make public its political guidelines, or the CIEEMG could also provide more information about its decisions, as Germany's Federal Security Council does. France could also propose steps to advance bilateral dialogue and consultations in order to increase mutual trust. The Aachen Treaty appendix already contemplates the creation of a joint consultation body as a potential way forward.[51]

Franco-German political friction on arms exports reflects the EU's larger difficulties in the realm of foreign and security policy. Assuming that both governments are committed to developing deeper and better-integrated European defence, as they have indicated, each needs to move towards compromise, and not to insist on concessions that will be unacceptable to the other. This kind of cooperation would strengthen European defence.

Notes

1 Stockholm International Peace Research Institute (SIPRI), *The Arms Trade with the Third World* (Stockholm and New York: Almqvist & Wiksell and Humanities Press, 1971), p. 17.

2 See Keith Krause, *Arms and the State: Patterns of Military Production and Trade* (Cambridge: Cambridge University Press, 1992).

3 Lucie Béraud-Sudreau, 'War in Yemen: European Divisions on Arms-export Controls', Military Balance Blog, 20 March 2018, https://www.iiss.org/blogs/military-balance/2018/03/war-yemen-european-arms-export; and Lucie Béraud-Sudreau, 'War in Yemen: European Divisions on Arms-export Controls Continue', Military Balance Blog, 25 October 2018, https://www.iiss.org/blogs/military-balance/2018/10/yemen-arms-export-divisions-continue.

4 Laurent Lagneau, 'Berlin met des bâtons dans les roues de Nexter', opex360.com, 22 December 2012, http://www.opex360.com/2012/12/22/berlin-met-des-batons-dans-les-roues-de-nexter/.

5 'Un premier pas', *TTU Lettre d'informations stratégiques et de défense*, 26 January 2015; Jean-Dominique Merchet, 'L'industrie française de l'armement est l'otage de la coalition allemande', *L'Opinion*, 27 October 2014, https://www.lopinion.fr/blog/secret-defense/l-industrie-francaise-l-armement-est-l-otage-coalition-allemande-17749; and Bertrand Slaski and Frederik Schuman, 'Coopération franco-allemande dans l'industrie de défense: Bilan et perspectives', *Les notes stratégiques*, CEIS, June 2015.

6 Michel Cabirol, 'Eurofighter, A330 MRTT, Casa C295, H145 … bloqués à l'export: Berlin fragilise Airbus', *La Tribune*, 25 February 2019, https://www.latribune.fr/entreprises-finance/industrie/aeronautique-defense/eurofighter-a330-mrtt-casa-c295-h145-bloques-a-l-export-berlin-fragilise-airbus-808239.html.

7 Anne-Marie Descôtes, 'Vom "German-free" zum gegenseitigen Vertrauen', Bundesakademie für Sicherheitspolitik, Arbeitspapier no. 7/2019, March 2019, https://www.baks.bund.de/de/arbeitspapiere/2019/vom-german-free-zum-gegenseitigen-vertrauen.

8 See 'Accord entre le Gouvernement de la République Fédérale d'Allemagne et le Gouvernement de la République Française sur les exportations vers les pays tiers des matériels d'armement développés et/ou produits en coopération', available (in French) at http://www.assemblee-nationale.fr/rap-info/i2334.asp, as an appendix to Jean-Claude Sandrier, Christian Martin and Alain Veyret, 'Contrôle des exportations d'armement', Rapport d'information déposé par la Commission de la Défense Nationale et des Forces Armées, Assemblée Nationale, 25 April 2000.

9 Assemblée Nationale, 'Audition de Monsieur Stéphane Mayer, président-directeur général de Nexter', 15 May 2019, http://www.assemblee-nationale.fr/15/cr-cdef/18-19/c1819034.asp.

10 This section builds on work the author undertook with Samuel Faure and

Michael Sladeczeck in 2015. See Lucie Béraud-Sudreau, Samuel B.H. Faure and Michael Sladeczeck, 'Réguler le commerce des armes par le Parlement et l'opinion publique. Comparaison du contrôle des exportations d'armement en Allemagne, France, Royaume-Uni et Suède', *Politique européenne*, no. 48, 2015/2, pp. 82–121.

11 'Framework Agreement Between the French Republic, the Federal Republic of Germany, the Italian Republic, the Kingdom of Spain, the Kingdom of Sweden, and the United Kingdom of Great Britain and Northern Ireland Concerning Measures to Facilitate the Restructuring and Operation of the European Defence Industry', Farnborough, 27 July 2000, https:// assets.publishing.service.gov. uk/government/uploads/system/ uploads/attachment_data/file/518178/ TS0033_2001.pdf.

12 'Report by the Government of the Federal Republic of Germany on Its Policy of Exports of Conventional Military Equipment in 2017', September 2018, https://www.bmwi. de/Redaktion/EN/Publikationen/ Aussenwirtschaft/2017-military-equipment-export-report. pdf?__blob=publicationFile&v=2.

13 SIPRI Arms Industry Database, 'SIPRI Top 100 for 2002–17', https://www. sipri.org/databases/armsindustry.

14 French companies listed in the Military Balance+ include ACMAT; Areva TA; Arianespace; Armaris; Arquus (formerly Renault Trucks Defense); Astrium; ATR; Babcock Mission Critical Services France (BMCSF); Cegelec Défense et Naval Sud-Est; CFM International; Chantiers de l'Atlantique; CNN MCO; Constructions Industrielles de la Méditerranée (CNIM); Constructions Mécaniques de Normandie (CMN); Couach; Dassault Aviation; DCI; ECA Group; Europrop International; Eurosam; EuroTorp; GME; H2X; Helicopter Engines Maintenance, Repair and Overhaul Services (HE-MRO); Kership; MAURIC; Naval Group (formerly DCNS); Nexter; NHIndustries; OCEA; Piriou; Plascoa; Raidco Marine; Rolls-Royce Turbomeca (RRTM); Sabena Technics; Safran; Safran Aircraft Engines (formerly Snecma); Safran Helicopter Engines; Sagem; Sapura Thales Electronics (STE); Socarenam; Sofema; STX Europe; STX France; Texelis; Thales; Thales Alenia Space; ThalesRaytheonSystems; and Volvo-Renault Trucks. German companies listed in the Military Balance+ include Abeking & Rasmussen; Aerodata; Airbus DS Optronics; ARTEC; Atlas Elektronik; Blohm+Voss; Deutz; Diehl; Diehl Aerosystems; Diehl Defence; Ecarys; Eurofighter; EuroJet Turbo; EuroSpike; Fassmer; Ferrostaal; Flensburger Fahrzeugbau Gesellschaft (FFG); German Naval Yards Kiel; Grob Aircraft AG; Hensoldt; Howaldtswerke-Deutsche Werft (HDW); IBD Deisenroth Engineering; Krauss-Maffei Wegmann (KMW); Lürssen Werft; MAN Energy Solutions (formerly MAN Diesel & Turbo); MTU Friedrichshafen; OHB System AG; Projekt System & Management (PSM); RAM-System; Raytheon Anschütz; RENK; Rheinland Air Service (RAS); Rheinmetall; Rheinmetall MAN Military Vehicles (RMMW);

Siemens; Stemme; TAURUS Systems; Thales Deutschland; ThyssenKrupp Marine Systems (TKMS); and ZF Friedrichshafen.

15 Emmanuel Macron, 'La Défense de la France: Le Prix de la Liberté', pp. 43–8, in 'Présidentielle: Questions de Défense', *Revue Défense Nationale*, no. 799, April 2017, p. 47.

16 Leaked campaign email, WikiLeaks, 24 October 2016, https://wikileaks.org/macron-emails/emailid/55103. There is an accompanying note on arms exports: see https://wikileaks.org/macron-emails//fileid/50541/18127.

17 Amnesty International France, 'Les engagements des candidats', 11 April 2017, https://www.amnesty.fr/actualites/candidats-2017.

18 Benoît Hamon, 'Mon projet pour la politique de défense de la France', speech in Strasbourg, 23 March 2017, https://www.benoithamon2017.fr/wp-content/uploads/2017/03/Benoit-Hamon-Mon-projet-pour-la-politique-de-la-Defense-de-la-France.pdf.

19 France Info, 'Ventes d'armes à l'Arabie saoudite: "Je ne vois pas pourquoi ce serait interdit", explique Richard Ferrand, qui évoque "des relations de confiance"', 9 April 2018, https://twitter.com/franceinfo/status/983600013233278976/video/1; Europe 1, 'Les ventes d'armes à l'Arabie saoudite, "un intérêt clair" pour la France, selon Griveaux', 9 April 2018, http://www.europe1.fr/economie/les-ventes-darmes-a-larabie-saoudite-un-interet-clair-pour-la-france-selon-griveaux-3622352.

20 CDU/CSU, 'Für ein Deutschland, in dem wir gut und gerne leben',

Regierungsprogramm 2017–2021, July 2017, https://www.cdu.de/system/tdf/media/dokumente/170703regierungsprogramm2017.pdf?file=1; Alternative für Deutschland, 'Programm für Deutschland. Wahlprogramm der Alternative für Deutschland für die Wahl zum Deutschen Bundestag am 24. September 2017', April 2017, https://www.afd.de/wp-content/uploads/sites/111/2017/06/2017-06-01_AfD-Bundestagswahlprogramm_Onlinefassung.pdf; Die Linke, 'Wahlprogramm der Partei Die Linke zur Bundestagswahl 2017', June 2017, p. 96, https://www.die-linke.de/fileadmin/download/wahlen2017/wahlprogramm2017/die_linke_wahlprogramm_2017.pdf; and Bündnis 90/Grünen, 'Zukunft Wird Aud Mut Gemacht. Bundestagswahlprogramm 2017', June 2017, p. 101, https://www.handelsblatt.com/downloads/20108316/1/buendnis_90_die_gruenen_bundestagswahlprogramm_2017_barrierefrei.pdf.

21 SPD, 'Hamburg Programme, Principal Guidelines of the Social Democratic Party of Germany', 28 October 2007, p. 14, https://www.spd.de/fileadmin/Dokumente/Beschluesse/Grundsatzprogramme/hamburger_programm_englisch.pdf.

22 Konrad-Adenauer-Stiftung e.V., 'Shaping Germany's Future: Coalition Treaty Between CDU/CSU and SPD', 18th legislative period, February 2014, pp. 7, 9, non-official translation available at https://www.kas.de/c/document_library/get_file?uuid=d58641a0-02ab-935a-c295-1148b45cc426&groupId=252038.

23 SPD, 'Zeit für mehr Gerechtigkeit. Unser Regierungsprogramm für Deutschland', pp. 104–5, https://www.spd.de/fileadmin/ Dokumente/Regierungsprogramm/ SPD_Regierungsprogramm_ BTW_2017_A5_RZ_WEB.pdf.

24 'Ein neur Aufbruch für Europa, eine neue Dynamik für Deutschland, eine neuer Zusammenhalt für unser Land, Koalitionsvertrag zwischen CDU, CSU und SPD, 19 Legislaturperiode', March 2018, p. 149, https://www.cdu. de/system/tdf/media/dokumente/ koalitionsvertrag_2018.pdf?file=1.

25 Béraud-Sudreau, Faure and Sladeczek, 'Réguler le commerce des armes par le Parlement et l'opinion publique: Comparaison du contrôle des exportations d'armement en Allemagne, France, Royaume-Uni et Suède', pp. 99–103.

26 The German newspapers selected were the *Frankfurter Allgemeine Zeitung*, *Süddeutsche Zeitung* and *Tages Zeitung*. The French ones were *Le Figaro*, *Le Monde* and *Libération*.

27 In 2018, a coalition of NGOs (including Action des Chrétiens pour l'Abolition de la Torture, Amnesty International France) asked for legal advice on French arms transfers in the context of the war in Yemen, between April 2015 to March 2018. The report was made public. See Joseph Breham and Laurence Greig, 'Les transfers d'armes de la France dans le cadre du conflit au Yémen, à compter d'avril 2015 jusqu'à la période actuelle', *Ancile Avocats*, 16 March 2018, https://amnestyfr.cdn.prismic. io/amnestyfr%2Fb2bf59b9-cd8e-471f-a689-e8e84f151b17_etude+juridique_

cabinet+ancile_transfert+d%27arme s+de+la+france+dans+le+cadre+du+ conflit+au+y%C3%A9men.pdf; and Disclose, 'Made in France', https:// made-in-france.disclose.ngo/en/.

28 Author interview, French NGO representative, April 2013.

29 Commission de la défense nationale et des forces armées, 'Audition de Mme Florence Parly, ministre des Armées, sur le rapport au Parlement sur les exportations d'armement de la France', 4 July 2018, http:// www.assemblee-nationale.fr/15/ cr-cdef/17-18/c1718070.asp; and Commission de la défense nationale et des forces armées, 'Audition de Mme Florence Parly, ministre des Armées, sur les opérations en cours et les exportations d'armement', 7 May 2019, http://www.assemblee-nationale.fr/15/ cr-cdef/18-19/c1819032.asp.

30 AFP, 'La gauche réclame la "transparence" sur la vente d'armes au Yémen', *L'Obs*, 15 April 2019, https://www.nouvelobs.com/ politique/20190415.OBS11593/ la-gauche-reclame-la-transparence-sur-la-vente-d-armes-au-yemen.html.

31 'Schriftliche Fragen', Waffenexporte. org, October 2017, http:// www.waffenexporte.org/ category/deutscher_bundestag/ schriftliche_fragen/.

32 Bundesverfassungsgericht, 'Right of Bundestag Members to Be Informed of Exports of Military Equipment After the Federal Security Council Has Granted Permits', Press Release No. 91/2014, 21 October 2014, https:// www.bundesverfassungsgericht. de/SharedDocs/Pressemitteilungen/ EN/2014/bvg14-091.html.

33 BMWi, 'A Restrictive, Responsible Policy on the Export of Military Equipment', https://www.bmwi.de/Redaktion/EN/Dossier/export-controls-for-military-equipment.html.

34 Assemblée Nationale, 'Proposition de résolution tendant à la création d'une commission d'enquête sur le respect des engagements internationaux de la France au regard des autorisations d'exportations d'armes, munitions, formations, services et assistance accordées ces trois dernières années aux belligérants du conflit au Yémen', 6 April 2018, http://www.assemblee-nationale.fr/15/propositions/pion0856.asp.

35 See Assemblée Nationale, 'Contrôle des exportations d'armement', http://www2.assemblee-nationale.fr/15/commissions-permanentes/commission-des-affaires-etrangeres/missions-d-information/controle-des-exportations-d-armement/(block)/55065.

36 Manon Rescan, 'A l'Assemblée, des élus s'invitent dans le débat miné sur les ventes d'armes à l'Arabie saoudite', Le Monde, 8 June 2019, https://www.lemonde.fr/politique/article/2019/06/08/l-assemblee-s-invite-dans-le-debat-mine-sur-les-ventes-d-armes_5473357_823448.html.

37 Assemblée Nationale, 'Rapport d'information no 2334, déposé par la Commission de la Défense Nationale et des Forces Armées, sur le contrôle des exportations d'armement, et présenté par MM. Jean-Claude Sandrier, Christian Martin et Alain Veyret', 25 April 2000, http://www.assemblee-nationale.fr/rap-info/i2334.asp. For the CIEEMG export-control criteria, see pp.

30–3. See also Louis Gautier, La défense de la France après la guerre froide (Paris: Presses Universitaires de France, 2009), pp. 506–8.

38 'Twentieth Annual Report According to Article 8(2) of Council Common Position 2008/944/CFSP Defining Common Rules Governing the Control of Exports of Military Technology and Equipment', Official Journal of the European Union, C453/1, 14 December 2018, p. 521, https://eur-lex.europa.eu/legal-content/EN/TXT/PDF/?uri=OJ:C:2018:453:FULL&from=EN; and Assemblée Nationale, XIIIème Législature, 'Session ordinaire de 2010–2011, 161e séance, Compte-rendu intégral, 1ère séance du mardi 12 avril 2011', p. 2,462, http://www.assemblee-nationale.fr/13/pdf/cri/2010-2011/20110161.pdf.

39 John Nicolas Tecumseh Helferich, 'Arms Export Controls Under Siege of Globalisation: Defeated Nation States or Voluntary Surrender?', Master's thesis, Sciences Po, Paris, 2019.

40 Federal Government of Germany, Bundersministerium für Wirtschaft und Energie, 'Politische Grundsätze der Bundesregierung für den Export von Kriegswaffen und sonstigen Rüstungsgütern', April 2009, https://www.bmwi.de/Redaktion/DE/Downloads/A/aussenwirtschaftsrecht-grundsaetze.html.

41 French Ministry of Foreign Affairs, 'Traité entre la République française et la République fédérale d'Allemagne sur la coopération et l'intégration franco-allemandes', p. 5, https://www.diplomatie.gouv.fr/IMG/pdf/traite.aix-la-chapelle.22.01.2019_cle8d3c8e.pdf.

42 Douglas Barrie, 'Europe's Big Three

Manufacturers Expose Defence-export Discord', Military Balance Blog, 26 February 2019, https://www.iiss.org/blogs/military-balance/2019/02/europe-big-three-manufacturers.

43 'Deutsch-französisches Geheimpapier regelt Waffenexporte neu', *Der Spiegel*, 15 February 2019, https://www.spiegel.de/politik/deutschland/ruestungsexporte-deutsch-franzoesisches-geheimpapier-a-1253393.html; Jean-Dominique Merchet, 'Export d'armement: vers un seuil franco-allemand de 20%', *L'Opinion*, 18 February 2019, https://www.lopinion.fr/blog/secret-defense/export-d-armement-vers-seuil-franco-allemand-20-178252; and 'Joint Armaments Projects: German–French Secret Paper Reorganises Arms Exports', Defense-aerospace.com, 15 February 2019.

44 Federal Government of Germany, 'White Paper on German Security Policy and the Future of the Bundeswehr', July 2016, p. 74.

45 Barrie, 'Europe's Big Three Manufacturers Expose Defence-export Discord'.

46 Hugo Meijer, 'Transatlantic Perspectives on China's Military Modernization: The Case of Europe's Arms Embargo Against the People's Republic of China', *Paris Papers*, no. 12, October 2014.

47 Sibylle Bauer, Mark Bromley and Giovanna Maletta, 'The Further Development of the Common Position 944/2008/CFSP on Arms Exports Control', European Parliament, 16 July 2018, http://www.europarl.europa.eu/thinktank/en/document.html?reference=EXPO_STU(2018)603876.

48 French Ministry of the Armed Forces, 'Rapport au Parlement 2018 sur les exportations d'armement', July 2018, p. 92, https://www.defense.gouv.fr/actualites/articles/rapport-au-parlement-2018-sur-les-exportations-d-armement.

49 United States Defense Security Cooperation Agency, 'Arms Sales: Congressional Review Process', https://www.dsca.mil/resources/arms-sales-congressional-review-process.

50 Inspektionen för strategiska produkter, 'Våra råd', https://isp.se/om-isp/vara-rad/.

51 'A Franco-German Joint Parliament for Better EU Coordination', Euractiv, 21 March 2019, https://www.euractiv.com/section/politics/news/a-franco-german-joint-parliament-for-better-eu-coordination/.

Visions of Omani Reform

James Fromson and Steven Simon

Oman's place on the Arab world's periphery has long been its defining characteristic. Geographically, it is far removed from the calamities roiling the Levant. The conflict in Yemen is next door but feels worlds away from pristine Muscat. Oman's physical distance from the historic centres of Arab power made it a refuge for religious dissidents in Islam's early days; the country's majority Ibadi sect descends from the *khawarij*, Muslim puritans who rejected caliphal authority in favour of their own, more stringent inter-pretations. Since then much has changed, but Ibadism remains distinct from mainstream Sunnism. What is more, Oman's cultural imprint on the Arab world is light: the stereotype of a muted 'Omani nice', akin to Americans' putative appreciation of Minnesotans, is generally the limit of other Arabs' view of Omanis.

Unlike their flashier neighbours in Riyadh, Doha and Abu Dhabi, Omanis often wear this marginal status as a badge of honour. It has enabled Oman to maintain relative political neutrality in the region and to serve effectively and usefully as an honest broker in various disputes and negotiations, including the Joint Comprehensive Plan of Action – that is, the Iran nuclear deal.[1] Although Oman has cautiously granted the US Navy limited access to strategically important ports, the United States and Europe continue to

James Fromson is an MPA candidate at Princeton University's Woodrow Wilson School of Public and International Affairs, and held a David L. Boren Fellowship in Oman. **Steven Simon** is the John J. McCloy '16 Visiting Professor of History at Amherst College and served as a senior director on the National Security Council in the Clinton and Obama administrations.

Survival | vol. 61 no. 4 | August–September 2019 | pp. 99–116   DOI 10.1080/00396338.2019.1637117

value Oman's substantially neutral, mediatory role.[2] Yet the country's de facto foreign minister, Yusuf bin Alawi, has downplayed that role, calling reports of Omani facilitation of diplomatic contacts between Iran and the United States 'exaggerated'.[3] The government's overall aim is seemingly to cultivate Oman's 'sleepy sultanate' reputation so that little news – in either English or Arabic – emerges about the country.

The dearth of scholarly attention to Oman is notable, even by the minimal standards of research on Gulf monarchies. That political scientists and journalists face major official hurdles securing approvals from the Omani government is no coincidence; projects that touch on politically sensitive questions (a broadly defined category in the sultanate) are as unwelcome as they are in Saudi Arabia or the United Arab Emirates (UAE). The result is that very little of note is reported. Accordingly, our analysis depends on dozens of conversations with Omanis and expatriates in Muscat – from both government and the private sector – all of whom preferred to speak off the record due to their concerns about government reprisal.

Appearances can be deceiving. Despite Oman's cultivated quiet, the country holds more policy relevance than meets the eye. Existing journalism and think-tank analysis on Oman tends to focus on political epiphenomena – above all, the psychodrama of a possible leadership transition.[4] Academic work, by contrast, explores the country's social depth and history, but rarely attempts to draw conclusions of broader applicability. Both camps have largely missed the point that Oman's domestic politics and efforts at economic reform also have implications for its Gulf neighbours and, more broadly, for Western policy towards the Gulf.

Oman has, for years, been quietly confronting many of the same challenges of reform now faced by Saudi Arabia, Bahrain and others. Oman's fast-dwindling oil reserves have forced its government to acknowledge the need for reducing the economy's oil dependence. The country's struggle to do so is ominous both for its own prospects and for the longer-term trajectories of its supposedly reform-minded neighbours. The dynamics of Oman's political economy do shed light on the problematic scenarios the country may face, but they also illuminate the difficulty of reforming Gulf rentier states writ large. Thus, the stakes of understanding Oman are higher than commonly understood. A close American and British partner, Oman faces potentially dire consequences if it fails to adapt to its impending challenges. The mere possibility of such a result should grab the attention of Oman's more comfortable neighbours and remind Western policymakers that the seemingly surest of bets may not be so.

Origins

The historical process of Omani state-building reveals the architecture of Oman's development since 1970, while also showing why economic and political reforms have proven so difficult. One point, in particular, is essential: Sultan Qaboos bin Said Al Said's intensely personalistic form of autocracy and the country's economic dependence on oil rents are symbiotic, and were baked into the Omani state from the start. Together, they make Oman's political dispensation an archetypal example of the rentier social contract, in which the ruler as symbolic 'father' to the nation distributes non-tax wealth in exchange for political quiescence.[5]

After seizing power in 1970 with the help of British commandos, the young Sultan Qaboos faced twin challenges, lacking personal legitimacy as a ruler and having inherited a territory without a functioning state. Oman, at this point, was more an archipelago of regional, tribal and sectarian loyalties than an integrated nation. The country's southern Dhofar province was in the midst of a separatist insurgency, while the interior around Jabal Akhdar retained latent resentment toward the sultans of Muscat for having ended the political primacy of the Ibadi imams. What is more, having grown up virtually confined to his father's southern palace in Salalah, Qaboos had never set foot in Muscat and lacked the kinds of political and patronage networks required to corral Oman's fractious tribes and merchant elites. The state he inherited, such as it was, had almost no administrative capacity and ill-defined borders, and was dirt poor.

Oil-driven state-building offered Qaboos a solution to his twin problems of governance and legitimacy. Between 1969 and 1970, Omani state revenues increased nearly 40-fold from their early-1960s level.[6] (It is not coincidental that British interest in Oman and the value of Shell's concession in the country also peaked at this moment.) Although the oil revenues of richer neighbours dwarfed Oman's, its new wealth still enabled the young sultan to build an all-encompassing welfare state that provided government jobs to those who wanted them, new infrastructure in places that had seen little development for centuries and lucrative opportunities for Oman's commercial elite. By monopolising the distribution of oil rents, Qaboos ensured that Omanis' older loyalties – *asabiyyat* in Ibn Khaldun's formulation – had little chance of securing the benefits that siding with the emerging state would bring. That the central government was now most Omanis' primary source of sustenance and employment had an important homogenising effect on the population: being Omani became defined by one's interaction with the Omani state. As important, the handful of merchant elites who could have stymied Qaboos's ascent were successfully integrated into the new patronage machine. As loyal contractors to the sultan, they became the state's core.[7]

Expanding the reinvented Omani state's administrative reach was sufficient to break down older political reference points, but Qaboos needed to personalise this process if he were to legitimise his power. More than any other Gulf monarch, the sultan achieved this by building a weak bureaucracy in which all decision-making flowed through him. Unlike his royal peers in other Gulf countries, he also quietly but completely distanced his family from the levers of power. By becoming the state itself – arrogating to himself the positions of prime minister, commander of the armed forces, foreign minister and finance minister – Qaboos ensured that the benefits of state development would be seen as flowing exclusively from his magnanimity. Hefty payments made tribal and commercial elites personally invested in Qaboos's rule; their service to the ruler guaranteed more cash and government contracts. In 1970, the British consul general in Bahrain laid out the basis of Qaboos's legitimacy: 'Sayyid Qaboos made clear that his voice would predominate in military, financial and external affairs, and, he stressed, in the award of large commercial contracts.'[8] This is precisely what happened. The so-called *nahda* ('renaissance') narrative of Qaboos's rule held that the nation itself was redeemed through the sultan's generosity and guidance.

Over the years, the Omani government has made efforts to further legitimise the sultan's rule using the precepts of Ibadism, the Al Said family legacy and a cult of personality highlighting his unique traits as a ruler. Yet the fact remains that the modern Omani state and the basis of the sultan's power both depend on oil rents, which constituted the lifeblood of the state-building process on which Qaboos's legitimacy has always rested.

The discourse of reform

Oman's breakneck development throughout the 1970s, fuelled by an embargo-driven oil-revenue windfall, physically transformed the country. Gleaming new infrastructure reached towns where life had changed little for centuries; increased Omani life expectancy and exploding birth rates followed accordingly. Yet, as prices crashed in the 1980s, Oman's trajectory and spending became unsustainable. Government jobs could no longer meet the demands of educated youth for employment and a continually rising standard of living. Oil output, which peaked at about one million barrels per day, looked to run out after 15–20 years with the extraction technology of the day. Dramatically increased standards of living throughout the 1980s began to reduce birth rates, but Oman – having had the second-highest birth rate in the world as recently as the 1970s – retained a rapidly growing demographic 'youth bulge'.[9] In short, Oman's good luck appeared to be dissipating almost as abruptly as it had arrived.

Out of what appeared to be a sense of enlightened self-interest, the Omani government responded by rallying around the discourse of reform – above all, the notion that Oman would have to disassemble its rentier state and build a market economy. According to a contemporaneous British press report, Omani policymakers had decided on 'diversification and Omanization' as the only path forward.[10] The reduction of the public-sector workforce, the expansion of the private sector and the curtailment of subsidies were identified as particular priorities. What Hazem Beblawi described as the 'rentier mentality' – by which the assurance of state largesse crowds out innovation and competition – became anathema.[11] Yet the technocratic jargon used to describe the reforms belied their revolutionary implications: movement towards a purely market economy would imply completely upending the political–economic bargain upon which the sultan's rule rested. With less coming from on high, it was unclear whether the population would remain quiescent.

It helped to keep timelines for reform long. Oman pioneered the now-ubiquitous 'Vision' framing of neoliberal economic reform. Oman's version – enacted in 1995 – was known as 'Vision 2020'. It laid out a series of steps that, together, were supposed to provide the country with 'suitable conditions for take-off' by focusing on economic diversification through non-extractive industries, labour-market reform and the development of Oman's human capital.[12] It also set ambitious timelines for the reduction of the country's oil dependence: by 2020, oil revenue was to fall from 41% of GDP to 9%. In parallel, non-oil industries were to reach nearly 81% of GDP by the target date. Most remarkably, the share of citizen labour in the private sector was to jump from a mere 7.5% in 1996 to at least 75% by 2020.[13]

Even as it held out the salutary effects of reform, Vision 2020 was also remarkable in the degree to which it pathologised Omanis for their embrace of the benefits of rentierism. A representative passage reads: 'The low level of productivity of labour resources [is a major challenge to reform]. The reluctance of Omanis to join certain professions and occupations has led to [the] reduction of their capacity to face future challenges, affected their integration with the world economy, and at the same time hindered the substitution of expatriate labour.'[14] Omanis' seemingly rational response to the economic incentives before them – who would reject a job that promised high pay and easy hours? – was instead portrayed as the principal obstacle to state-led reform. The Vision 2020 statement unabashedly treats the logical result of Oman's social contract as the system's principal threat.

Even as the government blamed its subjects for not engaging in 'market' behaviour, the proposed remedies – to improve human capital through education and training – stood only to change the parameters and discourse of the rent-seeking game. Robin Steiner and others have convincingly identified the ways in which insider connections and performative displays of so-called market values have subverted the meritocratic pretensions of the effort to build a culture of 'innovation' and 'competition' in Oman.[15] Even as Vision 2020 levelled implicit criticisms of Omanis' complacency, it promised to intensify the state-led development – just of a different kind – that produced the very behaviour it was condemning.

A decade after Vision 2020's promulgation, it was clear that Oman not only would fail to meet these targets but had actually regressed on many of the relevant indicators. By 2010, oil revenues, buoyed by high prices, represented a higher proportion of GDP than in 1995. Labour-market reform had fallen far short; the private sector was only about 15% Omani by 2008 – a far cry from the desired 75% share laid out more than a decade earlier.[16]

This failure is not surprising, given the underlying contradiction between Vision 2020's diagnosis of the country's rentier malaise and the steps proposed to tackle it. Yet it is worth asking why the government even bothered to put forward a document so manifestly unequal to its stated goal of disciplining Omanis with 'market values'. Changing Omanis' behaviour would have required a total revision of the basis upon which the Omani state was built – in particular, the quid pro quo of patronage for obedience. The studiously economic language of Vision 2020 reform circumvented politics entirely; the kinds of political changes implicit in truly reforming Oman's political–economic bargain were clearly off the table. Instead, the discourse of permanent reform presented a useful complement to the narrative of Oman's ongoing renaissance under the sultan's rule. Just as it played well domestically, so too did talk of reform appeal to Oman's international backers at the moment of peak influence of the Washington Consensus. In short, the plan was good branding.

'The people want the reform of the regime'

By the late 2000s, Oman's Vision 2020 appeared an afterthought. The highest sustained oil prices since the 1970s made the idea of reforming the patronage system disconnected from political reality. Omani elites and, in particular, regime insiders were profiting handsomely from the status quo, with most government ministers directly involved in private-sector profiteering that depended on government contracts or other access. There was little apparent pressure to undertake labour-market and state-welfare reforms that would eat into profits or threaten a popular backlash.

This is not to say that all Omanis were benefiting equally. The children of the 1980s and 1990s were, by 2011, arriving at adulthood and finding that state largesse was unable to uphold the implicit promise of jobs and a livelihood. Youth unemployment reached at least 30%.[17] The rise of social media also made Omanis more aware of the kleptocratic activities of elite insiders and growing perceived inequality (although the country's Gini coefficient remains unavailable). Promises that major infrastructure projects – above all, the development of the town of Sohar as the centrepiece of Omani economic diversification – would bring jobs to thousands of Omanis gave way to the luxurious gated communities built to accommodate the new facilities' expat managers (as well as decidedly less luxurious housing built for foreign labourers).

When, in February 2011, protests erupted in Sohar and spread across the country, the Omani elite was in shock. According to knowledgeable insiders, the sultan himself was in a state of denial about the prospect that Oman could be subject to the same kinds of protest that arose in Tunis and Cairo. Yet thousands of young people flooded the streets of Sohar, torching the local outlet of a supermarket chain owned by a top regime insider and raising the slogan: 'The people want the reform of the regime'.[18] That protesters did not call for the end of the sultan's rule did suggest a qualitative difference from their counterparts in Egypt and elsewhere: they retained hope that they could improve their end of the rentier bargain. If the regime did not uphold its end by providing stable livelihoods, it implicitly should not expect permanent quiescence. The majority of demonstrators made specifically economic demands centred on job opportunities, limiting price increases and fighting corruption.

Unlike his autocratic peers in Arab 'republics', the sultan had the benefit of being able to meet the protesters' demands for more government benefits. Within weeks, the government drastically raised the citizen minimum wage, instituted a monthly allowance for job seekers and promised the creation of 50,000 new public-sector jobs. Led by Saudi Arabia, the other Gulf Cooperation Council (GCC) states stepped in with more than $10 billion in aid to Oman to support this massive new programme.[19] As oil prices plummeted throughout 2015, Oman also issued new sovereign debt to further pad its financial buffer.[20] Although protesters' demands primarily concerned benefits and corruption, the sultan also took symbolic steps toward political liberalisation. The powers of the appointed Majlis al-Shura were expanded, though they did not approach anything resembling those of an empowered legislative body.

These inducements allowed the sultan to avoid the militarised repression witnessed elsewhere in the region, but they also exposed the stark tension between neoliberal economic reforms of the kind put forward in Vision 2020 and political stability. By doubling down on state benefits to buy off dissent, the sultan ensured that reform would be all the more politically painful if implemented. What is more, in the protests' aftermath, the Omani state increased its repression of dissidents and control of the country's media. Thousands were arrested as protests continued to smoulder throughout 2011 and, according to the Gulf Centre for Human Rights, 'torture [became] the state's knee jerk response to political expression'.[21] While more limited in scope and kind than the punishment meted out by the likes of Syria's Bashar al-Assad or Egypt's Abdel Fattah Al-Sisi, Oman's securitised response was the country's most significant political repression since the early days of the sultan's rule.

This combination of carrots and sticks was sufficient to enforce a tenuous calm, but 2011 revealed the potential brittleness of Oman's system even as it highlighted an essential dilemma: the steps needed to transform the country's economy – labour-market reform, privatisation and subsidy reduction – were precisely those that could lead to greater income inequality and attendant popular anger. Paroxysms of violence and state collapse around the region gradually invalidated the more salutary interpretations of the Arab Spring and reminded protesters of how bad things could get, but Omani elites were aware that they had, at best, bought themselves a temporary reprieve.

Duelling narratives

Since 2011, two narratives of Oman's post-uprising trajectory have emerged. The first, which dominates Western media coverage, holds that Oman weathered the storm of popular discontent and has made strides toward political and economic liberalisation. Proponents cite the country's relatively high scores on measures of good governance, as well as Oman's regional role as a diplomatic intermediary, as prima facie evidence that the country must be doing something right. The second view of Oman's trajectory looks at the discourse of economic reform as something akin to *Groundhog Day*, with the same ineffectual platform being periodically rebranded for public-relations purposes. This more pessimistic perspective is favoured by those – including international credit-ratings agencies – who focus on the country's economic fundamentals. Each view contains elements of truth, but the latter discerns the political–economic dynamics most likely to shape Oman in the long run.

Omanis' pride in the country's development under Sultan Qaboos is clear to any visitor. Most middle-aged people have seen their material standards of living improve by orders of magnitude since childhood. Prosperity has trickled down over the years, as many Omanis were brought into the middle class. Amid the discourse of reform and diversification, it is important for outsiders to remember that oil has not, in fact, hindered Omani growth, as some scholars of rentier political economy had predicted.[22] Representatively, Michael Ross found that, since 1960, Oman had witnessed the highest per capita economic growth rate of any oil producer.[23] Moreover, the party may continue for a while, with the International Monetary Fund (IMF) forecasting that Oman is likely to enjoy the fastest economic growth in the GCC in 2019.[24] Government-subsidised land, housing, services and infrastructure – to say nothing of jobs – have made loyalty to the sultan easy for many Omanis who benefit from the status quo.

Oman has also shown an ability to take limited steps towards disassembling parts of its welfare state while maintaining political stability. As oil prices plummeted in 2015 and 2016, the Omani government took what the IMF called 'bold measures' to reduce expenditures on wages and benefits, while also limiting new capital outlays.[25] Although budget-deficit growth still outpaced the cuts, the state manifested some ability to enforce spending discipline on citizen benefits. In the depths of the 2016 oil-market tumble, Oman also made tentative progress in cutting wasteful fuel and electricity subsidies. Electricity-subsidy cuts were targeted at the largest industrial consumers, while the roughly 20% reduction in fuel subsidies hit consumers accustomed to American-style gas-guzzlers.[26]

Fortifying the sunnier view of Oman's economic prospects is the air of official confidence regarding the country's fiscal balance. In particular, there appears to be increasing optimism about Oman's ability to put off hard choices as global oil prices stabilise. At the April 2018 Oman Economic Forum, panellists – including a senior Omani Central Bank official – appeared convinced that pessimistic assessments of Oman's economic prospects were based purely on future projections of oil-market weakness. Once oil prices improved, the thinking went, the boom times would return.[27] The jocular tone of Omani policymakers suggests a latent conviction – despite the talk of economic diversification – that oil exporters' struggles in recent years have been an aberration from a future of further oil-driven growth.

Contrary to such sentiments, however, ratings agencies and international financial institutions indicate that their pessimism – rather than stemming from gloomy oil-price projections – is due fundamentally to a lack of confidence in the Omani government's ability to make necessary economic reforms. Two of the three major credit-ratings agencies have downgraded Omani sovereign debt – which stood at a record 40% of GDP in 2017 – to non-investment grade (that is, 'junk').[28] Moody's, the gentlest, gives Omani bonds the

Agencies have downgraded Omani debt

lowest possible investment-grade rating and maintains a negative outlook, suggesting further downgrades in the offing. Its justification is instructive: 'Moody's does not foresee a significant nominal reduction of non-interest government spending over the medium term.'[29] The agencies describe Omani efforts at belt-tightening since the downturn in oil prices, including slowing the increase of public wages, as fundamentally insufficient to meet the scope of Oman's impending fiscal challenges.

As a result, the agencies forecast growing budget deficits, halting progress in economic diversification and steadily increasing borrowing costs. Estimates of Oman's break-even oil price, under current fiscal conditions, range from the IMF's more conservative $75 per barrel to as high as $110; there are few signs that oil markets are sustainably headed for even the lower bound of that range.[30] Despite the technocratic language, the forecast is one of potential economic crisis. The crux of this pessimism is that the scope of Oman's economic challenges and the inadequacy of the proposed reforms have only grown since the 1990s. Above all, youth unemployment remains endemic: an April 2018 World Bank paper put the rate as high as

49% (even higher than in the 1990s).[31] Accurate estimates are hard to come by, but this one is plausible, given that Oman retains the highest birth rate in the GCC. The flow of new college graduates into the labour market is still above 40,000 per year, and the creation of public-sector jobs – those most desired by graduates for their social prestige, relative cushiness and high wages – does not approach that level.

Even as the unemployment rate creeps upward, the contours of the bargain reaffirmed in the 2011 uprising's aftermath remain unchanged. Oman's public discourse still centres on finding employment for job-seekers, as promised. (For example, Oman's daily newspapers – all of which are de facto state-controlled – often include front-page stories with a running tally of public-sector jobs provided.) The expansion of the welfare state required to mollify protesters has taken on a life of its own. As Steffen Hertog has noted about this dynamic, 'expectations are easy to raise but difficult to curb'.[32]

Vision 2040 is remarkably similar to Vision 2020

This political context is the lens through which to view 'Vision 2040', Oman's new economic-reform plan that is key to any discussion of the country's prospects. Above all, it is the state's primary attempt to grapple with a core dilemma: the need to meet citizen expectations of welfare provision while creating an economy that can withstand an impending post-oil era.

Superficially, Vision 2040 is a candid and bracing document, in that it acknowledges areas where reform previously stalled. Yet it is still remarkably similar to Vision 2020. The new plan refers to 'moving forward [on] economic diversification and mobilizing other sustained sources for [government] revenue', and emphasises the 'necessity of … continually upgrading capabilities and qualifying Omani workers to achieve a productive take-off in the various sectors'.[33] In fact, its main pillars – economic diversification and citizen private-sector employment – are so close to those laid out in Vision 2020 that stylistic tics appear to have been transferred directly into the new document. (For instance: the repeated use of 'take-off' to describe improvements to the citizen workforce.) Overall, it aims to reduce extractive industries' contribution to GDP to 30%, a target that is plausible given price fluctuations.

More striking, however, is the document's failure to mention spe-cific targets for reducing the growth of the overall government wage bill. Since government jobs are the primary means by which Oman distributes the country's oil rents, decreased reliance on resource wealth can only be demonstrated by reducing the public-employment burden. After spend-ing the 1990s and 2000s moving toward greater expatriate employment in the private sector (and away from the desired reduction), the new plan's drafters appear to have been more cautious about affixing specific goals to labour-market transformation.

Sidestepping the specifics of labour-market reform may have been politically expedient, but it also suggests that Vision 2040 will fare no better than its predecessor in forging fundamental change. The new plan posits that improving the quality of Oman's labour supply will incentivise private-sector employers to hire citizens over expatriates. Yet it fails to explain how this squares with the existing structure of Oman's economy. In particular, expatriate labour – representing almost 90% of Oman's private-sector workforce and nearly half the country's population – is the productive engine upon which the country's non-extractive industries depend.[34] Since the country's founding, cheap labour has functioned as a subsidy for the country's private sector, much of which is controlled by ruling elites. In the wake of 2011, the Omani government actually issued significant numbers of new work permits for foreign workers to ensure the profit margins – and loyalty – of elite-controlled businesses.[35] Eliminating this implicit private-sector subsidy could cause much of Oman's non-extractive-industry growth to stall. This is the central dilemma facing Omani policymakers: sustainable private-sector growth may require continued depressed wages and massive numbers of guest workers, while employing citizens in the private sector requires interventions to raise wages, enforce the hiring of Omani citizens and limit foreign-labour flows.

Many Omanis will only work in the private sector if the wage approaches that of a government job. Most public events in Oman that purport to discuss economic reform are, in fact, glorified marketing events showcasing a handful of Omani start-ups for powering Oman's putative emerging 'knowledge economy'. The urge to celebrate private-sector employment, particularly in high-tech industries, sometimes reaches a state of near-parody, as when extended discussion at economic conferences focuses on Oman's minuscule domestic drone industry as an avenue for job creation.[36] Little evidence of these efforts' effectiveness is needed beyond the fact that, in 2011, the creation of tens of thousands of new government jobs caused more than 30,000 Omanis working in the private sector to leave their employers in hope of snaring a sinecure.[37]

Despite the implicit tension between the liberalisation of Oman's economy and the imperative of citizen employment, it is clear that the government prioritises the latter. Omanisation has been in place for decades but has become particularly urgent in recent years, as the government fights to stave off unemployment. In practice, the policy involves curtailing visas for foreign workers, limiting entire professions to Omanis exclusively, and forcing businesses to accept quotas of Omani employees in proportions fixed to their expatriate hiring. Functionally, Omanisation serves as a further subsidy to Omani citizens and an implicit tax on businesses; without the force of law, the jobs for them would not exist. It is no surprise that regime elites made this decision, as the private sector is far more easily controlled than massive numbers of unemployed youth. Nevertheless, the policy's most notable feature is that it works directly against Vision 2040's stated goal of sustainably building Oman's private sector. Managers at firms doing business in Oman admit that they accept their quota of citizen labour in order to be seen as cooperating with government priorities and to access major contracts. Even so, the government often touts progress in Omanisation as a step towards the diversification of Oman's economy. In reality, however, Omanisation is underpinned by precisely the kinds of subsidies to citizen employment that it is meant to reduce. This sleight of hand bodes ill for Vision 2040's prospects.

A perfect storm?

Oman's political–economic future has intrinsic importance to Western policymakers because it is a strategic partner that hosts significant numbers of American and British troops and materiel. Crisis in Oman would be a shock to those who count on stability in the region's wealthy states to balance chaos in many of the rest. More broadly, Oman offers insight into the challenges of reforming other Middle Eastern rentier states. It will be the first major oil-dependent economy in the region forced to transition back to non-rentier modes of production, and the difficulties it has faced may have broad implications for policymakers and academics thinking about other GCC states. This is particularly true of Saudi Arabia, which shares with Oman a slow-motion power transition of uncertain outcome and a latently fractious population.

Western diplomats in Muscat, expatriates in the private sector and Omani elites themselves typically fall into one of two camps. The main one predicts general continuity. In this view, Oman may be able to make its oil reserves last longer than expected and thus preserve the most important features of its social contract. This contingent does not hold much hope for significant rollback of the rentier state or progress in moving away from state-led development, but implicitly incorporates confidence that the government will be able to rely on its regional and international patrons should the going, once again, get tough. When such a moment comes, the thinking runs, Oman may have a better chance at transforming its economy since its population has already been primed with the notion that dwindling oil reserves will require material sacrifices. A more realpolitik version of this argument holds that Oman's comfortable and disarmed population could be easily contained in the event of renewed instability. Its proponents typically view concerns about an impending power transition upon the sultan's death as exaggerated, and instead believe that the Omani elite will engineer a pacted transfer of power to the next generation of the Al Said.

A well-informed minority – including diplomats, academics and others with whom we spoke – sees potential for significantly more turmoil and disruption. In this 'perfect storm' scenario, a cascade of political and economic shocks could overwhelm a system that is brittle and unable to reform itself. This camp, while viewing the immediate future as largely stable, focuses on Oman's medium- to long-term trajectory. In the medium term, it expects the deterioration of Oman's ability to sustain its welfare state and more dire consequences if it fails to do so. Proponents regard the anger that flared in 2011 as lurking just below the surface, as suggested by increasing instances of small-scale protest over jobs and living conditions throughout 2017 and

2018.[38] While they agree that the transition from Qaboos will likely proceed smoothly in the near term, they anticipate that the sultan's successor will have fewer resources at his disposal for restoring an elite governing consensus. Fiscally, in this scenario the trend lines are generally negative, with sustained low break-even oil prices possibly a thing of the past and Oman's cost of debt servicing set to jump when previously issued bonds mature in the early years of the next decade. An unsteady new ruler could find himself facing increasing demands with diminished resources. Although this camp rarely predicts outright state collapse, it sees the re-emergence of 2011-style popular unrest as possible, if not likely. The Omani state's putative 'niceness' would then be truly put to the test.

Adjudicating these conflicting views is difficult, given the many unknowns on which they depend, but the pessimists should not be dismissed out of hand. Few believed that Omanis would rise up as they did in 2011. Many, perhaps most, Middle Eastern states face greater immediate fiscal challenges than Oman, but Omanis also have vastly greater demands and expectations than do, for instance, Egyptians. There is little apparent indication either that Omanis will stop expecting state largesse or that the ruling elite will cede its political monopoly any time soon. As Oman's fiscal landscape deteriorates, one side or the other of this rentier bargain will likely be forced to adjust its demands. This adjustment could produce explosive results.

*   *   *

Oman's domestic trajectory has regional implications. Oman was the first in the region to systematise plans for rentier reform in a way that has now become de rigueur among its neighbours. With 'Vision' plans of reform proliferating across the Gulf (and benefiting from massive public-relations efforts in Western capitals), do Oman's struggles suggest that other states will face comparable challenges? States such as the UAE, Qatar and Kuwait that benefit from extremely high resource rents per capita will, in the near term, have their cake and eat it too; they have reform plans on the books – lending them the reputational benefits and aura of reform – but lack fiscal pressure to implement them.

Saudi Arabia's 'Vision 2030' may benefit from comparison with the Omani paradigm. Saudi Arabia's population is equally accustomed to a comprehensive social safety net. The increasingly insular Saudi elite, cowed by Crown Prince Muhammad bin Salman (MBS)'s ambitious authoritarianism, appears even less likely than Oman's to renegotiate the terms of its political control. As in Oman, the discourse of reform advanced by MBS has been a useful tool for shaping domestic and international perceptions, but there is little reason to believe that the Saudi government is willing to take the political risks that would come with true labour-market reform. Part of the reason MBS appears to have support among the Saudi middle class is that his 'reforms' have been limited to the social sphere, while leaving direct and implicit state subsidies largely intact.

Caution is warranted in drawing too direct a comparison between Oman and other Arab oil-rentier states, since there are many ways in which Oman is meaningfully different. The fact remains that Oman's rulers and ruled have consistently preferred the kabuki of reform to truly giving up their prerogatives. This reality should worry those who hope to see Gulf rentier states make smooth transitions away from unsustainable models of development.

Notes

[1] See, for instance, Editorial Board, 'Oman's Guiding Hand in a Churning Middle East', *Christian Science Monitor*, 31 October 2018; and Shohini Gupta, 'Oman: The Unsung Hero of the Iranian Nuclear Deal', *Foreign Policy Journal*, 23 July 2015.

[2] See, for example, Camille Lons, 'Onshore Balancing: The Threat to Oman's Neutrality', European Council on Foreign Relations, 3 April 2019.

[3] 'Oman Says Role in Iran Deal "Exaggerated"', *Gulf News*, 1 December 2013.

[4] See Marc Junyent, 'Do Not Take Oman's Stability for Granted', Open Democracy, 12 December 2018.

[5] Marc Valeri, *Oman: Politics and Society in the Qaboos State* (Oxford: Oxford University Press, 2013), p. 71.

[6] *Ibid.*, p. 72.

[7] Marc Valeri, 'Oligarchy vs. Oligarchy', in *Business Politics in the Middle East* (London: Hurst & Co., 2013), p. 20.

[8] D.G. Crawford, Consul General Muscat, to M.S. Weir, Political Resident, Bahrain, 2 November 1970, reproduced in *Records of Oman 1966–1971*, vol. 5 (Cambridge: Archive Editions), p. 158; cited and quoted in Sarah G. Phillips and Jennifer S. Hunt, '"Without Sultan Qaboos, We Would Be Yemen": The Renaissance Narrative and the Political Settlement in Oman',

Journal of International Development, vol. 29, no 5, July 2017, p. 656.

9   Alasdair Drysdale, 'Population Dynamics and Birth Spacing in Oman', *International Journal of Middle East Studies,* vol. 42, no. 1, February 2010, pp. 123–44.

10   Valeri, 'Oligarchy vs. Oligarchy', p. 18.

11   Hazem Beblawi, 'The Rentier State in the Arab World', *Arab Studies Quarterly,* vol. 9, no. 4, Fall 1987, pp. 383–98.

12   'The Vision for Oman's Economy: Oman 2020', p. 127.

13   Oxford Business Group, 'The Report: Oman 2009', p. 45.

14   'The Vision for Oman's Economy: Oman 2020', p. 146.

15   Robin Steiner, *Between Oil Pasts and Utopian Dreams,* PhD dissertation, University of Arizona, 2018, p. 51.

16   Kristian Coates-Ulrichsen, *Insecure Gulf: The End of Uncertainty and the Transition to the Post-oil Era* (New York: Columbia University Press, 2011), p. 99.

17   Crystal Ennis and Ra'id al-Jamali, 'Elusive Employment', Chatham House Research Paper, September 2014, p. 3.

18   Marc Valeri, 'Simmering Unrest and Succession Challenges in Oman', Carnegie Endowment for International Peace, 28 January 2015.

19   *Ibid.*

20   'Oman Returns to International Bond Markets', Oxford Business Group, 22 July 2016.

21   Gulf Centre for Human Rights, 'Torture in Oman', January 2014.

22   Michael L. Ross, *The Oil Curse: How Petroleum Wealth Shapes the Development of Nations* (Princeton, NJ: Princeton University Press, 2013), p. 117.

23   *Ibid.,* p. 199.

24   'IMF Raises Growth Forecasts for GCC states', Gulf News, 9 October 2018.

25   'IMF Staff Completes 2016 Article IV Mission to Oman', IMF Press Release no. 16/205.

26   Tom Moerenhout, 'Energy Pricing Reforms in the Gulf: A Trend But Not (Yet) a Norm', Global Subsidies Initiative Report, International Institute for Sustainable Development, January 2018.

27   Oman Economic Forum, 'Oman's Economy in Light of the Global Economic Recovery', YouTube.com, April 2018.

28   'Oman Government Debt to GDP', Trading Economics, https://tradingeconomics.com/oman/government-debt-to-gdp.

29   Moody's Investor Service, 'Moody's Downgrades Oman's Rating to Baa3, Outlook Negative', 16 March 2018.

30   IMF, 'IMF Executive Board Concludes 2018 Article IV Consultation with Oman', Press Release no. 18/280, 6 July 2018.

31   World Bank, 'Oman's Economic Outlook – April 2018', 16 April 2018.

32   Steffen Hertog, 'The Costs of Counter-revolution in the GCC', *Foreign Policy,* 31 May 2011.

33   Sultanate of Oman Supreme Council for Planning, 'A Brief of The Ninth Five-Year Development Plan', September 2016.

34   National Center for Statistics & Information, 'Statistical Year Book', issue 45, p. 103.

35   Coates-Ulrichsen, *Insecure Gulf,* p. 64.

36   'Ayn Wajha al-Iqtsad al-Omani?' [Where is the Omani economy heading?], Sultan Qaboos University, 9 October 2018.

37   *Ibid.*

38   Economist Intelligence Unit, 'Government Offers 25,000 Jobs to Avert Protest', 23 October 2017.

What Kind of Japan? Tokyo's Strategic Options in a Contested Asia

H.D.P. Envall

Japan faces significant strategic uncertainty. China's growing assertiveness and the unpredictability introduced into Asian affairs by US President Donald Trump could leave Japan isolated. Unsurprisingly, therefore, analysts of Japanese security have sought to understand how Japan might respond to these challenges so as to retain a central place in the Asian security order.[1] Japanese Prime Minister Shinzo Abe has rejected the notion of Japan as a 'tier-two country',[2] but there is long-standing ambiguity about Japan's role in international affairs.[3] It is an issue that has attracted particular attention in Australia, given Canberra's increasingly close security partnership with Japan.[4] The Australian discussion has usefully focused on two possible Japanese trajectories, depending on whether Tokyo chooses a 'hard' or 'comfortable' future.

At least according to the Australian debate, a Japan that opts for a hard future would compete with China and rebuild its military power. This would not preclude engagement, but the focus would inevitably shift towards balancing. This would be Japan choosing, finally, to be a 'normal' nation. Conversely, a Japan that plumps for a comfortable future would be essentially pacifist, accommodate China and maybe even decouple from the United States. But would Japan really stand its ground in this way? Would

H.D.P. Envall is a fellow and senior lecturer in the Department of International Relations at the Australian National University.

Survival | vol. 61 no. 4 | August–September 2019 | pp. 117–130   DOI 10.1080/00396338.2019.1637126 it readily accept its strategic decline and China's rise? Would it seek to build up its military power and so become a more normal nation? Or would a more 'comfortable' Japan emerge, accepting of its strategic decline and China's rise to hegemony in Asia?[5] How Japan answers such questions will affect whether the region becomes even more strategically contested.

Tokyo is likely to steer a path somewhere between the comfortable and hard scenarios. Japan's policy shifts in recent years, along with current strategic uncertainties, point towards a national strategy designed to present a counterweight to China without necessarily contesting Beijing's regional primacy. It will likely mix deterrence with engagement in a more complex, and possibly riskier, strategy, so as to hedge against the challenges presented by both partners and adversaries. This is the strategy of a regional power.[6]

Japan's growing strategic isolation

Japan's strategic environment is characterised by broad and specific security threats, alliance-management challenges and ongoing domestic limitations on its security role. The country's 2017 Defense White Paper notes that the 'security environment surrounding Japan grows increasingly severe'.[7] Most obviously, North Korea threatens Japan directly with its nuclear and missile programmes and indirectly as a trigger for a wider war on the Korean Peninsula.[8] Tokyo has long viewed North Korea as a significant security threat. Pyongyang's 1998 launch of a *Taepodong* missile over Japan was a catalyst for a round of security reforms and, in particular, efforts at developing ballistic-missile defence. Notwithstanding the tentative calming effects of the summit between Trump and North Korean leader Kim Jong-un in June 2018, Tokyo sees North Korea's rapid push towards a thermonuclear-tipped, long-range missile capability as a major disruption. This is not so much because it changes Japan's assessment of North Korea's threat, but more because it challenges the credibility of the US security commitment to Japan and thus the core of the US–Japan alliance.[9]

China represents both a specific security threat and a broader strategic problem. The security threat is a result of the dispute between Japan and China over the sovereignty of the Senkaku/Diaoyu islands in the East China

Sea. Chinese activities in the area, including collisions, regular incursions and some near-military confrontations, as well as several diplomatic crises since 2010, have substantially heightened Japanese threat perceptions of China. More broadly, China is supplanting Japan as the leading power in East Asia in terms of trade relationships, infrastructure-building around the region and investment activities, as well as institutional and diplomatic influence. In Tokyo, therefore, China is increasingly seen as engaging in 'creeping expansionism' and 'coercive behaviour'.[10]

Under Trump's leadership, the US has also become a significant strategic concern for Japan. By conducting foreign policy erratically and unpredictably, Trump has undermined regional confidence in the US as a security partner and, in Japan's case, as a security guarantor. In short order, Trump has managed to stoke both abandonment and entrapment fears in Tokyo. On the one hand, by suggesting that Japan continues to 'free ride' on the alliance or even arguing that Tokyo should pursue its own nuclear-weapons capacity, Trump has implied that the US may be less willing to bear the burden of the alliance. On the other hand, by countenancing unilateral actions in the region, such as a pre-emptive strike on North Korea or a trade war with China, Trump has raised the prospect of Japan being drawn into US-instigated crises.[11]

Japanese policymakers also face domestic challenges that have wider strategic implications. Demographic changes – specifically Japan's ageing and declining population – along with the long-term difficulty of achieving sustainable economic growth, improving wages, overcoming deflation-ary pressures, addressing growing inequalities and managing the national debt will over time hinder Japan's ability to deal with its external problems. There also remain substantial doubts as to whether Japan's political system, with its weak opposition and increasingly fragmented party politics, can address domestic issues effectively.[12]

These factors make Japan's strategic context one of threat, vulnerabil-ity and potential isolation. Beijing is now arguably Tokyo's most serious security problem; Japan cannot rely on the US with the same level of confi-dence to be its security guarantor; and Japan's relations with other powers in the region, notably Russia and South Korea, are in a poor state due to territorial disputes, differing historical understandings and diverging strategic objectives. Japan, as Shogo Suzuki and Corey Wallace argue, 'is exposed more than ever to various and intersecting forms of military and economic coercion'.[13]

Comfortable or hard Japan?

This question is hardly new. It lay at the heart of Japanese debates about becoming a 'normal nation' in the 1990s, as pursued by political figures such as Ichiro Ozawa. Yoshihide Soeya's promotion of Japan as a 'middle power' in the mid-2000s also implied a reorientation of the country towards a more modest strategic role.[14] Indeed, the regular recurrence of such debates is a sign of the unfinished and unsettled nature of Japan's post-Cold War security reforms. But what a hard versus comfortable Japan means in the uncertain context of today's contested Asia remains unclear.

Under a comfortable-Japan scenario, resisting China is too demanding because Japan would struggle to build a containing coalition or develop the necessary hard power (in particular, nuclear weapons). This argument echoes the 'middle power' stance of Soeya, suggesting that Japan will move towards a 'comfortable' strategic posture via a gentle decline in power. Limited by its strategic marginalisation, such a Japan would re-embrace its pacifism and the idea of being a civilian power. It would also drift 'out of the US orbit' and instead turn towards China. In the end, as Graeme Dobell argues, the basis for this profound strategic reorientation would be a simple calculation: 'that the cost of resisting Beijing is too high'.[15]

Hugh White similarly contends that, rather than re-emerging as a great power, Japan will adopt a 'more modest course'. He sees Japan as having three choices. It could accept Chinese primacy but ensure that it could 'resist Chinese pressure on really vital issues by maintaining strong air and naval forces, backed by a minimum nuclear deterrent'.[16] This would still be consistent with a 'classic "middle power" posture', even if the idea of a more comfortable middle power possessing a nuclear deterrent stretches, perhaps beyond the breaking point, notions of Japanese pacifism or a comfortable Japan.[17] A modest or middle power in White's imagining, therefore, might not be a comfortable power in the sense used by Dobell.

White's second choice is the 'Canada option'. This would involve Tokyo accepting Chinese hegemony and developing a relationship with China similar to the traditional one between Canada and the US – a kind of 'small power' posture. Whether Japan could or would establish this kind of relationship with the one-party authoritarian state of China is highly doubtful, however. At a minimum, it would likely entail significant concessions on Japan's part regarding the Senkaku/Diaoyu islands, as well as wider Japanese cooperation in Chinese-led institutions such as the Asian Infrastructure Investment Bank (AIIB) or the Belt and Road Initiative (BRI).

Significantly, these distinctions – between a small, modest middle, and great power – rest on material capabilities and on coalition-building capacity. If Japan were intent on avoiding the Canada option, it would need to develop an independent nuclear deterrent simply to retain a modest role in the regional power balance. To become a great power again, it would need to do still more – namely, to demonstrate that it could build regional coalitions to balance China. As a great power, Tokyo would not 'bend to Beijing' but would instead return to 'normal nation' status. It would continue to rebuild its military power, remain the key Asian ally for the US and lead the region 'in balancing against and engaging China'. Such balancing might, for instance, involve establishing a more robust quadrilateral 'alliance of democracies' to link Japan not only with the US but also with India and Australia.[18]

A hard-Japan scenario, therefore, would constitute the most significant break with past Japanese policy. Pursuing it would require Japan to abandon the domestic political and legal restrictions on its security role. These would include Article 9 of the constitution (already substantially weakened) and the three non-nuclear principles barring Japan's possession of nuclear weapons, its production of such weapons and their presence in the country. This option would also require Japan to invest substantially more in its military and to show a willingness to actively participate in a potential regional conflict. Even then, as White's second condition highlights, Japan would have to demonstrate that it is a regional leader and be accepted as such. White is justifiably sceptical as to whether this last condition could be met.

It is outside Japan's direct control, and would be complicated by the fact that the potential partner countries all have their own interests in positive relations with China. Indeed, this twist highlights the ongoing importance of the US to Japan, not only as an alliance partner but also as a regional coalition builder. The US remains crucial to all of Tokyo's strategic choices, even the hard-Japan option.[19]

Changes, continuities and constraints

Japan has undergone substantial reform since 2012 under the leadership of Abe. Changes have been implemented in three broad areas: defence capabilities, the US–Japan alliance and regional diplomacy. On defence, Japan has pursued change on different fronts under the banner of making a 'proactive contribution to peace' (*sekkyokuteki heiwashugi*).[20] It has sought to reform the country's security institutions, reassess its strategic environment and upgrade its military capacity. Institutional reforms have included the establishment of the National Security Council and the development of a national security strategy. The Japan Self-Defense Forces (JSDF) have become much more versatile and formidable, and the constitution has been reinterpreted to allow for the right to collective self-defence (that is, to defend allies). Within the alliance, Japan and the US have updated their bilateral defence guidelines in order to improve inter-operability, including on such matters as intelligence-gathering, missile defence and joint training. In terms of regional diplomacy, Japan has loosened previous restrictions on arms exports, signed technology-transfer deals, emphasised the strategic dimension of its overseas development-aid programmes and deepened its strategic partnerships in the region.[21]

There is much in these reforms to suggest that Abe has been pursuing a hard-Japan strategy. Indeed, Dobell views that strategy as Abe's 'vision for Japan' and argues that a hard Japan can be seen in Abe's active response to Trump's decision to abandon the Trans-Pacific Partnership, the prime minister's commitment to revise the Japanese constitution and his pursuit of a quadrilateral partnership. The hard-Japan idea is closely associated with Abe's nationalist vision and would accord with the view that Japan has indeed arrived at a 'watershed moment' in its security transformation.[22]

A return to a more comfortable Japan, by contrast, would indicate that the reforms to Japan's security policies under Abe have already reached their limit and that Abe has been a political outlier unlikely to be followed by future Japanese leaders. However, an important distinction arises in the context of the comfortable-versus-hard-Japan debate. While Abe's individual policy vision and ideas are strongly nationalist, historically revisionist and controversial, the actual, concrete policy prescriptions enacted by his government have been much more modest and demonstrate substantial continuities with past practice.[23] The boost in defence capabilities through increased spending has been measured. Likewise, work on increasing US–Japan defence cooperation has been focused on practical, low-level developments and incremental change. Abe's regional diplomacy follows a well-established pattern of regional engagement. Much established defence policy has been retained, including 'defensive defence' (*senshu boei*) and the three non-nuclear principles.[24]

The key area of transformation has been in collective self-defence. Japan is now much less restricted in its international security role and, particularly, in coming to the defence of allies. As Christopher Hughes notes, Japan has made it 'hard to opt out of U.S.–Japan alliance operations involving the use of force'.[25] As the Abe government has retained the three non-nuclear principles, however, Japan cannot legally develop an independent nuclear-weapons capability. Instead, it must continue to rely on American extended nuclear deterrence. This dispensation underscores the limited scope of Abe's reforms. The implication is that Japan will move towards a small, comfortable strategic future almost by default or, at least, as a result of domestic political opinion and a continuing nuclear taboo. Although this taboo is now open to public discussion, as demonstrated by senior Liberal Democratic Party (LDP) figure Shigeru Ishiba having raised the issue recently, it remains influential. There are also strong reasons why such a shift remains unlikely. The technological and infrastructural obstacles Japan would face cover everything from a lack of appropriate launch vehicles and missile technology to the challenges of miniaturising warheads and developing associated infrastructure.[26]

Moreover, the Abe reforms are premised on a reliable US commitment to Asia. Buttressing American power in the region, with a view to further constraining China, has been a key goal of the Abe government.[27] Prioritising this objective has moved Abe to practise a highly personal and ingratiating style of diplomacy vis-à-vis Trump – for example, presenting the new president with a gold-coloured golf club that retailed for $3,755.[28] Yet Japan was subsequently marginalised over North Korea and subject to Trump's trade protectionism.[29] More substantively, the need to ensure US support has rendered Japan less concerned about entrapment in US-led conflicts, as illustrated by the decision on collective self-defence.[30] But at the same time, Trump's 'America First' approach to security in Asia has heightened Japan's fear of American abandonment with respect to a range of Japanese interests, including the South China Sea, global trade and North Korea's threat.

The tension between abandonment and entrapment was evident during the nuclear crisis on the Korean Peninsula in 2017–18. In the first half of 2018, Trump contrived to make both dangers seem plausible. Initially, war seemed more likely than at any time since 1953.[31] Later, Trump left Japan stranded on the sidelines as he met with North Korean leader Kim Jong-un in Singapore, dropping Tokyo's preferred 'maximum pressure' strategy towards Pyongyang and paying little regard to Japanese interests.[32] In Japan, concerns were expressed over the abstract nature of the summit agreement, its lack of attention to the intermediate-range missile threat, and the presumption that Japan would inevitably be the central player in providing economic support to North Korea following denuclearisation.[33] The fact remains that Japan has no plausible short- or medium-term alternative to America's security guarantee and wider strategic support. Japan's ability to deter adversaries turns on cooperating closely with the US, while its regional diplomacy, including its expanding relationship with Australia, has been deliberately aligned with US preferences.[34]

A realist outlook

The comfortable–hard dichotomy has obvious limitations, especially in terms of clearly delineating a set of specific policies. The idea of a nuclear Japan still being only a comfortable or a middle power significantly strains current understandings of these terms. Yet even a much stronger Japan could still struggle to be a hard power assuming alliance-building is a necessary condition thereof. In any case, it is clear that Japan under the Abe government is not seeking a comfortable strategic position in Asia, but is focusing instead on boosting deterrence. Indeed, Japan has never really advocated a comfortable strategic position vis-à-vis China. Although then-prime minister Yukio Hatoyama entertained the idea of engaging Beijing and setting Japan up as a 'bridge' between China and the US in 2009–10, the subsequent deterioration of Sino-Japanese relations rendered it infeasible.[35] In this respect, Abe is not an outlier in pushing for a harder Japan, but rather is acting in a way consistent with both past LDP policies and the policies of the governments led by the Democratic Party of Japan post-Hatoyama.

In effect, Abe is reinforcing a putative realist approach. Accordingly, his policies should be understood not in terms of nationalism or revisionism, but as purposeful means of building up Japan's defence capabilities, enhancing its principal alliance and improving Japan's regional cooperation in the face of specific threats. They suggest a country that no longer views itself as a potential great power but instead sees itself as a possible regional power that can shape its regional order but does 'not extend much beyond' that order, as Barry Buzan and Ole Wæver put it.[36]

Likewise, Japan's established threat perceptions, focusing on North Korea and China, have been affirmed over the past year. This dictates a continued emphasis on deterrence, which remains a primary objective of the country's security strategy.[37] But Japan's recent efforts to strengthen deterrence appear to turn more on its perceptions of America's future reliability than on any revised assessment of North Korean and Chinese threats. Given Trump's demonstration that America's commitment to the region cannot be taken for granted, those efforts constitute both balancing against China and hedging against the risk of US strategic decline or withdrawal. A US withdrawal from Asia would clearly place pressure on Japan to boost its independent deterrence capacity, and signal Japan to consider a nuclear capability of its own. These eventualities seem unlikely. But Japan is still seeking to boost its independent deterrent in a less radical way by developing a conventional counter-strike capability with the acquisition of long-range missiles.[38]

While Japan will continue to prioritise deterrence, it will also likely need to revisit hedging through regional engagement with China to offset the risk of a decline in US support. Indeed, the Abe government has indicated that it may reconsider whether Japan should become more engaged in the AIIB and the BRI, even as it has also pushed for a US–Japan–Australia regional investment fund.[39] It has also agreed to establish direct lines of communication between the JSDF and the Chinese military in order to avoid clashes between the two countries in the East China Sea.[40] There are, of course, clear limitations to the possible scope of greater engagement with China. The Senkaku/Diaoyu dispute involves fundamental differences over sovereignty and regional influence that cannot be easily resolved. Furthermore, Japan is unlikely to pursue greater economic engagement with China if this means abandoning its goal of developing a more open, rules-based economic order or conceding victory to China in the two countries' broader competition over Asia's economic and trade architecture.[41]

*   *   *

Japan's emerging strategy is one of deterrence with engagement. It fits at best uneasily in the comfortable–hard framework, and is potentially confusing and even contradictory in that it mixes balancing and bandwagoning aspects against both adversaries and allies. This makes the collapse of such a strategy a significant risk. The upshot is that Japan, in practice, is unlikely to move too far towards either a comfortable strategy based on comprehensive engagement or a hard strategy entailing a fully independent (and nuclear) deterrence capacity and successful coalition-building.

On balance, therefore, White's modest middle-power model is the most probable actual outcome. But Japan would not be a middle power in the accepted sense – that is, a niche diplomatic player or an internationalist voice. Instead, it is likely to become increasingly realist and regionally focused. As a regional actor in Asia, it would seek to resist Chinese primacy, build a range of strategic partnerships around the region and attempt, as far as possible, to keep the US engaged.

Notes

1   See Brendan Taylor, 'Asia's Century and the Problem of Japan's Centrality', *International Affairs*, vol. 87, no. 4, July 2011, pp. 871–85. See also, more recently, Eric Heginbotham and Richard J. Samuels, 'Active Denial: Redesigning Japan's Response to China's Military Challenge', *International Security*, vol. 42, no. 4, Spring 2018, pp. 128–69.

2   Shinzo Abe, 'Japan is Back', policy speech at the Center for Strategic and International Studies (CSIS), 22 February 2013, https://www. mofa.go.jp/announce/pm/abe/ us_20130222en.html.

3   Jacob M. Schlesinger, 'Identity Confusion: Is Japan Now a "Great Power"?', *Wall Street Journal*, 18 July 2014, https://blogs.wsj. com/japanrealtime/2014/07/18/ identity-confusion-is-japan-now- a-great-power/. See also Masaru Tamamoto, 'Ambiguous Japan: Japanese National Identity at Century's End', in G. John Ikenberry and Michael Mastanduno (eds), *International Relations Theory and the Asia-Pacific* (New York: Columbia University Press, 2003), pp. 195–7.

4   Hugh White, 'Without America: Australia in the New Asia', *Quarterly Essay*, no. 68, 2017, https://www. quarterlyessay.com.au/essay/2017/11/ without-america/extract.

5   See Graeme Dobell, 'Hard Japan Versus Comfortable Japan', *Strategist*, 26 February 2018, https://www. aspistrategist.org.au/hard-japan- versus-comfortable-japan/; and Graeme Dobell, 'Asia's Rise: The Rules and the Rulers', *Inside Story*, 15 February 2018, http://insidestory.org. au/asias-rise-the-rules-and-the-rulers/.

6   On regional powers, see Barry Buzan and Ole Wæver, *Regions and Powers: The Structure of International Security* (Cambridge: Cambridge University Press, 2003).

7   Japan Ministry of Defense, 'Defense of Japan 2017', p. 43, https://www.mod. go.jp/e/publ/w_paper/2017.html.

8   On the Korean Peninsula's role as Asia's 'crucible', see Brendan Taylor, *The Four Flashpoints: How Asia Goes to War* (Carlton: La Trobe University Press, 2018), pp. 23–62.

9   Bruce Bennett, James Dobbins, Jeffrey W. Hornung and Andrew Scobell, 'After the Summit: Prospects for the Korean Peninsula', *Survival*, vol. 60, no. 4, August–September 2018, p. 26. See also Brendan Taylor and H.D.P. Envall, 'A Nuclear Arms Race in Northeast Asia?', in *Nuclear Asia, Paradigm Shift No. 2* (Canberra: ANU College of Asia and the Pacific, 2017– 18), p. 24.

10 See Masashi Nishihara, 'Japan Should Stand Firm on the Senkaku Islands Dispute', *AJISS Commentary*, no. 164, 6 November 2012; and '"Seiji no Genba", Nichu Reisen (3): Yasukuni ni Genin Surikaeru' ['Politics on Site', the Sino-Japanese Cold War, Part 3: Sidestepping Yasukuni as a Cause], *Yomiuri Shinbun*, 6 February 2014. See also Jeffrey W. Hornung, 'Japan's Growing Hard Hedge Against China', *Asian Security*, vol. 10, no. 2, June 2014, pp. 97–122.

11 H.D.P. Envall, 'Can Japan's Golden

Golf Diplomacy Win Over Donald
Trump?', in Australian National
University, *The Trump Administration's
First 100 Days: What Should Asia Do?*
(Canberra: ANU College of Asia and
the Pacific, 2017), pp. 16–17.

[12] Jonathan Webb, 'Japan's Demographic
Disaster: Looming Crisis Threatens
US Power and Asia-Pacific
Regional Stability', IISS Analysis,
4 August 2017, https://www.
iiss.org/blogs/analysis/2017/08/
japan-demographic-disaster.

[13] Shogo Suzuki and Corey Wallace,
'Explaining Japan's Response
to Geopolitical Vulnerability',
International Affairs, vol. 94, no. 4, July
2018, p. 711.

[14] See Ichiro Ozawa, *Blueprint for a New
Japan: The Rethinking of a Nation*, trans.
Louisa Rubinfien (Tokyo: Kodansha
International, 1994); and Yoshihide
Soeya, *Nihon no 'Midoru Pawa' Gaiko:
Sengo Nihon no Sentaku to Koso* [Japan's
'Middle Power' Diplomacy: Postwar
Japan's Choices and Conceptions]
(Tokyo: Chikuma Shinsho, 2005).
See also Yoshihide Soeya, 'Prospects
for Japan as a Middle Power', *East
Asia Forum*, 29 July 2013, http://
www.eastasiaforum.org/2013/07/29/
prospects-for-japan-as-a-middle-
power/.

[15] Dobell, 'Hard Japan Versus
Comfortable Japan'. This is not dis-
similar to the strategic approach
adopted by the Japanese government
of Yukio Hatoyama in 2009–10. See
H.D.P. Envall, 'Clashing Expectations:
Strategic Thinking and Alliance
Mismanagement in Japan', in Yoichiro
Sato and Tan See Seng (eds), *United
States Engagement in the Asia-Pacific:*

Perspectives from Asia (Amherst, NY:
Cambria Press, 2015), pp. 61–88.

[16] White, 'Without America', p. 60.

[17] Hugh White, 'Japan's Tough Choice',
Straits Times, 31 October 2017, https://
www.straitstimes.com/opinion/
japans-tough-choice.

[18] Dobell, 'Hard Japan Versus
Comfortable Japan'.

[19] White, 'Without America', p. 60.

[20] Government of Japan, 'National
Security Strategy', 17 December 2013,
p. 1.

[21] H.D.P. Envall, 'The "Abe Doctrine":
Japan's New Regional Realism',
International Relations of the Asia-Pacific,
June 2018, https://academic.oup.
com/irap/advance-article-abstract/
doi/10.1093/irap/lcy014/5033025?redir
ectedFrom=fulltext, pp. 12–16.

[22] Christopher W. Hughes, 'Japan's
Strategic Trajectory and Collective
Self-Defense: Essential Continuity
or Radical Shift?', *Journal of Japanese
Studies*, vol. 43, no. 1, Winter 2017, p.
93. See also Karl Gustafsson, Linus
Hagström and Ulv Hanssen, 'Japan's
Pacifism is Dead', *Survival*, vol. 60, no.
6, December 2018–January 2019,
pp. 137–58.

[23] Envall, 'The "Abe Doctrine"', pp. 7–16.

[24] See Adam P. Liff, 'Japan's Defense
Policy: Abe the Evolutionary',
Washington Quarterly, vol. 38, no. 2,
Summer 2015, pp. 89–92; and Leif-
Eric Easley, 'How Proactive? How
Pacifist? Charting Japan's Evolving
Defence Posture', *Australian Journal of
International Affairs*, vol. 71, no. 1, July
2016, pp. 78–80.

[25] Hughes, 'Japan's Strategic Trajectory
and Collective Self-Defense', p. 98.

[26] 'Hikakusangensoku Minaoshi Teiki

Ishiba shi Kokunai ni Bei Kakuheiki Giron Shucho' [Ishiba Raises Review of Three Non-Nuclear Principles, Advocates Introduction of US Nuclear Weapons into Japan], *Yomiuri Shinbun*, 7 September 2017. See also Mike Mochizuki, 'Three Reasons Why Japan Will Likely Continue to Reject Nuclear Weapons', *Washington Post*, 6 November 2017, https://www.washingtonpost.com/news/monkey-cage/wp/2017/11/06/japan-is-likely-to-retain-its-non-nuclear-principles-heres-why/?utm_term=.fd3325ef0b5e. For a discussion on the technological challenges, see Richard A. Bitzinger, 'Does Japan Really Want Nuclear Weapons?', *Asia Times*, 8 September 2017, https://www.asiatimes.com/2017/09/opinion/japan-really-want-nuclear-weapons/.

27 H.D.P. Envall, 'Japan's "Pivot" Perspective: Reassurance, Restructuring, and the Rebalance', *Security Challenges*, vol. 12, no. 3, December 2016, pp. 18–19.

28 E. Michael Johnson, 'Donald Trump Receives $3,755 Driver from Japan's Prime Minister', *Golf Digest*, 20 November 2016, http://www.golfdigest.com/story/donald-trump-receives-dollar3755-driver-from-japans-prime-minister; and Envall, 'Can Japan's Golden Golf Diplomacy Win Over Donald Trump?', p. 16.

29 See Glen S. Fukushima, 'Is Trump Stringing Abe Along?', *East Asia Forum*, 3 June 2018, http://www.eastasiaforum.org/2018/06/03/is-trump-stringing-abe-along/. See also 'Trump's Short-sighted Mistreatment of Japan', *Financial Times*, 19 April 2018, https://www.ft.com/content/3dd4773a-42f6-11e8-93cf-67ac3a6482fd.

30 H.D.P. Envall, 'Japan: From Passive Partner to Active Ally', in Michael Wesley (ed.), *Global Allies: Comparing US Alliances in the 21st Century* (Canberra: ANU Press, 2017), p. 29.

31 'Donald Trump May be Bluffing Over a Pre-emptive Strike on North Korea', *The Economist*, 27 January 2018, https://www.economist.com/briefing/2018/01/27/donald-trump-may-be-bluffing-over-a-pre-emptive-strike-on-north-korea.

32 'Dealing with North Korea, Trump Puts Showmanship First', *The Economist*, 16 June 2018, https://www.economist.com/leaders/2018/06/16/dealing-with-north-korea-trump-puts-showmanship-first.

33 See 'Beicho Shuno Kaidan Kita no Kaku Hoki Jitsugen e Kosho Tsuzuke yo' [US–North Korea Leaders Summit: Negotiations Must Continue to Achieve North's Denuclearisation], *Yomiuri Shinbun*, 13 June 2018; and Soichiro Tahara, 'Beicho Kaidan o Oe, Nihon Seifu ga Daita Ke'nen' [Japanese Government Holds Concerns after US–North Korea Summit], *Nikkei Bijinesu Online*, 15 June 2018.

34 Tomohiko Satake and Yusuke Ishihara, 'America's Rebalance to Asia and its Implications for Japan–US–Australia Security Cooperation', *Asia-Pacific Review*, vol. 19, no. 2, November 2012, pp. 6–25.

35 Envall, 'Clashing Expectations', pp. 72–3.

36 Buzan and Wæver, *Regions and Powers*, p. 34.

37 Japan Ministry of Defense, 'Defense of Japan 2017', p. 218.

38 Itsunori Onodera, 'Press Conference by Defense Minister Onodera', 8 December 2017, http://www.mod.go.jp/e/press/conference/2017/12/08.html. See also Shinichi Fujiwara, 'Japan Deploying Longer-range Missiles to Counter China', *Asahi Shimbun*, 30 April 2019, http://www.asahi.com/ajw/articles/AJ201904300006.html.

39 See 'Japan Would Consider Joining China-led AIIB if Doubts Are Dispelled, Abe Says', *Japan Times*, 16 May 2017, https://www.japantimes.co.jp/news/2017/05/16/business/japan-consider-joining-china-led-aiib-doubts-dispelled-abe-says/; and Jonathan Pryke and Richard McGregor, 'The New US–Japan–Australia Infrastructure Fund', *Interpreter*, 31 July 2018, https://www.lowyinstitute.org/the-interpreter/the-new-us%E2%80%93japan%E2%80%93australia-infrastructure-fund.

40 'Japan, China Agree on Hotline to Avoid Clash in East China Sea', *Asahi Shimbun*, 7 December 2017.

41 See Saori N. Katada, 'East Asia's Rising Geoeconomics and the Strategy for Japan', Chicago Council on Global Affairs, January 2018, https://www.thechicagocouncil.org/sites/default/files/east-asias-rising-geonomics-and-strategy-japan_skatada_20180124.pdf.

After His Holiness: Tibet, Reincarnation Politics and the Future of Sino-Indian Relations

Iskander Rehman

The relationship between China and India is widely considered one of the most consequential of the twenty-first century. A vibrant literature on the complex ties between these civilisational powers has blossomed over the past decade – with a spate of recent confrontations in remote Himalayan border regions only heightening international interest. Foreign observers have, thus far, primarily focused on the military, economic and diplomatic aspects of this increasingly pan-Asian great-power competition. The Tibetan issue – insofar as it receives more than a passing mention – is viewed primarily through the lens of the long-standing Sino-Indian territorial dispute, and of Beijing's obsessive, authoritarian quest for dominion over its restive border regions.

Yet one could argue that there is another, more spiritual dimension to this multifaceted rivalry, one that gets short shrift in many Western analyses, perhaps precisely because of its seemingly esoteric nature. This is the ongoing struggle to shape the future of Tibetan Buddhism. It is a battle that involves arcane ceremonies, ancient history and godly reincarnations. Like most internationalised confessional disputes over the centuries, it is also deeply political in nature, involving a range of non-state and state actors, from extremist sects to state intelligence agencies. There is a strange, almost Kafkaesque quality to this shadow war, with a nominally atheist state,

Iskander Rehman is a Senior Fellow at the Pell Center for International Relations and Public Policy, and an Adjunct Senior Fellow at the Center for a New American Security.

Survival | vol. 61 no. 4 | August–September 2019 | pp. 131–156   DOI 10.1080/00396338.2019.1637127

the People's Republic of China, endeavouring to regulate, and in some cases redefine, the recondite rituals governing the reincarnation of 'living buddhas' or *tulkus*.

At the heart of this theological tussle lies the question of 14th Dalai Lama Tenzin Gyatso's succession, and what it might mean for the future not only of Tibetan Buddhism, but also of the Tibetan people's historic struggle for greater self-rule. It is also, to a certain extent, a new front in a Sino-Indian battle for Buddhist soft power in Asia. As the otherwise redoubtable Tenzin has begun to show signs of ageing and fatigue, this issue has become more pressing. The purpose of this essay is to explore the many ramifications of reincarnation politics for Sino-Indian relations. It argues that more atten-tion needs to be devoted to this issue, at the crux of which lies Beijing's ambition to cement its control over the Himalayan border regions and to permanently extinguish any organised form of religious opposition to communist rule. Indeed, over the past few decades, Chinese intelligence agencies have waged a relentless covert campaign to foment regional and sectarian divisions within the overseas Tibetan community, with the hope that the movement will fracture after the passing of the 14th Dalai Lama.

The centrality of the Tibetan issue

The Sino-Indian rivalry is deeply rooted and complex. As academic observ-ers of the relationship have noted, it can best be described as a 'compound' rivalry – a form of competition which spans several areas and involves mul-tiple issues, all of which bleed into each other.[1] It is positional, ideological and spatial, and draws on several interlocking mutual grievances, from China's history of military and diplomatic support to Pakistan, to India's growing proximity to the United States and its democratic allies.[2] At the knotty heart of Sino-Indian discord, however, lies the border issue, at the centre of which, in turn, features the question of Tibet.

The Tibetan issue generates friction on multiple levels. It embodies com-peting conceptions of history, state security, religious freedom and human rights. Disputes over control of Tibet's perceived historic boundaries and peoples fuelled the Sino-Indian antagonisms that led to open conflict in 1962 and 1967. These disputes continue to pollute the bilateral relationship.[3]

For Indian security managers, the Himalayas have traditionally been seen as something of a northward defensive glacis. China's absorption of the Tibetan plateau in 1950 was associated with the loss of what had been a vital buffer zone.[4] For the Chinese, the 'repossession' of Tibet and its vast, mineral-rich territories was both a means of recouping prestige after the so-called 'century of humiliation' and an opportunity to permanently anchor Chinese state power deeper within Southwestern and Central Asia.[5]

Although Sino-Indian relations have been officially normalised for more than three decades, Beijing has not forgotten India's history of support for Tibetan insurgent movements. Nor has it forgiven the Indian government's decision, under Jawaharlal Nehru, to shelter the Dalai Lama and host the Tibetan government-in-exile. To this day, whenever severe disturbances erupt in the Tibet Autonomous Region (TAR) or in ethnically Tibetan regions, Chinese state media and officials do not hesitate to imply that 'outside powers' – invariably the India-based 'Dalai clique' and their Western sympathisers – are fanning the flames of domestic discord.[6] Similarly, Beijing regularly lodges diplomatic protests when high-ranking Indian government officials or the Dalai Lama visit disputed territory, and Arunachal Pradesh in particular.[7] Indeed, as Raja Mohan has noted, 'When Tibet is relatively quiescent, it is possible for India and China to keep their fundamental disagreements on the backburner and move forward with the normalization of bilateral relations. When Tibet is restive, as it was during 2008 and since, it comes back to cast a big shadow on Sino-Indian relations.'[8]

As we shall see in more depth below, the Chinese state has vastly expanded the reach, scale and sophistication of its security apparatus in ethnic border regions such as Tibet, Inner Mongolia and Xinjiang – regions which have, in the words of some observers, morphed into high-tech 'laboratories for social control'.[9] Yet despite China's crushing, almost panoptical, presence, its leaders are still riven with concerns over mass unrest, internal fragmentation and 'fissiparous tendencies'.[10]

New Delhi, for its part, remains wary of the prospect of renewed Chinese meddling in its troubled northeast, and frets over Beijing's aggressive attempts to coax its smaller Himalayan neighbours, ranging from Nepal to Bhutan, away from India's perceived sphere of influence. Chinese actions in

Tibet also affect Indian public opinion. Indeed, the subcontinent's ancient ties to Tibet and Mahayana Buddhism precondition the Indian populace, as well as its vibrant strategic community, to view Beijing's repressive policies in a profoundly negative light.[11]

Perhaps most importantly, the absence of a resolution to the long-standing Sino-Indian border dispute – or even of a shared consensus on where much of the border lies – is tied to significant differences of opinion and interpretation over what constitutes 'greater' Tibet; over the validity of the McMahon Line, which Beijing rejects as an imperialist artifice; and over past areas of Tibetan sovereignty. For instance, China's dogged insistence on naming the Indian state of Arunachal Pradesh 'Southern Tibet' is undergirded by the argument that any region that once fell under Lhasa's writ should now be folded into a greater China. This is a controversial position for many reasons. Indeed, if one were to religiously follow such a linear historical logic, present-day China might have to be ruled from Ulaanbaatar or the steppes of Outer Manchuria.[12] Tibet's own early medieval past – when it dominated the Silk Road and its armies cowed the Tang Empire into submission – provides another empirical basis for rejecting the Chinese state-sanctioned narrative underlying its expansive territorial claims.[13]

The main historiographical challenge, however, lies in the fact that many of the Himalayan borderlands in dispute have traditionally been characterised by a great degree of fluidity, in terms of both human settlement and political control. As the French historian Bérénice Guyot-Réchard observes in an excellent recent study,

> the eastern Himalayas were historically a world of active (if not always large-scale) movement and interaction between many ethnic, linguistic, and cultural groups. The formidable landscape did not preclude these exchanges but shaped them in specific ways. Political interaction and conceptions of space and authority followed complex logics. This was a world where different actors could share, at different times and for different aspects, ownership and use of a place, its produce, and its people. Authority tended to be located in socio-economic relations, in control over people, rather than over territory. This interaction should

not be romanticised. Conflict, tensions, competition, prejudice and civilising missions were present. But this was a world articulated in ways starkly different from Western frameworks of sovereignty and 'international' relations.[14]

Due to the rugged nature of the terrain and the difficulties posed by harsh climatic conditions, pre-modern states exerted little true sovereignty in these remote regions.[15] Even at the height of the Raj, British forces rarely ventured beyond the so-called 'inner line' that separated the plains from the densely wooded hills of the Himalayan northeast.[16]

Nevertheless, evidence of past religious, or at least monastic, authority over regions such as Arunachal Pradesh has been leveraged by China as a means of asserting its claims over large tracts of Indian territory.[17] This brings us to another, often overlooked, aspect of the Sino-Indian border dispute, which is its profoundly religious character. Not only is the history of religion weaponised in order to affirm sovereignty over a contested space, much of the territory along the border is considered in and of itself to be sacred ground for a variety of religious groups. This is the case most famously for Mount Kailash and Lake Manasarovar in the TAR, which are major *yatra* or pilgrimage destinations for Hindus, Buddhists and Bonpos, but also for places such as Mount Kanchenjunga, which is revered as a deity by the local Sikkimese.[18] Among the mosaic of tribes and ethnicities that dwell along the Indian side of the border, many subscribe to shamanistic belief systems, whereby key elements of the local landscape – rivers, forests and mountain peaks – are infused with spirituality and believed to host supernatural beings and spirits.[19] With regard to the Tibetan people more specifically, Laura G. Rubio has noted that:

> the emergence of spatial referents in Tibet was determined in great measure by a pre-Buddhist religious lore centred on mountain cults, the introduction and assimilation of Buddhism and the establishment of a Lhasa-centred polity in the seventeenth century, which set up a regime in Central Tibet based on a combination of religion and politics ... The establishment of a sacred geography, and the development of Tibet's unique social and

political system generated strong attachments to the Tibetan land. The presence of (Buddhist) Tantric yogis and lamas, a rich Buddhist textual tradition, the projection of the Tibetan mandala principle into the Tibetan landscape, and the notion of 'hidden lands' (Tib. sbas-yul) as well as the idea that Tibet is the special field of activity of the Buddhist deity Chenrezig (spyan-ras-gzigzs; Skt. Alokitesvara), embodiment of compassion, and that Tibetans are his descendants, all contributed to the shaping of religious conceptions of territory, and of attachment to the homeland.[20]

International-relations theorists such as Anthony Smith have noted that it is essential to complement our more secular and 'state-centered modernist approaches' to territorial conflict with a 'perspective that highlights the importance of popular beliefs and sentiments about landscape and territory'.[21] Political scientist Ron Hassner has suggested that the 'sacred' quality of a territory under dispute, 'combined with the historically contingent conditions that may accompany the creation and management of sacred places', can impede efforts toward dispute resolution.[22]

This is quite clearly a key aspect of the long-standing Sino-Indian border dispute, which involves two multi-ethnic and multi-religious states (albeit ones that display varying degrees of diversity) that have diametrically different approaches to religious toleration and freedom of expression. New Delhi does not seek solely to shield its fertile lowlands from future Chinese encroachment – it is also safeguarding territory that hundreds of thousands of its own citizens have vested with deep spiritual meaning. Looking beyond the issue of spatial control, however, there is a deeper and almost equally fraught religious struggle under way. It is a clash over the complex rules and rituals governing an organised religion, but also an eminently political contest. Ultimately, as we shall see, it is a dispute driven by Beijing's desire to eradicate religiously inspired opposition to communist rule.

Reincarnation politics

The rules governing the *tulku* system of reincarnate lamas are highly complex, and have varied through time. As one Tibetologist notes, while this system draws on specific 'Buddhist concepts and ideals that were already present in Mahayana Buddhism in India', the 'social position of reincarnated enlightened persons, regarded as emanations of transcendent divinities, is a genuine Tibetan development'.[23] The Dalai Lama has existed as a formalised politico-religious institution since the sixteenth century, when the third Dalai Lama, Sonam Gyatso, entered into a priest–patron relationship with the Mongol ruler Altan Khan. Believed to be the reincarnation of Avalokitesvara, a bodhisattva of compassion, the Dalai Lama is the highest-ranking figure within the Gelugpa or 'yellow hat' religious tradition – the largest and most powerful sub-sect of Tibetan Buddhism. The Dalai Lama shares a unique, almost symbiotic spiritual relationship with the Panchen Lama, the second-most important figure in the Gelugpa school. In Tibetan religious folklore, the two are frequently referred to as the 'Sun and Moon in the Tibetan Buddhist spiritual firmament'.[24] Their smooth functioning as a duo is deemed critical as 'each lama', according to the Central Tibetan Administration, 'is not only involved in the search for each other's reincarnation, but also assumes the interchangeable role as Disciple and Teacher to each other'.[25] Over the past decades, however, this long-standing, deeply ritualised interdependency has been irredeemably fractured. In 1995, the 11th Panchen Lama was abducted by the Chinese authorities at the age of six, and has not been seen since. He was subsequently replaced by a Chinese-selected candidate that the Dalai Lama and Tibetan government-in-exile have refused to recognise.

The abduction of the young Panchen Lama was one of the first clear signs of Beijing's ruthless determination to exert control over the entirety of the *tulku* system, even at the cost of widespread international opprobrium. As University of Westminster professor Dibyesh Anand has noted, it was only natural that following the Chinese occupation of Tibet in 1951, tensions between the *tulku* system and territorial control would emerge, as 'traditionally, politico-religious legitimacy in Tibet flowed through the institution of reincarnation and not absolutist dominance of territory and population in the form of sovereignty'.[26] The figure of the Dalai Lama, in particular, is viewed as a threat to Chinese Communist rule. Although the ageing monk formally relinquished his political role in 2011, he continues to be revered as a living god by millions of Tibetans and Buddhists around the world. He is also the most immediately recognisable and charismatic symbol of the Tibetan people's travails under communist rule. Most importantly – and this is something that Western commentators sometimes fail to fully appreciate – he has proven to be a remarkably canny leader, fostering unity among a deeply diverse and factionalised Tibetan overseas community.[27]

It is frequently assumed that China's principal goal is to prevent the reincarnation of the Dalai Lama in an area outside its sovereignty, for fear that a new, more ethno-nationalistic leader might emerge – one less inclined to pursue his predecessor's 'Middle Way' policy toward Tibet. This is only partially true. In reality, the Chinese Communist Party's ambitions are more wide-ranging. In addition to forestalling such an eventuality, Beijing harbours a more long-term objective of shattering the Tibetan community into feuding factions by eroding or delegitimising the religious institutions and figures which help provide it with greater structure and unity. Indeed, the Chinese leadership considers the emergence of any form of pan-Tibetan consciousness, whether ethnic or religious, to be a threat.[28] A subsidiary objective is thus to isolate Tibetan Buddhists within China from their foreign-based counterparts.

In September 2007, the Chinese government introduced new legislation which laid out strict rules governing reincarnations. Entitled 'Measures on the Management of the Reincarnations of Living Buddhas in Tibetan Buddhism', the law specifies that 'reincarnating living Buddhas should respect and protect the principles of the unification of the state', and that all applications for reincarnations should be submitted to 'the local religious affairs departments at the level of people's government above county-level'. The law also specifies that, once a 'living Buddha permit' is approved, the deity should also undergo a government-sanctioned 'training plan'.[29] After being educated in the merits of Chinese government policies, living Buddhas are expected to 'play an important role in stabilizing social order in Tibetan areas'. This has occasionally taken on somewhat outlandish dimensions, with government-approved living Buddhas lecturing their followers on the benefits of family planning and birth control, for example.[30]

That a nominally atheist government should seek to involve itself in the arcane intricacies of the *tulku* system might appear somewhat bewildering. Yet the Chinese government has rather improbably cast itself as the guardian of Tibetan tradition in the face of attacks by outside forces of disruption.[31] A series of bureaus and organisational affiliates nested within China's shadowy United Front Work Department 'manage' Tibetan religious affairs, including the complex issue of reincarnate lamas. According to some reports, the United Front Work Department has compiled a database of more than 1,300 'officially approved living Buddhas' who reside within Tibet, and 'who will be called on when the time comes' to endorse Beijing's choices.[32] Naturally, the most important of these choices is that of the next Dalai Lama.

China has repeatedly stressed that the Dalai Lama's reincarnation should be conducted according to the Qing Dynasty-era tradition of drawing lots from a golden urn in front of Jokhang Monastery in Lhasa.[33] Tibetans have objected to this argument on several grounds. The most obvious disagreement is procedural in nature: the lottery would only include pre-screened candidates, and the Chinese Communist Party would most likely rig the process. This is what the Tibetan government-in-exile claims occurred with the party's selection of 'their' Panchen Lama in 1995. Chen Weijian, the vice-president of the Sino-Tibetan Friendship Association, New Zealand, has accused the Chinese government of placing an 'ivory lot bearing Gyaltsen Norbu's name a tad taller than the others' into the urn, thus turning the 'sacred process of selecting a reincarnation … into a chicanery'.[34] Another argument is more historically grounded. Many Tibetans consider the golden-urn ceremony as something of a foreign import. Initially a Chinese bureaucratic means of assigning administrative posts, the ceremony was introduced into Tibet by Emperor Qianlong in 1792 in circumstances that differ substantially from those surrounding its use today.[35] As Peter Schwieger has noted:

> During the Qing Dynasty, the emperor and the Dalai Lama were bound
> together by the priest–patron relationship … The ideological roots of this
> relationship were found in sophisticated concepts of Tibetan Buddhism,
> accepted by both parties to legitimize power and status. These concepts
> allowed for a mutual instrumentalization by both sides, the Gelugpa
> and the Qing Emperor, that suited their own individual purposes.

But the end of the Qing Dynasty also brought an end to this mutually accepted, common ideological ground. Seen in this light, the efforts of the government of the People's Republic of China to control Tibetan religious affairs by acting in the tradition of the Qing Empire in relation to Tibetan reincarnations look like a flimsy attempt to use old rituals – long bereft of a mutually accepted ideological base – for new ends.[36]

Rather than countering Beijing's reincarnation politics by laying out an equally rigid set of rules governing his own rebirth, the current Dalai Lama has deftly kept the world – and the Communist Party – guessing. On some occasions, he has argued that it would be 'logical' for his reincarnation to be another exile; on others, he has suggested that he might be reincarnated as a woman, or that he might not even reincarnate at all, adding that 'There is no guarantee that some stupid Dalai Lama won't come next, who will disgrace himself or herself. That would be very sad. So, much better that a centuries-old tradition should cease at the time of a quite popular Dalai Lama.'[37] This last suggestion, in particular, has provoked China's ire, with one Communist Party official claiming that the Dalai Lama was 'profaning religion and Tibetan Buddhism' by putting his own reincarnation in doubt.[38] A potential driver behind any decision not to reincarnate would be the desire to avoid a chaotic situation similar to that of the Western schism in the fourteenth century – when there were rival papal courts in Rome and Avignon – with two Dalai Lamas, one in Lhasa and one in Dharamsala.[39] Few of the Tibetan refugees and monks residing in India with whom I spoke, however, considered this to be a likely option. One monk suggested that the Dalai Lama might be 'raising such a possibility in order to keep the Chinese guessing and us Tibetans united', while another lama confided that, in his opinion, 'As long as the Tibetan people were suffering, the Dalai Lama, as the embodiment of compassion, would reincarnate.'[40]

A final possibility, first floated by the Dalai Lama in 2011 and recently reiterated by Lobsang Sangay, the elected president of the Tibetan government-in-exile, is that he will 'emanate' rather than reincarnate,[41] meaning that the Dalai Lama could formally identify a successor who shares his 'mind stream' and to whom he could begin the alleged transfer of his consciousness before he dies.[42] As Tibetologist Robert Barnett has noted, these varied announcements may constitute a means of signalling to the Chinese government that by claiming rigid control over all reincarnations, it has boxed itself into a theological (and political) corner.[43]

Ramifications for Sino-Indian relations

How might the question of the Dalai Lama's reincarnation affect Sino-Indian relations? Due to the sensitivities involved, India's management of the Tibetan issue has required a great degree of caution and finesse. Above all, the emphasis has been on predictability and on preventing, as much as possible, Beijing's stance on the Dalai Lama and the Tibetan government-in-exile from completely derailing an already fraught Sino-Indian relationship. Occasionally, these concerns have led the Indian government to crack down on Tibetan protests or self-immolations during visits from Chinese officials, or on the anniversary of the 1959 uprising.[44] More recently, growing tensions with China prompted the Indian Ministry of External Affairs to issue a controversial note advising political leaders and high-level civil servants to distance themselves from Tibetan gatherings, citing 'very sensitive times' in Sino-Indian relations.[45]

At the same time, and despite these occasional sensitivities, the Indian state remains firmly attached to the protection of the Tibetan-exile community's religious rights, and segments of India's security establishment continue to view China's fear of ethnic unrest as a potential vulnerability to be exploited in the event of conflict. Young Tibetan men are still quietly encouraged to join the Special Frontier Force (SFF), which recently revamped its pay and conditions in a bid to attract more recruits.[46] The pursuit of a military career in units composed of ethnic Tibetans or Himalayan peoples – whether the Ladakh Scouts or the SFF – provides a source of pride and financial stability to young Tibetan men who might otherwise seek to channel their youthful energy elsewhere.[47] Indeed, New Delhi is not eager to see a more ardent brand of Tibetan nationalism develop on Indian soil. This is for two main reasons. Firstly, such a development might have severely negative consequences for Sino-Indian relations, with Chinese officials intensifying their critiques of India's alleged 'fuelling of tensions' and 'political meddling' in Tibet. Secondly, Indian security managers do not wish to redirect Tibetan nationalism by stoking the flames of separatist militancy, potentially spawning another Gorkhaland-type movement on their own soil.[48] The Dalai Lama's Middle Way or *Umaylam* approach, which was formally adopted in the late 1980s and which seeks greater Tibetan autonomy rather than formal independence, has played an important role in sustaining the process of Sino-Indian normalisation. Were it to be jettisoned, or to become a minority position, this might generate all manner of difficulties – both internally and externally – for India.

The uncertainties surrounding the Dalai Lama's reincarnation bring an unwelcome degree of unpredictability to the Sino-Indian rivalry. One of the main mysteries is where the next Dalai Lama may emanate or reincarnate, and whether this might occur on Indian soil. Tibetologists, journalists and government officials have been eagerly scrutinising the Dalai Lama's travel plans and parsing his sometimes cryptic statements in their search for clues. Within India, commentators often point to the state of Arunachal Pradesh, and to the town of Tawang, which hosts the most significant Tibetan Buddhist monastery outside Tibet, as potential sites for emanation or reincarnation. There would be a precedent for the selection of Tawang, given that the sixth Dalai Lama originated from the town's environs. During the Dalai Lama's most recent visit to Arunachal Pradesh in April 2017, rumours swirled that his successor would be chosen from that region. Both the Dalai Lama and the Tibetan government-in-exile are keen to ensure that the Tibetan community remains united across tribal and ethnic lines following his passing, and it has been suggested that selecting an 'emanated' spiritual leader from the Monpa community in Arunachal Pradesh might prove politically astute.[49] Comments made by Sangay close to a decade ago are particularly revealing:

> The Chinese hardliner strategy is to wait for the passing of HH [His Holiness] the Dalai Lama (whom we all hope lives very, very long into the future) but the appointment of the Fifteenth Dalai Lama could foil their strategy. Of course the Chinese government will try to raise political objections but they will do that even if Tibetans follow the traditional protocol of reincarnation. To settle the Fifteenth Dalai Lama, the Chinese

government will spend billions of dollars, because to legitimize their candidate would fatally wound the Tibetan movement. To prevent such exploitation, as mentioned in interviews by His Holiness himself, it would be wise for HHDL [His Holiness the Dalai Lama] to appoint a young man of fifteen or twenty years of age, perhaps with part Monpa heritage in view of the importance of the state of Arunachal Pradesh in the dispute between India and China.[50]

These comments are significant for the following reasons: they acknowledge that the decision regarding the Dalai Lama's reincarnation is inherently political; that it is significantly shaped by sectarian and ethnic dynamics; and, most importantly, that it is inherently linked to the Sino-Indian border dispute. As a former secretary of the Indian Ministry of External Affairs has noted, China 'realises that the Sino-Indian boundary is, in actual fact, largely the Tibet–India boundary, except for a short length that abuts Xinjiang'.[51] This helps explain the vehemence of China's reaction to the Dalai Lama's visit to Arunachal Pradesh in 2017, during which Pema Khandu, the chief minister of that state, claimed that Tibet, rather than China, was India's northern neighbour.[52] The politics surrounding the Dalai Lama's reincarnation are thus inextricably bound to the Sino-Indian border dispute, and, by feeding China's frustration over its continued inability to corral the Tibetan Buddhist hierarchy into subservience, have in many ways delayed its resolution.

Of course, there is a possibility that the next Dalai Lama could surface elsewhere, far from India. For some in New Delhi, this might constitute a secret source of relief, as it would, to a certain extent, help to 'decouple' Sino-Indian territorial disputes from the Tibetan issue. The candidate could perhaps be drawn from the Tibetan diaspora in the West, or from Mongolia. Of the two options, the latter seems somewhat more likely, due to the deep-rooted historical ties between Tibet and Mongolia. As mentioned earlier, it was a Mongolian khan who created the position of Dalai Lama in the sixteenth century, and the fourth Dalai Lama, Yonten Gyatso, was a Mongolian. During the Dalai Lama's 2016 visit to Mongolia, there were rumours that the landlocked nation could host his successor.[53] Still, it should be noted that when such hypotheses have been raised in the past, the Dalai Lama himself has quashed them.[54] Two additional factors might militate against the selection of Mongolia as the birthplace or point of origin for the 15th Dalai Lama. The first of these is Mongolia's geographical distance from the spiritual heartland of Tibetan Buddhism and its associated sites of worship – an isolation which one Tibetan official said rendered 'the Mongolian option improbable'.[55] Secondly, Mongolia, as a sparsely populated, landlocked nation, is perceived as overly vulnerable to Chinese economic and military coercion. This was made painfully apparent following the Dalai Lama's visit to the country in 2016. In reaction to the religious leader's visit, a vengeful China closed a major border crossing with Mongolia for several days, imposed tariffs on commodity shipments and cancelled all scheduled interactions with Mongolian officials.[56] Following these actions, a chastised Mongolian foreign minister pledged to never again host the Dalai Lama, eliciting a statement from China that it 'hoped that Mongolia had learnt its lesson'.[57] The rapidity with which Ulaanbaatar bowed to Chinese pressure reduces the likelihood of Mongolia being chosen as the 'reincarnation spot' for the 15th Dalai Lama. Indeed, all options considered, the next Dalai Lama – provided the position is preserved – will most likely originate from India.

A vengeful China closed a border crossing

As the selection of the 15th Dalai Lama looms ever closer, a recrudescence of Chinese pressure along the Sino-Indian border should be expected, especially in areas featuring important religious 'nodes' for Tibetan Buddhism, such as Sikkim, Ladakh or Arunachal Pradesh. An intensification of the shadow war that Chinese intelligence has historically waged against the Tibetan diaspora and exile community should also be anticipated. Indian domestic-security agencies will thus have to contend with an increase in cyber attacks and cyber espionage against Tibetan leaders and websites, along with heightened Chinese human-intelligence activity, not just in neighbouring countries with sizeable Tibetan and Buddhist populations such as Nepal and Bhutan, but also within India itself.[58] Indeed, Indian intelligence professionals have indicated that Dharamsala is 'crawling with Chinese spies and informers', and that many of the monasteries of the four main Tibetan religious orders have been 'heavily penetrated by Chinese intelligence operatives'.[59] On occasion, India's suspicions regarding the growing ubiquity of Chinese 'plants' have generated friction with the Tibetan refugee community. For instance, the officially recognised 17th incarnation of the Karmapa Lama, Ogyen Trinley Dorje, who fled Tibet as a 14-year-old in December 1999, was suspected by some in India's Research and Analysis Wing of being a spy after large amounts of Chinese currency were found hidden in his monastery.[60] Although this particular cloud of distrust now seems to have been dispelled, Indian counter-intelligence's wariness is easy to understand.

Indeed, China's United Front Work Department has focused heavily on penetrating, subverting and disrupting Tibetan religious groups, and has proven reasonably successful at fomenting sectarian strife. A prime example of this 'divide and rule' strategy is Beijing's covert support of the Dorje Shugden movement, an extremist sect of purist yellow hats who revile the Dalai Lama and are suspected of having committed acts of lethal violence against members of his entourage. Leaked Communist Party documents reveal that 'the Shugden issue is an important front in our [China's] struggle with the Dalai clique', and officials from India's Intelligence Bureau have tracked flows of Chinese government funding to the Shugden sect via Nepal.[61] Theological disagreements among religious subgroups provide fertile ground for Chinese intelligence, which has been suspected of working to exacerbate the split within the Kagyu school over the true identity of the 17th Karmapa Lama (a minority group within the Kagyu school supports Trinley Thaye Dorje's claim to the title against Ogyen Trinley Dorje's).[62] As these intra-religious disputes have led to sporadic bursts of violence between groups of Kagyu monks, the Indian army has been obliged to provide permanent armed security at holy sites such as Rumtek Monastery in Sikkim. This can only be perceived as a net plus for China, as it generates tensions and frustrations between the Tibetan exile community and its Indian security guarantor. More recently, India's Intelligence Bureau reported that China has been actively recruiting 'disgruntled Tibetan refugees' in Arunachal Pradesh, in order to 'create a channel through which it can constantly receive relevant strategic information'.[63]

As analysts such as Jayadeva Ranade have observed, Buddhism has become a new frontier in the China–India rivalry, with both nations seeking to promote Buddhism as a means of enhancing their regional influence.[64] Beijing's activism on this front – most notably its financially extravagant offers to fund sects and monasteries that are hostile to the Dalai Lama or supportive of China's territorial claims – allows it to better monitor and control communities sprinkled across the Himalayan borderlands. For instance, Ranade notes that:

> there are many Tibetan Buddhist monasteries strung across the entire length of the Indo-Himalayan belt that exercise almost unmatched influence on the local populations in their jurisdictions. Monasteries like Hemis in Ladakh and Tawang in Arunachal Pradesh own considerable property and large tracts of land. The latter could at some stage become a nettlesome issue in negotiations between India and China. Viewed together with China's attempts to set up a monastery, seminary and nunnery in Lumbini [Nepal] to educate and train young monks free of cost, there is a real possibility that China will use them to try and increase its influence along India's northern borders.[65]

China's influence in Nepal is such that it has become increasingly difficult for Tibetans to escape via the Nepalese route into India. Indeed, Nepalese police, trained by Chinese operatives, have become adept at hunting down refugees and returning them into Chinese hands in exchange for a bounty.[66]

Should the Dalai Lama's reincarnation or emanation take place on Indian soil, some Indian observers fear that the current Dalai Lama's commitment to non-violence could be abandoned and that an increasingly factionalised Tibetan-exile community could splinter. Grounds for this fear are found in the frustration of a younger generation of Tibetans in India, who believe that the Middle Way approach has yielded little in the way of strategic dividends.[67] As China's economic and political clout has continued to grow, fewer international actors, from nation-states to Hollywood studios, are willing to risk incurring Beijing's wrath by expressing sympathy for the Tibetan cause.[68] Younger Tibetans, it is posited, may be more willing, out of sheer desperation over their brethren's plight and general international apathy, to engage in spectacular acts of violence.

Yet this outcome is unlikely for a number of reasons. Recent academic studies of the Tibetan-exile community suggest that, despite their very real frustration, very few young Tibetans would be willing to take up arms.[69] This was borne out by my numerous conversations with Tibetan youth in India. In addition, there is a sinking realisation that times have changed since the Tibetan guerrilla campaigns of the 1960s, and that China has vastly improved its internal security apparatus in the TAR, rendering the prospect of staging a successful large-scale revolt ever more chimeric.[70] The 14th Dalai Lama has also devolved his political role to the Tibetan government-in-exile, which has repeatedly confirmed its own adherence to the Middle Way approach.[71] His successor would inherit this reduced political role, and it is unlikely that he or she would seek to reverse what has become, in essence, a shared and secularised policy toward China.

That said, there is a very real possibility that the next Dalai Lama will prove a lot less successful in uniting various sects and factions than his shrewd predecessor. In the absence of one overarching source of moral authority, Tibetan politics could become increasingly polarised and rambunctious, and it is not inconceivable that certain factions might seek to rile up anti-China sentiment for political gain.[72]

Indeed, one of the most puzzling aspects of Beijing's intense hostility toward Tenzin Gyatso and his Middle Way policy is the fact that, in many ways, China has been fortunate that such a pragmatic figure has exerted such influence for so long.[73] As *The Economist* astutely pointed out more than three years ago:

> The great mystery about China's policy is why it seems to have decided that its best hope lies with the next Dalai Lama, not this one. Unlike many Tibetans, he has accepted Chinese sovereignty. He has used his enormous prestige to urge Tibetans to refrain from violent resistance. China faces a far more serious threat from the mainly Muslim ethnic Uighurs in the neighbouring region of Xinjiang. To safeguard its internal security, placate its disgruntled Tibetan citizens and improve its international reputation,

common sense suggests China should start talking seriously to the 14th Dalai Lama.[74]

There may also be certain bureaucratic compulsions behind Chinese officials' reluctance to reinitiate formal contacts with the Tibetan government-in-exile. Indeed, since the last round of talks ended in an impasse in 2010, China's violently antagonistic approach to the government-in-exile has not shifted. Barnett has suggested that this may be because the United Front Work Department has maintained its prestige within the Communist Party, as well as its control over Tibet policy, precisely by continuing to advocate for a hardline approach toward ethnic-minority areas. As a result, if the Chinese leadership were to roll back its policies in Tibet, many of which are similar to those being applied in Xinjiang, China 'would risk looking weak and susceptible to pressure from foreigners or from Tibetan activists within Tibet', possibly triggering 'further demands in other minority areas'.[75] The last point seems consistent with the Chinese leadership's interpretation of the sudden disintegration of the Soviet Union in the early 1990s, a phenomenon it attributes, in part, to Moscow's relaxation of its minorities policy.[76]

*   *   *

Over the past few decades, China has succeeded in resolving a number of its most contentious land-border quarrels, including with former foes such as Russia and Vietnam. With regard to its trans-Himalayan neighbour, however, the situation appears far less promising. Despite more than 20 rounds of intense bilateral negotiations, any permanent, mutually acceptable solution to the Sino-Indian border remains elusive.

With its inherent linkage to the Tibetan issue, the Sino-Indian border dispute is fundamentally a 'two-level game', in which both international and domestic considerations are at play.[77] The territories in dispute are inextricably intertwined with the Communist Party's perception of its 'core interests' and its long-standing fears of ethno-religious separatism, internal instability and foreign subversion. It is for this reason that otherwise esoteric topics, such as the rules, traditions and debates surrounding a living god's reincarnation, are of critical importance for gauging the future trajectory of Sino-Indian ties. As the 14th Dalai Lama has grown more frail, Beijing has become ever more shrill on the issue of his reincarnation, and has arguably behaved more assertively along its Himalayan borderlands. These developments should not be viewed in isolation. Indeed, the Sino-Indian border dispute extends far beyond the issue of state sovereignty and territorial control. It is also a struggle between two competing notions of nationhood, a battle for the preservation of a sense of pan-Tibetan identity and a conflict over the future of Tibetan Buddhism.

Acknowledgements

The author would like to thank Kate Saunders, Isaac Stone Fish, Elizabeth Clarke and Tenzin Loden Bhutia for their kind assistance in organising the fieldwork for this article.

Notes

1   For a seminal study of the nature and drivers of great-power rivalries, see William R. Thompson (ed.), *Great Power Rivalries* (Columbia, SC: University of South Carolina Press, 1999). For a discussion of why the Sino-Indian relationship should be considered a 'compound' rivalry, see Manjeet S. Pardesi, 'China and India: The Evolution of a Compound Rivalry', in Sumit Ganguly et al. (eds), *The Routledge Handbook of Asian Security Studies: Second Edition* (New York: Routledge, 2018), pp. 164–78.

2   For two thoughtful overviews of the various challenges India faces in its competition with China, see Rajesh Rajagopalan, *India's Strategic Choices: China and the Balance of Power* (New Delhi: Carnegie India, September 2017), http://carnegieindia.org/2017/09/14/india-s-strategic-choices-china-and-

balance-of-power-in-asia-pub-73108; and Jeff M. Smith, *Cold Peace: China–India Rivalry in the Twenty-First Century* (Lanham, MD: Lexington Books, 2014).

3   For a discussion of how the Tibetan issue exacerbated early tensions in the Sino-Indian relationship, see John Garver, 'China's Decision for War with India in 1962', in Alastair Iain Johnston and Robert S. Ross (eds), *New Directions in the Study of China's Foreign Policy* (Stanford, CA: Stanford University Press, 2006), pp. 86–130; and Sulmaan Wasif Khan, *Muslim, Trader, Nomad, Spy: China's Cold War and the People of the Tibetan Borderlands* (Chapel Hill, NC: University of North Carolina Press, 2015).

4   For an excellent overview of this line of thinking – largely inherited from the Raj – see Peter John Probst, *The Future of the Great Game: Sir Olaf Caroe,*

India's Independence, and the Defense of Asia (Akron, OH: University of Akron Press, 2005), p. 45.

5 For a classic discussion of China's view of Tibet as a door into Central and Southern Asia, see Owen Lattimore, *Inner Asian Frontiers of China* (New York: Oxford University Press, 1988). For a detailed study of imperial precedents to such thinking, see Peter C. Perdue, *China Marches West: The Qing Conquest of Central Eurasia* (Cambridge, MA: Belknap Press, 2005).

6 See 'China's Premier Blames Dalai Lama "Clique" for Violence in Tibet', CNN, 18 March 2008, http://edition.cnn.com/2008/WORLD/asiapcf/03/17/tibet.unrest/index.html.

7 For details of a recent occurrence, see Suthirto Patranobis, 'China Protests PM Modi's Visit to Arunachal Pradesh, Says Will Lodge Stern Diplomatic Protest with India', *Hindustan Times*, 15 February 2018, https://www.hindustantimes.com/india-news/china-protests-pm-modi-s-visit-to-arunachal-pradesh-says-will-lodge-stern-diplomatic-protest-with-india/story-bpnRDP1wmdpKG35UOSxFRI.html.

8 C. Raja Mohan, *Samudra Manthan: Sino-Indian Rivalry in the Indo-Pacific* (Washington DC: Carnegie Endowment for International Peace, 2012), p. 19.

9 Josh Chin and Clement Burge, 'Twelve Days in Xinjiang: How China's Surveillance State Overwhelms Daily Life', *Wall Street Journal*, 19 December 2017, https://www.wsj.com/articles/twelve-days-in-xinjiang-how-chinas-surveillance-state-overwhelms-daily-life-1513700355.

10 These concerns are most vividly reflected in the considerable (and growing) financial efforts and technological resources the Chinese government is funnelling into domestic security, surveillance and censorship. See Frank Frang, 'China Continues Vast Spending on Domestic Security', *Epoch Times*, 7 March 2016, https://www.theepochtimes.com/china-continues-vast-spending-on-domestic-security_1984944.html.

11 See Bhavna Tripathy, 'The Tibetan Uprising and Indian Opinion of the Chinese: An Analysis of the Tibet Factor in Sino-Indian Relations, 1947–1959', *Journal of Defense Studies*, vol. 6, no. 4, 2012, pp. 27–54.

12 Christopher Ford has noted that 'The two dynasties that give rise to the most sweeping of [China's] modern territorial claims, the Yuan and Qing dynasties, were actually non-Chinese conquest dynasties, created when outside barbarian peoples – Mongols and Manchus, respectively – invaded and defeated China, thereafter ruling it as merely one component of their sprawling empires.' Christopher A. Ford, 'Realpolitik with Chinese Characteristics: Chinese Strategic Culture and the Modern Communist Party-State', in Ashley Tellis et al. (eds), *Strategic Asia 2016–2017: Understanding Strategic Cultures in the Asia-Pacific* (Seattle, WA: National Bureau of Asian Research, 2016), pp. 29–63.

13 On Tibet's military dominance in the eighth century, see Sam Van Schaik, *Tibet: A History* (New Haven, CT: Yale University Press, 2011), chapter two.

On China's rewriting of the past, see Howard W. French, *Everything Under the Heavens: How the Past Helps Shape China's Push for Global Power* (New York: Alfred A. Knopf, 2017).

14 Bérénice Guyot-Réchard, *Shadow States: India, China and the Himalayas, 1910–1962* (New York: Cambridge University Press, 2017), p. 11.

15 See Sara Shneiderman, 'Barbarians at the Border and Civilizing Projects: Analyzing Ethnic and National Identities in the Tibetan Context', in Christian Kleiger (ed.), *Tibetan Borderlands* (Leiden: Brill, 2006), pp. 9–34; and Matthew W. Mosca, *From Frontier Policy to Foreign Policy: The Question of India and the Transformation of Geopolitics in Qing China* (Stanford, CA: Stanford University Press, 2013).

16 See Boddhisattva Khar, 'Where Was the Postcolonial? A History of Policing Impossible Lines', in Sanjib Baruah (ed.), *Beyond Counter-Insurgency: Breaking the Impasse in Northeast India* (New Delhi: Oxford University Press, 2009), pp. 49–77.

17 Lucy Hornby and Aliya Ram, 'China and India Renew War of Words over Tibet', *Financial Times*, 20 April 2017, https://www.ft.com/content/e5d141b0-2584-11e7-8691-d5f7e0cd0a16.

18 Mount Kanchenjunga is so closely tied to local religious sentiment that the Sikkimese government has forbidden mountaineering expeditions from 'defiling' its peak. See Luke Harding, 'Climbers Banned from Sacred Peak', *Guardian*, 12 July 2000, https://www.theguardian.com/world/2000/jul/13/lukeharding.

19 This is true, for instance, of the Lepcha people. For an interesting exploration of the role landscape plays in the Lepchas' religious practices, see Jenny Bentley, 'Narrations of Contest: Competition Among Representatives of Local Lepcha Belief and Guru Rinpoche in Sikkim', *Bulletin of Tibetology*, vol. 46, no. 1, 2010, pp. 135–61.

20 Laura G. Rubio, *Displacement, Territoriality and Exile: The Construction of Ethnic and National Identities in Tibetan Refugee Communities*, PhD dissertation, University of Manchester, 2014, pp. 14–15.

21 Anthony D. Smith, 'Sacred Territories and National Conflict', *Israel Affairs*, vol. 5, no. 4, 1999, p. 29.

22 Ron E. Hassner, 'To Halve and to Hold: Conflicts over Sacred Space and the Problem of Indivisibility', *Security Studies*, vol. 12, no. 4, 2003, p. 8.

23 Peter Schweiger, *The Dalai Lama and the Emperor of China: A Political History of the Tibetan Institution of Reincarnation* (New York: Columbia University Press, 2015), p. 1.

24 *The Panchen Lama Lineage: How Reincarnation Is Being Reinvented as a Political Tool* (Dharamsala: Department of Information and International Relations, Central Tibetan Administration, 1996), p. 1, http://tibet.net/2015/12/the-panchen-lama-lineage-how-reincarnation-is-being-reinvented-as-a-political-tool/. For an accessible explanation of this complex relationship, see Jonathan Mirsky, 'A Lamas' Who's Who', *New York Review of Books*, 27 April 2000, https://www.nybooks.com/articles/2000/04/27/a-lamas-whos-who/.

25 See *The Panchen Lama Lineage*, p. 1.

26 *Ibid.*, p. 37.

27 For an excellent overview of these factional conflicts, see Carole McGranahan, *Arrested Histories: Tibet, the CIA, and Memories of a Forgotten War* (Durham, NC: Duke University Press, 2010).

28 See Ben Hillman, 'Unrest in Tibet and the Limits of Regional Autonomy', in Ben Hillman and Gray Tuttle (eds), *Ethnic Conflict and Protest in Tibet and Xinjiang: Unrest in China's West* (New York: Columbia University Press, 2016), chapter one.

29 See *Measures on the Management of the Reincarnation of Living Buddhas in Tibetan Buddhism* (Beijing: State Administration for Religious Affairs, 2007), English translation available at https://www.cecc.gov/resources/legal-provisions/measures-on-the-management-of-the-reincarnation-of-living-buddhas-in-0.

30 See Dawa Tsering, 'Contemporary Tibetans' Views of Tulkus (sprul-sku)', *China Tibetology*, vol. 1, no. 6, 2010, p. 7.

31 See 'China Tells Dalai Lama Again to Respect Reincarnation', Reuters, 10 September 2014, https://www.reuters.com/article/us-china-tibet/china-tells-dalai-lama-again-to-respect-reincarnation-idUSKBN0H50S T20140910?feedType=RSS.

32 James Kynge, Lucy Hornby and Jamil Anderlini, 'Inside China's Secret "Magic Weapon" for Worldwide Influence', *Financial Times*, 26 October 2017, https://www.ft.com/content/fb2b3934-b004-11e7-beba-5521c713abf4.

33 'China Says It Will Elect Next Dalai Lama by Draw of Lots from Lhasa Temple's Sacred Urn', *Firstpost*, 11 April 2017, https://www.firstpost.com/world/china-says-it-will-elect-next-dalai-lama-by-draw-of-lots-from-sacred-urn-3379818.html.

34 *The Panchen Lama Lineage*, p. 42.

35 See Max Oidtmann, *Forging the Golden Urn: The Qing Empire and the Politics of Reincarnation in Tibet* (New York: Columbia University Press, 2018).

36 Peter Schweiger, *The Dalai Lama and the Emperor of China: A Political History of the Tibetan Institution of Reincarnation* (New York: Columbia University Press, 2015), pp. 216–17.

37 Sean Silbert, 'Why the Dalai Lama Says Reincarnation Might Not Be for Him', *Los Angeles Times*, 20 December 2014, https://www.latimes.com/world/asia/la-fg-dalai-lama-reincarnation-20141219-story.html.

38 Quoted in 'The Golden Urn', *The Economist*, 19 May 2016, https://www.economist.com/china/2015/03/19/the-golden-urn.

39 This historical parallel was first made by an unnamed senior official within the Obama administration. See Evan Osnos, 'The Next Incarnation', *New Yorker*, 4 October 2010, https://www.newyorker.com/magazine/2010/10/04/the-next-incarnation.

40 Interview with a monk and head lama at Ghoom Monastery, West Bengal, 7 April 2017.

41 'Dalai Lama May Pick His Successor Soon: Lobsang Sangay', *Hindustan Times*, 20 May 2017, https://www.hindustantimes.com/india-news/dalai-lama-may-pick-his-successor-soon-lobsang-sangay/story-9Hy3SlnuUtpnznvw2sRFJI.html.

42 Amy Kazmin, 'An Exclusive Interview with the Dalai Lama', *Financial Times*, 7 November 2013, https://www.

ft.com/content/d49d13aa-4749-11e3-b4d3-00144feabdco.

43 See Didi Kirsten Tatlow, 'Dalai Lama Keeps Firm Grip on Reins of Succession', *New York Times*, 5 October 2011, https://www.nytimes.com/2011/10/06/world/asia/06iht-letter06.html.

44 See, for example, 'Delhi: Tibetans Try to Stage Protest Near Chinese Embassy on National Uprising Day, More than 70 Detained', *Indian Express*, 11 March 2017, https://indianexpress.com/article/india/tibetans-protest-india-national-uprising-day-chinese-embassy-4564145/; and Jason Burke, 'India Cracks Down on Tibetan Protests During Chinese Leaders' Visit', *Guardian*, 28 March 2012, https://www.theguardian.com/world/2012/mar/28/india-cracks-down-tibetan-protests-china.

45 See 'India Claims Its Policy on Tibet Hasn't Changed Amid Reports of Government Asking Leaders to Avoid Tibetan Events', *Firstpost*, 2 March 2018, https://www.firstpost.com/india/india-claims-its-policy-on-tibet-hasnt-changed-amid-reports-of-govt-asking-leaders-to-avoid-tibetan-events-4373477.html; and Prashant Jha, 'After Government's Red Card, Tibetans Shift Dalai Lama Event from Delhi to Dharamshala', *Hindustan Times*, 6 March 2018, https://www.hindustantimes.com/india-news/after-govt-s-red-card-tibetans-shift-dalai-lama-event-from-delhi-to-dharamshala/story-dQB4Ak8BjwZuoiCqht6l3H.html.

46 Conversation with a Central Tibetan Administration official, Tibetan Settlement Office, Darjeeling District, 7 April 2017.

47 See 'U.S. Embassy Cables: Widening Generational Divide Between Tibet's Leaders and Youth', *Guardian*, 16 December 2010, https://www.theguardian.com/world/us-embassy-cables-documents/160094.

48 On the Gorkhaland movement, see Amiya K. Samanta, *Gorkhaland Movement: A Study in Ethnic Separatism* (New Delhi: A.P.H. Publishing Corporation, 2000).

49 See Tshering Chonzom Bhutia, 'The Politics of Reincarnation: India, China, and the Dalai Lama', *Diplomat*, 20 April 2017, https://thediplomat.com/2017/04/the-politics-of-reincarnation-india-china-and-tibet/.

50 See Lobsang Sangay, 'Agenda for the Special Meeting in Dharamsala', 14 November 2008, http://tibet.ca/en/library/wtn/4587.

51 Ranjit S. Kalha, 'The Politics of Reincarnation Will Be the Next Crisis in Sino-Indian Relations', *Wire*, 14 April 2017, https://thewire.in/external-affairs/dalai-lama-china-india-tibet.

52 Rahul Karmakar, 'Arunachal Borders Tibet, Not China: CM Pena on Beijing's Protest Over Dalai Lama', *Hindustan Times*, 5 April 2017, https://www.hindustantimes.com/india-news/arunachal-borders-tibet-not-china-cm-pema-on-beijing-s-noise-over-dalai-lama-visit/story-cDE3x2Nl45uRz14YmMVQwO.html.

53 Interview with Dr Alicia Campi, 1 November 2017, Washington DC. See also Edward Wong, 'Mongolia, with Deep Ties to Dalai Lama, Turns from

Him Toward China', *New York Times*, 30 December 2016, https://www.nytimes.com/2016/12/30/world/asia/china-mongolia-dalai-lama.html.

54 'Dalai Lama: My Successor Has Not Been Found in Mongolia', Niigem News, 11 November 2011.

55 Interview with Tibetan official, Tibetan Refugee Center, Darjeeling, 28 March 2017.

56 'China "Blocks" Mongolia Border After Dalai Lama Visit', Al-Jazeera, 10 December 2016, https://www.aljazeera.com/news/2016/12/china-blocks-mongolia-border-dalai-lama-visit-161210060313417.html.

57 'China Says Hopes Mongolia Learned Lesson After Dalai Lama's Visit', Reuters, 24 January 2017, https://www.reuters.com/article/us-china-mongolia-dalailama/china-says-hopes-mongolia-learned-lesson-after-dalai-lama-visit-idUSKBN158197.

58 See James Griffiths, 'Chinese Hackers Spying on Tibetan Groups in India for Years, Experts Say', *South China Morning Post*, 21 August 2015, https://www.scmp.com/tech/social-gadgets/article/1851099/chinese-hackers-spying-tibetan-groups-india-years-experts-say.

59 Interview with retired Indian intelligence official, New Delhi, 4 April 2017.

60 See Ishaan Tharoor, 'Why India Is Investigating a Reincarnated Tibetan Lama', *Time*, 3 February 2011, http://content.time.com/time/world/article/0,8599,2046124,00.html; and Mian Ridge, 'How Tibet's Karmapa Lama Is Fueling China and India Border Tensions', *Christian Science Monitor*, 14 February 2011, https://www.csmonitor.com/World/Asia-South-Central/2011/0214/How-Tibet-s-Karmapa-Lama-is-fueling-China-and-India-border-tensions.

61 See David Lague, Paul Moone and Benjamin Kang Lim, 'China Co-opts a Buddhist Sect in Global Effort to Smear Dalai Lama', Reuters, 21 December 2015, https://www.reuters.com/investigates/special-report/china-dalailama/; and 'Murder in a Monastery', *Newsweek*, 4 May 1997, http://www.newsweek.com/murder-monastery-172992. On the Dorje Shugden movement more broadly, see Georges Dreyfus, 'The Shukden Affair: History and Nature of a Quarrel', *Journal of the International Association of Buddhist Studies*, vol. 21, no. 2, 1998, pp. 227–71.

62 For more on this issue, see 'Who's the Real Karmapa?', *Newsweek*, 4 February 2000, https://www.newsweek.com/whos-real-karmapa-157915.

63 Ananya Bhardwaj, 'China Luring Tibetan Refugees in India to Work as Its Spies, Intelligence Bureau Warns', *Print*, 5 January 2018, https://theprint.in/defence/china-luring-tibetan-refugees-india-to-spy-intelligence-bureau-warns/26613/.

64 Jayadeva Ranade, 'Buddhism: A New Frontier in the China–India Rivalry', Carnegie India, 17 March 2017, https://carnegieindia.org/2017/03/17/buddhism-new-frontier-in-china-india-rivalry-pub-68326.

65 *Ibid.*

66 See Tibet Justice Center, 'Tibet's Stateless Nationals III: The Status of Tibetan Refugees in India', June 2016, http://www.tibetjustice.org/wp-content/uploads/2016/09/

TJCIndiaReport2016.pdf.

67 See 'U.S. Embassy Cables: Tibetan Frustration with the Middle Way', *Guardian*, 16 December 2010, https://www.theguardian.com/world/us-embassy-cables-documents/248429.

68 On China's growing economic clout in Hollywood and its effect on the Tibetan cause, see Tatiana Siegel, 'Richard Gere's Studio Exile: Why His Hollywood Career Took an Indie Turn', *Hollywood Reporter*, 18 April 2017, https://www.hollywoodreporter.com/features/richard-geres-studio-exile-why-his-hollywood-career-took-an-indie-turn-992258.

69 See Mark Owen, 'Preparing for the Future: Reassessing the Possibility of Violence Emanating from Tibetan Exile Communities in India', *India Review*, vol. 13, no. 2, 2014, pp. 149–69.

70 On the growing challenges associated with conducting special-warfare campaigns in the TAR, see Iskander Rehman, 'A Himalayan Challenge: India's Conventional Deterrent and the Role of Special Operations Forces Along the Sino-Indian Border', *Naval War College Review*, vol. 70, no. 1, 2017, pp. 104–42.

71 See Central Tibetan Administration, 'CTA President Reaffirms Kashag's Commitment to the Middle Way Approach', 21 September 2017, https://tibet.net/2017/09/cta-president-reaffirms-kashags-commitment-to-the-middle-way-approach/.

72 The most recent Tibetan elections were remarkably contentious, although no candidate openly questioned the pertinence of the Middle Way approach. See Greeta Anand, 'Mudslinging Trumps the Middle Way in Tibetan Exiles' Election', *New York Times*, 23 March 2016, https://www.nytimes.com/2016/03/24/world/asia/dalai-lama-tibet-dharamsala.html.

73 Beijing has condemned the Dalai Lama's Middle Way policy as a cover for gaining independence and 'creating a state within a state'. See Atul Aneja, 'White Paper on Tibet Denounces Middle Way', *Hindu*, 16 April 2015, https://www.thehindu.com/news/international/white-paper-on-tibet-denounces-middle-way/article7106400.ece.

74 'The Golden Urn'.

75 Robert Barnett, 'Imagining the Borderlands: Managing (to Prolong) Conflict in Tibet', *Nations and Nationalism*, vol. 22, no. 4, 2016, p. 716.

76 See, for instance, Minglang Zhou, 'The Fate of the Soviet Model of Multinational State-Building in the People's Republic of China', in Hua-Yu Li and Thomas P. Bernstein (eds), *China Learns from the Soviet Union, 1949–Present* (Lanham, MD: Lexington Books), pp. 477–505.

77 On two-level games, see Peter B. Evans, Harold K. Jacobson and Robert D. Putnam, *Double-Edged Diplomacy: International Bargaining and Domestic Politics* (Berkeley, CA: University of California Press, 1993).

Review Essay

War Powers

Russell Crandall

Presidents of War: The Epic Story, from 1807 to Modern Times
Michael Beschloss. New York: Crown, 2018. $35.00. 752 pp.

> The Constitution supposes, what the History of all Gov[ernmen]ts demonstrates, that the Ex[ecutive] is the branch of power most interested in war, & most prone to it. It has accordingly with studied care, vested the question of war in the Legisl[ative].
>
> James Madison to Thomas Jefferson, 1798

When James Madison, the fourth president of the United States (1809–17) and one of the nation's Founding Fathers, addressed Congress on 1 June 1812, he listed numerous 'injuries and indignities' that he accused Great Britain of inflicting on Americans, such as using Indian tribes to harass American forces and settlements on the country's western reaches, and the impressment of Yankee sailors into the Royal Navy. Most loathed, however, were the 1807 Orders in Council which, while hatched as a naval blockade of Napoleonic France, led to the British practice of detaining neutral American ships sailing to or from France.

Russell Crandall is a professor of American foreign policy at Davidson College in North Carolina, and a contributing editor to *Survival*.

Survival | vol. 61 no. 4 | August–September 2019 | pp. 157–162   DOI 10.1080/00396338.2019.1637128

For Madison, the orders were nothing less than a 'war against the lawful commerce of a friend'. As he said to Congress, the US constitution 'wisely' gave the legislative branch the duty of determining 'whether the United States shall continue passive under these progressive usurpations and these accumulating wrongs, or, opposing force to force in defense of their natural rights, shall commit a just cause into the hands of the Almighty Disposer of Events'. Henry Clay, the speaker of the House of Representatives and one of its so-called 'War Hawks', scribbled, 'Let us give in return for the insolence of British cannon, the peals of American thunder' (p. 61).

Madison allowed himself to believe that America would prevail in a

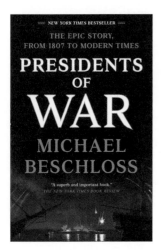

speedy conflict against an England preoccupied with its protracted fight against Napoleon, winning Canada as a prize of war. On 18 June 1812, he signed the congressional declaration of war. Ironically, the declaration came two days after Great Britain had cancelled the loathed orders. Given the speed of intercontinental communication at that time, Madison did not learn of the British move until almost two months later, the about-turn having been driven in no small part by domestic merchants who, tormented by an economic recession, wished to resume buying and selling with America. Even if Madison had known about London's rescission of the orders, it may well have made no difference: the once-circumspect president had by then 'adopted with gusto the identity of a majestic Commander-in-Chief' (p. 63).

Americans' confidence in their ability to swiftly defeat their militarily superior former colonial master was seen by some as delusional even at the time. Washington possessed only 16 war-ready vessels – most of them second-rate or small when compared to the Royal Navy's prodigious flotilla of several hundred ships. By August 1814, British forces were in Washington, the nascent republic's capital since 1790. Among other indignities, around 150 British troops – 'the most hellish looking fellows that ever trod God's earth', according to one terrified local – burnt the still-uncompleted US Capitol (p. 3). As redcoats ransacked the Senate, House and Supreme Court,

British Rear Admiral George Cockburn asked his men, 'Shall this harbor of Yankee "democracy" be burned? All for it will say, "Aye!"' (p. 3).

Having moved on to the Executive Mansion – which had started to be called the White House over the course of the war – Cockburn's elated men dined on Madison's Virginia meats and 'super-excellent Madeira' (pp. 3–4). Madison himself hastily departed the residence, 'still wearing formal knee breeches and buckled shoes' en route 'first by ferry, then by galloping horse' towards the relative safety of rural Virginia, lest he be hanged by the British (p. 1). Americans were apoplectic at the news that their commander-in-chief had fled the capital, the institutions of which the president had worked tirelessly to construct. Christening the conflict 'Mr. Madison's War', some pamphlets called him a 'coward' who went 'begging' for succour in Virginia, leaving his helpless wife Dolley to 'shift for herself' (p. 4). One citizen even threatened the president with 'dagger or poison' (p. 1).

Luckily for Madison's personal well-being (and historical legacy), Yankee forces won some key battles only a few weeks after his 'tail-between-the-legs return to Washington', first at Lake Champlain, then at the port of Baltimore and, by early January 1815, at New Orleans (p. 86).

The rise of 'presidential war'

As American presidential historian Michael Beschloss writes in his magisterial *Presidents of War*, even the reliably critical *Federal Republican* had to admit that the win at Baltimore's Fort McHenry had restored, 'in some degree, our national character from disgrace' (p. 86). By December 1814, the Treaty of Ghent had ended the war even if the communication time lag meant that Americans did not hear about it until mid-February 1815. Having been the first president to take the nation into an outright war, Madison tried to spin it as a victory despite not having secured Canada or even a formal pledge to honour US prerogatives in the Atlantic. Some of Madison's congressional partisans called it the 'second war for our independence', bragging that it was 'the most glorious war ever waged by any people' (p. 92).

As Beschloss tells it, Mr Madison's War was the first test of the US constitution's mechanisms for war fighting. During the Constitutional Convention in Philadelphia leading up to the successful 1788 ratification, Madison was anguished by the possibility that US presidents would, without popular support or consultation, cynically plunge the country into war in the way of the very European monarchs the American revolutionaries despised. Yet during his own presidency, 'however reluctantly, [he] succumbed to exactly that temptation', despite the 'absence of an immediate overwhelming danger, uneven support from Congress and the American people, and an overreaching mission that included a grab for Canada' (p. 585). We have lived with this legacy ever since, says Beschloss, as presidential control over war making has only increased over the years: 'By leading his country into a major war that had no absolute necessity or overwhelming support from Congress and the public, Madison, of all people, had opened the door for later Presidents to seek involvement in future conflicts that suffered from such shortcomings' (p. 5).

Beschloss reckons that US presidents have taken their nation to war 'roughly once in a generation' (p. vii). He offers riveting, exquisitely crafted case studies of eight presidents who went to war – Madison in 1812; James Polk in Mexico; Abraham Lincoln in the Civil War; William McKinley in Cuba; Woodrow Wilson in the First World War; Franklin Roosevelt in the Second World War; Harry Truman in Korea; and Lyndon Johnson in Vietnam – and one who did not: Thomas Jefferson during the *Chesapeake–Leopard* naval encounter with Britain in 1807.

Beschloss reminds us that the Founders intentionally designated Congress to be the 'sole power to declare war, and divided the responsibility to wage war between the executive and legislative branches' (p. viii). In 1848, Lincoln, then a member of Congress, wrote to his friend William Herndon that the framers had concluded that '*no one man* should hold the power' to plunge the country into war (p. viii, emphasis in original). Yet a mere half a century after the Constitutional Convention, storied New England politician Daniel Webster found it necessary to blast sitting president Polk's gratuitous 'presidential war' with Mexico (pp. 584–5). Beschloss is equally scathing, writing that 'James Polk lied and connived, creating a pretext for war that, despite his public claims, he designed to allow the United States to seize vast territory from Mexico' (p. 585). In February 1889, then-president McKinley 'showed how an outrageous offense that took American lives' –

in this case, the sinking of the USS *Maine* in Havana Harbor – 'could be employed to almost instantly unite the country for war' (p. 585). Roosevelt did the same following the surprise attack on Pearl Harbor in 1941. During the Cold War and after, presidents relied upon 'more modest forms of authorization', rarely bothering to have Congress 'fulfill its constitutional mandate to declare war'. Conflicts such as the Korean and Vietnam wars 'proved that the Constitution's demand for congressional war declarations could be ignored without serious penalty' (pp. 584–5).

Character and the constitution

Beschloss convincingly argues that the framers 'probably would have been thunderstruck' to learn that American commanders-in-chief now have the power to launch, on their sole authority, an attack that within a matter of minutes would incinerate millions of humans. The author also expresses concern at the prospect that a modern-day terrorist strike, much like the *Maine* sinking, 'could galvanize the country behind a President's demand for a war that it might otherwise shun' (p. 586). If Beschloss's presidential survey is any indication, this sort of cynical manipulation would likely generate even more acquiescence and a further transfer of power to the executive.

The most riveting part of the book deals with Johnson's idealistic, ambivalent venture into the Vietnam vortex, in which the author ably demonstrates how domestic political considerations and the doctrine of containment drew the United States into the war. (The quality of this discussion is not surprising, given that Beschloss has previously written on Johnson.) Yet, while the author does well in evaluating Johnson's wartime leadership, one quibble with the book might be that we do not get a profile of Richard Nixon (and, by extension, his foreign-policy guru Henry Kissinger), who also took the helm of this Southeast Asian conflagration. As a work of history, *Presidents of War* can be forgiven for not including the more recent case studies of George H.W. Bush in the Gulf War or his son (and later Barack Obama) in Afghanistan and Iraq.

In what is surely a thinly veiled jab at current US President Donald Trump, the author writes that the American Founders firmly believed that the office of the president would always be held by a person of 'sagacity, self-restraint, honesty, experience, character, and profound respect for democratic ideals' (p. 586). A bitter irony of the Trump presidency is that, whatever his sense of his wartime prerogatives vis-à-vis Congress, it is unlikely that he has read the US constitution or knows who William McKinley or James Polk were. Certainly, it has been widely reported that Trump does not read his daily intelligence briefings – a practice seen as near-sacred by the eight men immediately preceding him. Trump counters that he relies on an 'oral briefing' by aides, a format that fits his learning style. Beschloss is on solid ground when he concludes that the framers had no intention of giving war-making powers to the executive. One can only imagine the despair these wise patriots would have felt upon seeing an uncouth real-estate mogul and television celebrity take office without a hint of historical curiosity or professional duty.

Book Reviews

Politics and International Relations
Steven Simon

Who Fights for Reputation: The Psychology of Leaders in International Conflict
Keren Yarhi-Milo. Princeton, NJ: Princeton University Press, 2018. £26.00/$32.95. 357 pp.

Keren Yarhi-Milo gets personal in this book. She sets out to prove that the best predictor of a president's inclination to fight for reputation lies in his character, especially when character traits intersect in specific ways with views about the efficacy of the use of force. Borrowing from the field of psychology, Yarhi-Milo tells us that there are two kinds of people, low and high self-monitors. High self-monitors typically pay close attention to others' perceptions of them; are other-directed, in the sense that they instinctively tune their self-presentation to the expectations or needs of their interlocutors; and possess a strong social stage presence. They're the people everyone notices when they walk into a room. At the other end of the self-monitoring spectrum are low self-monitors, who couldn't care less about what others think of them, say what they believe to be true without regard for the preferences of their audience, and can circulate at a party for hours and leave without anyone having noticed they were there. Presumably, most people cluster toward the centre of the spectrum, and few exhibit all three crucial behaviours in equal measure. People are complicated.

This typology has been circulating for years, if not decades, and has informed constructivist models of international relations, but few scholars have made use of psychological insights because their application seemed too idiosyncratic, difficult to generalise, unsusceptible to scoring or tabulation and, in general, hard to squeeze into a parsimonious theoretical framework. Yarhi-Milo

     DOI 10.1080/00396338.2019.1637129

acknowledges these obstacles and has contrived a sensible, qualitative methodology that yields convincing results. There is a vast amount of information on presidents and, to a lesser degree, their principal advisers; a range of scholarly biographers and presidency specialists to poll on key attributes; and deep reservoirs of public statements, speeches, diaries and interviews that can be mined, along with a wealth of archival evidence, using word-search tools. The psychological literature itself provides indices designed to place subjects on the gamut of behavioural spectra. These sources are available for assessing presidential attitudes toward the use of force as well.

Although she covers a wider range in an online appendix, Yarhi-Milo focuses on just three presidents in the book: Jimmy Carter, a Democrat who served a single term (1977–81) as the successor and antithesis to the disgraced Republican Richard M. Nixon; Ronald Reagan (1981–89), a right-wing Republican; and Bill Clinton, the first post-Cold War president and a Democrat who served two terms (1993–2001) and who was impeached, but not convicted, in his second term. Carter was a low self-monitor, almost comically so, who was sceptical of the use of force and derided the notion that a reputation for resolve was something to kill for. When the Soviets invaded Afghanistan, Carter's view of force grew more favourable, but not as a tool to buttress his reputation for resolve. Rather, force would serve the material interest of keeping the Soviets away from the Persian Gulf. Reagan was the polar opposite, a high self-monitor, as his Hollywood career would suggest, and a believer in the utility of force, or the threat of it, to reinforce reputation. Clinton split the difference. He was, like Reagan, a high self-monitor, but, like Carter, unconvinced that reputation was best secured through the use of force.

In this book, Yarhi-Milo does not address the question of whether reputation is, in fact, important. (She does that elsewhere.) But her discipline on this score keeps the reader focused on her main point, which is that individuals matter, even in a world where systems rule.

Leap of Faith: Hubris, Negligence, and America's Greatest Foreign Policy Tragedy
Michael J. Mazarr. New York: PublicAffairs, 2019. $30.00. 528 pp.

Michael Mazarr, the author of this useful account of the second Iraq War, had several objectives. One reflected his sense that, despite the availability of numerous partial histories of the war, some of which are quite good, there was no overarching narrative that pulled all these threads together into a coherent tapestry. A second concern was to establish the motivation for the war. Lastly, he wanted to set forth lessons from the war that, if properly applied, would minimise the risk of another foreign-policy 'tragedy', to use his preferred term for this blood-soaked fiasco.

This book largely meets the first objective, recognising that much of the official documentation is still classified. Nonetheless, the cataract of memoirs, biographies, fly-on-the-wall reporting, leaked documents, reportage, interviews and declassified material, especially claims about Iraqi weapons of mass destruction, is sufficient for a satisfying, mostly chronological treatment of the war from its inception very nearly to the present. Thus, while not definitive, it will prove more than adequate, especially for younger readers who matured after the crucial decade, or those who were on another planet.

The second objective was more difficult to meet and therefore less successful. Mazarr believes that the root of the tragedy lay in the Bush administration's missionary zeal, which he situates in the broader historical context of American messianism. It is an interesting claim, but difficult to sustain in part because of definitional problems and in part because the evidence he so assiduously assembles runs counter to the reductionist thrust of his argument. Mazarr conflates missionary commitment with certainty, linking George W. Bush's tendency to insist that he was utterly confident that the invasion of Iraq and the 'global war on terror' were the right things to have done (and that he had no regrets) to the tendency of missionaries to be certain of their calling. That Bush frequently invoked God reinforced this apparent connection. But given the temper of the administration, the deranging effect of 9/11, the prevailing desire to get rid of Saddam Hussein, a belief in the efficacy of the use of force and towering ignorance about Iraq, locating the source of the invasion in the deeper swell of American messianism seems unnecessary and not particularly enlightening.

Mazarr's lessons learned are expressed in terms of the jurisprudence of criminal negligence. The indictment of the Bush administration for this felony is well argued, and Mazarr crisply converts the charges into rules for good foreign policy. There is something schizophrenic about this discussion, and about his overall assessment of the men and women in key policy positions in the run-up to the war and afterward. Even as he makes the case for criminal negligence, he emphasises the noble intentions of these officials, their brilliance, diligence and idealism. Yet his own very effective narrative underscores the mediocre performance of many players and their addiction to hubris juice, on which they had been drunk for years. Some of these individuals had pushed for war with Iraq in 1990–91, a foundational blunder that left no good options for the Clinton administration and, ultimately, for the second Bush presidency. Histories, like this one, that fail to treat the two Gulf wars as a single conflict punctuated by an awkward truce leave plenty of room for the comprehensive account that is yet to be written.

Why America Loses Wars: Limited War and US Strategy
From the Korean War to the Present
Donald Stoker. Cambridge: Cambridge University Press, 2019.
£22.00/$29.95. 344 pp.

This book is a plea for clarity where none is likely to be achieved, except perhaps in the theoretical literature on strategy. The author, Donald Stoker, served as professor of strategy and policy at the Naval Postgraduate School in Monterey, California, for nearly two decades. He is an authority on Karl von Clausewitz and has clearly read widely and thought deeply about why the US has lost wars since the Second World War. He is also a clear and vigorous prose stylist. He does not mince words.

Stoker's essential claim is that a war cannot be won if the objective is undefined and, perhaps obviously but nonetheless worth stating, if victory is not the objective. You cannot win if you do not know what you want, and you cannot win if you do not want to. In the years since Germany and Japan surrendered, General Douglas MacArthur's oft-mocked judgement that 'there is no substitute for victory' has been challenged by successive administrations for whom there were, in fact, substitutes for victory.

For Stoker, there are linguistic and conceptual barriers to understanding the nature of the problem. These were injected into strategic theory at the very outset of the Cold War, when fear of escalation engendered the notion of limited war. No one, apparently, could agree on what actually made a war limited: the means deployed? Constraints accepted? Questionable domestic support? Limited objectives? Using case studies ranging from Korea to Iraq, the argument demonstrates the difficulty, if not the impossibility, of reaching a comprehensive, definitive conclusion. One thing that is clear to Stoker is that definitional uncertainty has caused, or perhaps enabled, administrations fighting wars to characterise the violence in terms other than war, which in turn made the prospect of winning ever more remote.

The other large obstacle to victory is the failure to think through what happens when the guns fall silent. Stoker relates the reaction of General Colin Powell, then-chairman of the Joint Chiefs of Staff, to Fred Iklé's brilliant book *Every War Must End* as the administration was preparing to push Iraqi forces out of Kuwait in 1991. He was evidently thunderstruck by Iklé's insistence on the need to fashion the peace as the prerequisite for victory. He had sections of the book photocopied and distributed to key policymakers. (The National

Security Council staff sent a memo to the West Wing on this matter as well.) Yet the administration was utterly unprepared for what followed the ceasefire agreement signed by the US and Iraq at Safwan. Saddam remained in power, exploited a loophole in the armistice terms to suppress a rebellion, waged a war on the Kurds, impeded UN inspection efforts and corrupted sanctions enforcement. The Clinton administration, which had not started the war, had to deal with the unanticipated outcomes it produced.

The one issue that this engrossing book does not really grapple with is asymmetry of interest. If there is one reason that the US has lost wars, it is that Washington goes to war against actors whose need to avoid defeat is greater than American interest in victory.

The U.S. Army in the Iraq War, Volume I: Invasion, Insurgency, Civil War, 2003–2006
Colonel Joel D. Rayburn and Colonel Frank K. Sobchak, eds.
Carlisle, PA: United States Army War College Press, 2019. 696 pp. Available at https://publications.armywarcollege.edu/pubs/3667.pdf.

The U.S. Army in the Iraq War, Volume II: Surge and Withdrawal, 2007–2011
Colonel Joel D. Rayburn and Colonel Frank K. Sobchak, eds.
Carlisle, PA: United States Army War College Press, 2019. 668 pp. Available at https://publications.armywarcollege.edu/pubs/3668.pdf.

This comprehensive, two-volume work by two US Army officers, now retired, who are also diligent historians, might not prove to be the last word on the second Iraq War, but will do quite nicely until that last word is uttered. It is, of course, the history of the army in the war, but the war was quintessentially a ground war. At intervals, the US Air Force played an important role, in addition to army aviation, both by killing high-value targets, such as Abu Musab al-Zarqawi, the Jordanian psychopath who terrorised Iraqis in the early years of the war, and by providing close air support, intelligence and logistical needs throughout the conflict. But it was the infantry that bore the brunt of the fighting. The authors have a great deal of experience in Iraq and within the command that organised and directed combat operations. One of them, Joel Rayburn, now a mid-level State Department official after a brief stint on Donald Trump's National Security Council staff under Lieutenant-General I I.R. McMaster (who resigned in 2018 to make way for John Bolton), is a historian of Iraq and has written interestingly about British counter-insurgency strategy in the 1920s. It is worth recalling that one of the air bases used by US forces had already served as a Royal Air Force installation after the First World War, as Britain deployed its airpower to suppress a revolt against the Hashemite king imposed on Iraq by London. *Plus ça change.*

It took nearly two years for this important study to reach the public. This delay seems to have reflected persistent tensions within the army about the way the war was fought. The authors' key judgements might also have been controversial. Two of these stand out. The first is that there was indeed a winner and it was Iran; the second is that the 2007–08 surge might have won the war for the United States, if only the strategy had been pursued.

The first claim is largely undisputed. Saddam's Iraq had been the main bulwark against Iran's ability to project power in the region. For the most part, successive US administrations had favoured Iraq in the application of their intra-regional balancing strategy. They were encouraged to do so by the states on the Arab side of the Gulf, especially Saudi Arabia. (Others, such as Kuwait, which had been occupied and pillaged by Iraq in 1990 and had a large Shia population, felt differently.) Participants in decision-making during the First Gulf War, for example, are unanimous in identifying concerns about Iran as having been central to the US decision not to overthrow Saddam after ejecting his forces from Kuwait. The second Bush administration abandoned offshore balancing as a strategic imperative, betting that the US would win the war and enlist Iraq as an ally against Iran.

The second claim is somewhat idiosyncratic and recalls revisionist narratives about Vietnam. The surge was a strategy, perhaps a stratagem, devised by General David Petraeus to staunch the civil war by flooding contested areas with US troops, deploying in urban areas, walling off sectarian enclaves and establishing tactical alliances with Sunni tribes to help subdue radical violence. It worked. The level of violence declined substantially and, over time, a kind of political process got traction. But US forces had worn out their welcome, and a by-product of the new nationalist politics was an Iraqi demand that the US withdraw. The Bush administration bowed to the inevitable, pledging to pull out troops by 2011. It therefore fell to Barack Obama to fulfil the pledge. The resurgence of the Islamic State (ISIS) in 2014, according to the neo-revisionists, resulted from this withdrawal and, in their view, is Obama's fault. The authors of this study argue that the US should have kept the surge force in Iraq and widened the war to Iranian territory to give the US the freedom of action necessary to control Iraq and undermine Iran's influence in Baghdad.

It's a peculiar conclusion, however, given the scrupulous care the authors give to their account of the lunatic blunders that led to the US withdrawal.

These are well known, but Joel Rayburn and Frank Sobchak bring a special authority to the awful story. Lack of advance planning, wishful thinking, ignorance about Iraq, alienation of important constituencies, operational flip-flops, revolving-door command arrangements, strategic misconceptions, politicised management – the list, if not endless, is long. The question raised by the authors' strategic judgement regarding the victory the US could have won had it not lost its nerve is how success could have been achieved given this colossal level of malpractice. But the underlying issues – was the war a good idea that failed owing to human error? Or was it a bad idea not just because it was strategically misconceived, but because it misjudged US character and capacity? – demand serious discussion.

Russia and Eurasia
Angela Stent

Moscow Rules: What Drives Russia to Confront the West
Keir Giles. London: Royal Institute of International Affairs,
2019. £27.95/$34.99. 234 pp.

Keir Giles has written this insightful and sobering analysis 'for anybody who cannot understand why Russia and its leaders behave as they do' (p. xv). He explains why, after the Soviet collapse, many in the West mistakenly believed that post-Soviet Russia would seek to become more like the West and integrate with it, failing to understand that Russia is fundamentally not a European nation. In fact, as Russia has recovered from the 1990s and returned to the world stage, it has increasingly turned against the West.

Summing up the Kremlin's current world view, Giles argues that 'Russia's default view is that territory, political status, national prestige, and the requirements of hard security are valued more highly than the rights and quality of life of its citizens' (p. 160). If relations with the West are to improve, they cannot be based on the assumption that Moscow will change.

One problem is that Russia and the West have a fundamentally different understanding of how the Cold War ended. The West viewed the fall of the USSR as a liberation of Russia which Russians should have embraced; but this drastically underestimated the humiliation which many Russians felt at the loss of status and security that came with the end of Russia's domination of its neighbours. From Moscow's point of view, the failure to conclude a negotiated settlement to the end of the Cold War and to include Russia in Euro-Atlantic security arrangements is responsible for ongoing East–West tensions.

Giles argues that one reason for the incompatibility of Western and Russian views is Russia's expansive vision of what constitutes Russian territory, the product of centuries of absorbing its neighbours. For Moscow, Russia's security is guaranteed by the insecurity of its neighbours, as can be seen in today's Ukraine crisis, in which the Kremlin seeks to make it impossible for the government in Kiev to control its own territory and govern effectively. Moscow is insisting that the West respect its need for buffer states.

Giles stresses the continuity in Russian history from Peter the Great to Vladimir Putin, both in Russia's attitudes toward the West and in its treatment of its own people. 'Rather than constituting a break from Russian tradition, the Soviet regime co-opted, preserved, suspended or renamed permanent features of Russian life' (p. 118). One of these features is the use of the threat from abroad – especially from the West – to justify the economic hardship and political repres-

   DOI 10.1080/00396338.2019.1637130

sion that Russian citizens have had to endure for centuries. It has also entailed suppressing information about the real situation both inside and outside Russia, and attempts to isolate the population from the rest of the world.

Although Giles believes that it is possible for Russia and the West to work together on limited, strictly bilateral issues, his overall conclusion is not reassuring: the Russia–West 'relationship as a whole is not amenable to change through policy steps because it rests on the fundamental incompatibility between Russian interests and Western values' (p. 165).

In Putin's Footsteps: Searching for the Soul of an Empire Across Russia's Eleven Time Zones
Nina Khrushcheva and Jeffrey Tayler. New York: St. Martin's Press, 2019. £22.99/$28.99. 308 pp.

This lively and illuminating political exploration of Russia from Kaliningrad to Vladivostok vividly illustrates the adage: 'Putin has failed to build us a great future, so he has built us a great past' (p. 271). The authors travel the breadth of Russia to understand how much of Putin's plan to restore Russia's grandeur has spread from the major urban centres to the vast provincial hinterland. On their journey, they witness the myriad of contradictions that are today's Russia, where pride in the country's return to the world stage coexists with grinding poverty and doubts about Russia's future.

Putin has repeatedly stressed that Russia deserves to be a major world player because of its sheer size. But, as the authors point out, Russia's 11 time zones are excessive – there should only be seven, according to the generally accepted geographic markers of Greenwich Mean Time. By contrast, China's large landmass should span five time zones, but operates according to just one. For Russia's leaders, the fact that Russia has more contiguous time zones than any other country bespeaks its special status.

Wherever they travel, the authors encounter a conviction that Russia can only exist in opposition to the West. Putin, they argue, has increasingly staked his popularity on an image of the West as an enemy. He has 'surrendered to the traditionally xenophobic, inward-looking approach of what we might call "Byzantinism" – the attitude of "us versus them"' (p. 72).

The Putin restoration is reflected in the way the country portrays its Soviet past. The authors visit the Lenin Museum in his birthplace, Ulyanovsk. Four leaders dominate the museum – Vladimir Lenin, Joseph Stalin, Leonid Brezhnev and Vladimir Putin, all 'wise' leaders of a great Russia. But what about the reformers, ask the authors, one of whom is Nikita Khrushchev's granddaughter? Why are Khrushchev, Mikhail Gorbachev and Boris Yeltsin not featured in this museum? The guide's answer is very Soviet: 'There was no administrative order issued to set up such an exhibit' (p. 88). The authors speculate that the reformers are absent because 'they don't accord with the black-and-white view of Russian grandeur, as personified in firm leaders who must always appear unrepentant, despite the scale of the suffering they oversaw or caused' (p. 88).

Both Putin and Xi Jinping have touted their burgeoning personal and political partnership, but the authors experience the rather different reality of Sino-Russian relations on the level of ordinary people. They travel to Blagoveshchensk on the Chinese border, where author Nina Khrushcheva joins the throngs of Russian and Chinese shuttle traders on the ferry connecting the Russian city with Heihe on the Chinese side. The mutual animosity and suspicion is palpable, as the shuttle traders jostle with each other on a chaotic ferry ride.

The authors conclude that 'Russia does not constitute a separate civilization – it has borrowed too much from the West for that – but, in its own way, it seems a world of its own' (p. 279).

The Putin System: An Opposing View
Grigory Yavlinsky. New York: Columbia University Press, 2019.
£22.00/$28.00. 256 pp.

Grigory Yavlinsky, a democratic opposition politician in Russia who has run against both Yeltsin and Putin for president, presents a compelling view of the origins and development of the Putin system, challenging conventional analyses and questioning the impact of Western policies toward Russia over the past 30 years.

Characterising Russia as a peripheral authoritarian regime that has failed to integrate with the core industrial nations, Yavlinsky argues that 'many of Russia's policies stem from its leadership's resentment over being treated as a peripheral player, progressively marginalized within most international institutions and their decision-making on major global and regional issues' (p. ix). Russia's economically peripheral position and its authoritarianism, he says, are historically interconnected. But he also situates Russia's authoritarianism within the broader context of the weakening of Western democracies, and the growth of both corruption and income inequality in the West.

Yavlinsky blames the Yeltsin administration for not introducing far-reaching economic and political reforms. Partial measures led to the rise of the oligarchs, and to growing income inequality and pervasive corruption through the various privatisation schemes. 'Russia', Yavlinsky writes, failed in the 1990s 'to produce a class of autonomous and socially responsible wealth owners capable of collectively assuming the role of the advocate, organizer and driving force of active institutional transformation' (p. 8). It was under Yeltsin that the current system fusing governmental power with the ownership of economic assets emerged. Yavlinsky also blames the West for failing to give adequate support to post-Soviet Russia as it struggled to reinvent itself.

Moreover, the Yeltsin administration never undertook a thoroughgoing critical examination of the legacy of Bolshevism and Stalinism, although non-governmental organisations did. Thus, by the time Putin came to power, Russians were disillusioned with the chaotic 1990s and searching for answers in the Soviet past, something that Putin understood and exploited.

The system that Putin has created, argues Yavlinsky, has no real goals other than the inherent goal of self-perpetuation. It has only a 'fuzzy' ideology that is a hybrid of various ideas. Over time, the West has emerged as the main and virtually only foreign adversary of Russia, a theme incessantly repeated on state-run television channels. Hence, anyone who criticises the Russian government must be influenced by the West, which is portrayed as the main enemy of Russian statehood.

Yavlinsky enumerates the core features of the Putin system: exorbitant levels of endemic corruption; weak institutions and a lack of rule of law; a regime that is increasingly personalistic in nature; increasing stagnation; and social and economic ineffectiveness at accomplishing the tasks of development. 'On the whole,' he concludes, the Putin system 'has acquired the features of a mature autocracy organized on the principles of Mafia-like syndicates' (p. 203). But Putin enjoys support from below, and external threats have been reduced to a minimum.

The West's policies of sanctions, says Yavlinsky, intended to drive Russia further into the global economic periphery, are ineffective and likely to backfire by strengthening the regime.

Russia, BRICS, and the Disruption of Global Order
Rachel S. Salzman. Washington DC: Georgetown University Press, 2019. $32.95. 208 pp.

Rachel Salzman's analysis of Russia's role in creating and nurturing the BRICS organisation – comprising Brazil, Russia, India, China and South Africa – makes a valuable contribution to our understanding of how deteriorating ties with the West have led the Kremlin to seek allies in pushing for the creation of a 'post-West' global order. Although some observers question the importance of BRICS, Salzman makes a convincing case that the group stands as one of Putin's signature accomplishments, and that the group is slowly institutionalising itself, even though its long-term cohesion remains in question. Above all, BRICS has enabled Russia to create an organisation whose rules it can shape, unlike Western-dominated institutions, whose rules Russia has had to accept.

The term BRIC (Brazil, Russia, India, China) was first coined by Jim O'Neill of Goldman Sachs in 2001. Following the 9/11 terrorist attacks, O'Neill believed that in the future, 'globalisation' would no longer be synonymous with 'Americanisation'. He identified the four BRICs as future leaders in the global economy, predicting that they would eventually overtake the G7 countries. Even before these pronouncements, Russian foreign minister Yevgeny Primakov had in 1998 advocated a 'strategic triangle' of Russia, China and India as an alternative to the US-dominated global order.

Salzman traces Russia's growing tensions with the West throughout the late 1990s and into the early 2000s. The BRIC countries began meeting in 2005, but the group only coalesced in the wake of the 2008 financial crisis, when it became a subgroup within the G20. At the Pittsburgh G20 summit in 2009, the group was able to push through significant reforms on weights and quotas within the IMF. Since then, it has focused on strengthening relations among members. South Africa joined in 2010.

According to Salzman, the Ukraine crisis strengthened Russia's determination to ally itself with the economic non-West. Indeed, its four BRICS partners abstained in the UN General Assembly vote that condemned the annexation of Crimea, and none of them has joined the sanctions regime against Russia, providing support to Moscow even as the West has sought to isolate it. Moreover, in the past few years the organisation has created new institutions – a BRICS development bank and a contingency currency pool.

Despite Russia's positive rhetoric about BRICS and Moscow's insistence that it represents an alternative to the declining West, there are growing asymmetries within the organisation that call into question its future. China and India are both dynamic, modernising economies with populations many times that of Russia, whose population is shrinking. Russia, Salzman argues, is the only BRICS member that is not modernising; indeed, it appears to be regressing economically, if not militarily. Some have questioned whether Russia still belongs in the BRICS club.

So far, says Salzman, the BRICS group has not created a new model of global governance. But the organisation has given Russia an alternative to the Western-dominated institutions from which it has become increasingly alienated.

Politics Under the Influence: Vodka and Public Policy in Putin's Russia
Anna L. Bailey. Ithaca, NY: Cornell University Press, 2018.
£19.99/$24.95. 247 pp.

Legend has it that when Grand Prince Vladimir ruled Kievan Rus' and had to decide which religion to adopt for his subjects, he received a delegation of Muslim Bulgars who explained that alcohol was forbidden by Islam. Vladimir's response: 'Drinking is the joy of the Russes. We cannot exist without it' (p. 100). He adopted Christianity instead.

In this detailed analysis of the Russian state's ambivalent attitude toward vodka, Anna Bailey argues that excessive alcohol consumption has plagued Russian society for centuries (vodka distilling appeared in Russia sometime before the beginning of the sixteenth century). Yet successive Russian and Soviet governments have failed to recognise it as a public-health problem. Long periods of state monopoly over the production and sale of vodka, and the sizeable revenues that the monopoly produced, have been punctuated by brief forays into anti-alcohol campaigns and prohibition – all of which have failed. There are too many vested interests in maintaining robust alcohol production, and the state needs the revenues from sales.

The early Bolsheviks maintained that alcoholism was a product of capitalism, a way for members of the working class to escape the grim realities of their squalid lives. Hence, alcoholism would fade away under socialism. Alcohol was outlawed, but *samogon* (moonshine) flourished, and by 1925 the state restored its monopoly over the production and sale of alcohol. In 1930, Stalin instructed Vyacheslav Molotov to expand vodka production as much as possible to finance a major expansion of the Soviet army. Khrushchev half-heartedly tried to tackle the issue, but it was only in 1985, when Gorbachev came to power, that a concerted anti-alcohol campaign was launched – incurring the wrath of Soviet citizens. Production was restricted, prices were raised, and hours of sale and restaurant consumption were curtailed. However, by 1991 Gorbachev acknowledged that the loss of taxation revenue from anti-alcohol policies had contributed to the budget deficit, and he abandoned the campaign.

The Yeltsin government liberalised the alcohol market as part of its reforms, and newly established oligarchs and organised-crime syndicates moved into the market. When Putin came to power in 2000, he was determined to regain state control over the alcohol industry. He created a state holding company for alcohol production, Rosspirtprom, but there is no state monopoly over alcohol. Bailey also details how members of Putin's inner circle are themselves involved in the alcohol industry.

Dmitry Medvedev launched a new anti-alcohol campaign in 2009 after taking over the presidency. He cited public-health issues and Russia's demographic crisis – it was estimated that 26% of all deaths were associated with alcohol, and Russia's population was declining – as necessitating a reduction in consumption. Medvedev was joined by civic public-health advocates and the Russian Orthodox Church in urging temperance, to little avail.

Bailey concludes that it is impossible for Russia to pursue a rational policy toward alcohol consumption because of competing interest groups and the government's need to maintain a healthy state budget.

Asia-Pacific
Lanxin Xiang

Belt and Road: A Chinese World Order
Bruno Maçães. London: C. Hurst & Co., 2018. £20.00. 228 pp.

The Belt and Road Initiative (BRI) is a global development strategy first pro-posed by China in 2013. It had been mostly dismissed in the United States as unworkable until the administration of Donald Trump elevated it to a high-stakes challenge to its 'America First' world view, thus spurring some imaginative analysis, of which this book is a good example. In it, Bruno Maçães reveals his frustration that the 'Eurasian supercontinent' that emerged after the Cold War has become increasingly integrated, but 'not according to a Western model' (p. 2). He laments that the US has withdrawn from the region, leaving China to establish its own dominance. And he sensationally claims that the BRI is 'the Chinese plan to build a new world order replacing the US-led interna-tional system' (p. 5).

Having struck this alarmist note at the outset, it is no surprise that the rest of the book focuses on China's alleged geopolitical ambition to rival and eventu-ally defeat the Unites States. Key Chinese concepts are presented as propaganda masking sinister aims: the concept of 'connectivity' (*wu tong*), for example, which the Chinese actually borrowed from Europe, is twisted into something analo-gous to modern colonialism. Maçães claims that 'the traditional connectivity concept focuses on the end-points of the connection with limited consideration to what goes on between them', implying that the Chinese concept cares more about the spaces in between than it is prepared to admit. This, according to the author, 'is why the initiative speaks of a "belt" rather than a "road"' with respect to the land component of the initiative. 'On sea, only the end points are connected … but on land what is being envisioned is the fragmentation of production processes across different geographies' (p. 53). This stretches the facts a bit too far. The author is clearly seeking to imbue the BRI with territorial ambitions, but he seems to have forgotten his native Portugal's experience in the Asia-Pacific centuries ago. The Portuguese empire was not just concerned about Goa, Malacca and Macau. After it seized the Persian Gulf, its superior fleet encountered virtually no resistance. Clearly, the spaces in between have always been important.

Belt and Road's fundamental problem is its reliance on the Western concep-tion of international 'order', which stresses the mechanical distribution of power and the rise and fall of great powers. Maçães readily accepts Graham Allison's

Survival | vol. 61 no. 4 | August–September 2019 | pp. 177–182   DOI 10.1080/00396338.2019.1637131

Thucydides Trap theory, which predicts an inevitable confrontation between the US and China (pp. 7–8). But the traditional Chinese conception of 'order', which the author appears not to understand, has never been mechanical. The Chinese word for 'order', 治 (*zhi*), literally means 'flood control'. One cannot rely upon mechanical methods – that is, the building of dams – to contain floods. The most effective way is to build networks of connectivity that allow the water to find its own outlets. This is the philosophy that underpins the BRI, one that is easily misunderstood when the project is interpreted by Western concepts alone.

Japan Rearmed: The Politics of Military Power
Sheila A. Smith. Cambridge, MA: Harvard University Press,
2019. £21.95/$29.95. 333 pp.

Sheila Smith's analysis of Japanese security policies in *Japan Rearmed* is, as usual, brilliant and multidimensional. It is clear, she writes, that Japan has been pursuing, particularly under Prime Minister Shinzo Abe, a policy of rearmament despite the constitutionally mandated pacifism that has dominated Japanese debates on war and peace for more than 70 years. The question is why it has decided to rearm, and why the Japanese public has been so muted over this critical issue of constitutional change.

The answers supplied by most Japan experts are familiar: the country's external environment has been transformed, and Japan is now facing, for the first time in its post-war history, security challenges not only from a nuclear-armed North Korea, but also from China and its maritime ambitions. Smith, by contrast, stresses a more important dimension of Japanese concerns, the unreliability of the long-established alliance between Japan and the United States, which until recently has served as the cornerstone of Japanese national security. As Japan's perception of security threats has changed, the question of applying its military capability to war preparation has become urgent. However, unlike other US military alliances, such as NATO or the US–South Korea alliance, formal contingency planning that commits military force to combined operations has not been part of the US–Japan alliance. Therefore, Japan either has to integrate its forces into a combined command or rely upon itself to deter or repel an aggressor without US help.

Smith sees this dilemma as deriving from Japan's reliance on 'borrowed power' (p. 173). According to the original strategic bargain between Washington and Tokyo, Japan has no obligation to defend the United States. As long as Japan has no nuclear weapons, it has to rely upon the 'extended deterrence' offered by the US. As with France and Germany during the Cold War, there is some doubt in Japan about how fully the country is covered by the American nuclear umbrella. But whereas Germans could ask why the US would 'sacrifice Boston for Bonn' in the 1980s, the issue of extended deterrence is a sensitive one in Japan – a legacy of Hiroshima and Nagasaki – and the government cannot put the question to a public debate.

Today, there is a growing fear in Japan that it could be abandoned altogether by Washington. This fear started to take root during the Obama administration, when Washington retained the position of not entangling itself in sovereignty disputes over the Senkaku/Diaoyu islands in the East China Sea. Donald Trump's apparent lack of interest in strategic issues and suspicion of military alliances has only made this fear grow stronger. Ultimately, Smith concludes that 'the reliability of the United States, more than the military capabilities of its neighbors, will in the end decide the future of Japan's approach to military power' (p. 15).

Censored: Distraction and Diversion Inside China's Great Firewall
Margaret E. Roberts. Princeton, NJ: Princeton University Press, 2018. £24.00/$29.95. 271 pp.

The widespread use of the internet in authoritarian states has mostly been welcomed because of the common belief that the dissemination of information will ultimately triumph over any attempt to stop it. Margaret Roberts offers a dissenting opinion, warning that the power of governments to use the internet in the service of their own agendas should not be underestimated. In *Censored*, she demonstrates that both authoritarian regimes like China's and liberal democracies like the United States have erected barriers to the distribution of certain types of information. 'Every political entity', she writes, 'has incentives to promote particular types of information to their constituents' and 'reasons to control, slow down or prevent citizens from consuming other types of information' (p. 21). Laws in the name of national security have been adopted in most countries, and 'special interests … have been successful in a variety of democracies in advocating for lawmakers to pass laws that limit expression in particular issues' (p. 47).

This is not to say that governments face no costs in attempting to exert control over information. In democracies, attempts at censorship run into the problem of accountability. In authoritarian regimes, leaders face the 'dictator's dilemma'. According to the author, this dilemma can take the form of a backlash against the regime, as populations grow to suspect that government censorship is hiding dirty secrets. Consistent repression can create opportunities for discontent. Censorship can also restrict the information available to regimes as they try to gauge public sentiment. A third form of the dilemma can be seen in the costs of censorship. Modern censorship is very expensive, not only in terms of government expenditure, but also in terms of the way it can impede market operations, an important consideration in countries, like China, that rely upon e-commerce and foreign trade (pp. 23–4).

The Chinese approach to internet censorship is to focus on the gatekeepers of information rather than individuals. Thus, censorship rarely disrupts the daily life of citizens. Internet access is widespread in China, and social media is ubiquitous. As the former internet tsar of China's Communist Party, Lu Wei, put it, with 30 billion pieces of information being generated every day in China (as of 2015), 'it is not possible to apply censorship to this enormous amount of data' (p. 1).

Roberts concludes that, 'Though the digital era has made large strides toward bridging gaps between countries and cultures, censorship throttles cultural exchange between China and the West.' The author is particularly concerned with 'the bifurcation of media consumption between Chinese and Americans', which makes it difficult to foster cooperation on the basis of common ground (p. 235). This is a timely book that should be read by a wide audience.

To Build as Well as Destroy: American Nation Building in South Vietnam
Andrew J. Gawthorpe. Ithaca, NY: Cornell University Press, 2018. $45.00. 245 pp.

This fascinating book looks at the conceptual as well as the practical dimensions of American nation building. Despite its widespread usage, the term 'nation building' has multiple, competing definitions. It can refer to UN peacekeeping missions after civil wars, educational programmes intended to build a national identity, and even to the United States' exit strategies from its wars in places such as Iraq and Afghanistan. Andrew Gawthorpe prefers to think of this term as a 'metaphor' rather than 'a description of a particular, concrete set of processes or actions', adding that the term is 'malleable enough to refer to either wartime, peacetime, or a postwar period' (p. 9). Regardless of how it is defined, the success rate of US attempts at nation building remains dismal.

Gawthorpe uses South Vietnam as a case study, with good reason. As Henry Kissinger pointed out, it was the Vietnam War that first 'spawned … the notion of "nation-building"' (p. 9). In South Vietnam, the American government pursued a policy of pacification not only through military operations, but also by adopting a social–political approach. The creation of the Office of Civil Operations and Revolutionary Development Support (CORDS) in 1967 signalled the beginning of this effort. The agency was 'designed to allow the United States and the GVN [government of Vietnam] to work together on joint plans to strengthen the South Vietnamese regime', to build links with the rural population and to undermine the communist movement's influence on Vietnamese villagers (p. 67). Inspired by communist methods of rural mobilisation, CORDS came up with the idea of establishing a new village system to hinder communist activities and help reduce US casualties and the costs of rural pacification campaigns. From 1969 to 1972, CORDS began to implement its new village system by emphasising the so-called 'three selfs': self-government, self-defence and self-development (p. 18). In each case, success proved ephemeral. Self-governance required village elections, but these elections meant little as long as military officers remained in charge. Self-defence meant recruiting villagers into paramilitary units, which helped boost local security in a limited way, but did not help foster popular loyalty to the government or create a sense of mutual obligations between the government and rural citizens. The GVN was far too corrupt, weak and untrustworthy for that. The self-development scheme yielded negligible results, because central and provincial governments were unwilling to grant any serious power to village chiefs in economic affairs, either in agriculture, education or fishing (p. 184). Thus, although US nation-building efforts were part of its exit strategy, the hope being that the GVN would gain enough popular support that it would be able to withstand a communist assault after the American withdrawal, the result was quite the opposite. In his thoughtful conclusion, the author observes that 'the American experience of nation-building in South Vietnam … ought to be a humbling and sobering lesson for would-be nation builders' (p. 189).

Blaming China: It Might Feel Good but It Won't Fix America's Economy
Benjamin Shobert. Lincoln, NE: Potomac Books, 2018. $29.95. 212 pp.

Blaming others for one's own problems is a useful diversionary tactic that has been used by politicians since ancient times. It usually involves deploying some combination of half-truths, inaccurate data and distorted facts. In the last century, Adolf Hitler used this tactic to blame the Treaty of Versailles for Germany's domestic problems. More recently, US President Donald Trump has been blaming the Bretton Woods system for American problems. But whereas the Treaty of Versailles was in fact an unequal treaty imposed on Germany by foreign powers, the Bretton Woods system is a quintessentially American creation.

Benjamin Shobert ruthlessly dissects Trump's diagnosis of American economic problems, particularly as they relate to the supposedly unfair trade relationship between the US and China. He scrutinises the arguments of what he calls the 'Dragon Slayer Camp' – comprising men such as Peter Navarro, an adviser to Trump on trade who has long been insisting that the US has traded away its superiority to China for short-term economic gains (p. 13), and Aaron Friedberg, who has publicly questioned why the US has no Cold War-style containment strategy against China and claimed that he is 'puzzled and frustrated' by the fact that the inevitability of a US–China conflict is 'not something that serious people [speak] about in polite company' (p. 16).

Shobert demands that the members of the Slayer Camp be held accountable for their extreme views, arguing that they should be willing to shoulder the responsibility for US–China disengagement and even war; that they 'must be required to answer the question of what other option the world had when China first opened to the West'; and that they must provide evidence that all China's gains have been made by breaking the rules (p. 17).

As for the 'Panda Huggers' (those who sympathise with China), Shobert suggests that they too entertain some fantasies about China, such as their belief in 'convergence' theory – the idea that the Chinese and American systems will eventually move in one direction, something that has yet to take place. But the Huggers are at least sensitive to the historical and cultural consequences of China's experience of national humiliation, arguing that China should be seen as 'a particular type of rising power that has real security concerns based on recent history' (p. 42).

The most interesting part of the book is its discussion of the ideological roots of the current blame game against China. It originated during the Cold War, but was temporarily eclipsed by the collapse of the Soviet Union. Then, in the early 2000s, a small but radical 'neoconservative' movement captured key positions within the George W. Bush administration and tried to revive the Cold War China policy, which was based on two ideas: regime change for all authoritarian states, and the doctrine of pre-emption – that is, preparing for the unavoidable war with China before it takes place (pp. 117–19). Initially, Trump and the neocons did not see eye to eye on much, including China. But now that Trump's trade war is running into difficulties, the neocons seem to have sensed an opportunity to creep back into policymaking roles, National Security Advisor John Bolton being just one example. The trouble is, as Richard McGregor put it so well, 'America's problem is not that it does not work like China. It is that it no longer works like America' (p. v).

Closing Argument

The Special Fantasy

Dana H. Allin and Benjamin Rhode

I

In May 1903, Britain's King Edward VII arrived in France for a state visit. The two countries had been enemies and rivals for centuries. The devastation of the Hundred Years War ended in the mid-fifteenth century, but conflicts continued intermittently for another 250 years. By the late seventeenth century, France and England (later Great Britain) had commenced their 'second hundred-years war'. These struggles for supremacy spanned most of the long eighteenth century, determined that the language spoken in the future United States of America and Republic of India would be English, not French, and were capped by the cataclysmic Napoleonic Wars, often known until 1914 as the 'Great War'. Britain and its allies finally defeated Napoleon Bonaparte at Waterloo in 1815, but the Anglo-French antagonism lingered. Despite reaching a first *entente cordiale* in the 1840s, and fighting as allies against Russia in the Crimean War (1853–56), Britain and France remained wary of each other. Soon after that war, and despite ongoing bilateral cooperation in China, the ironclad warships built by Emperor Napoleon III – Bonaparte's nephew – sparked a naval race and an invasion scare in Britain.[1]

For the remainder of the century, France remained one of Britain's primary threats. The 'two-power standard' of 1889, under which Britain committed to maintain a navy as large as its next two rivals combined, was

Dana H. Allin is Editor of *Survival* and IISS Senior Fellow for US Foreign Policy and Transatlantic Affairs.
Benjamin Rhode is Editor of *Strategic Comments* and IISS Research Fellow for Transatlantic Affairs.

Survival | vol. 61 no. 4 | August–September 2019 | pp. 183–190   DOI 10.1080/00396338.2019.1637133

aimed at France and its soon-to-be ally Russia. In 1898, in an episode today largely forgotten by most Britons but which retains a certain resonance in France, a confrontation between British and French colonial forces at Fashoda, in what is now South Sudan, almost produced another war. In the face of a larger local British force led by Major-General Sir Herbert Kitchener (who was later immortalised in recruitment posters) and a far superior navy, the French were forced to withdraw. Many Frenchmen depicted the episode as a stain on national honour. (Charles de Gaulle, age eight at the time, would later list 'the surrender of Fashoda' as one of France's 'weaknesses and mistakes' that had 'saddened [him] … profoundly'.[2])

The mood was not improved by Britain's war the following year against the Boers in South Africa. The imperial superpower found itself mired in a bloody counter-insurgency against resourceful farmers, descendants of Dutch colonists, who had purchased modern German weapons. Thousands of Boer civilians died of disease and malnutrition in British concentration camps; Britain stood accused by much of Europe of committing atrocities. A few hundred Frenchmen seized the opportunity to fight the old enemy by joining the Boer forces. Some French diplomats cautiously explored the possibility of working with Germany to take their revenge on *perfide Albion*.[3]

Given the extent of their often adjacent imperial domains, it seemed quite possible that British and French forces might soon confront each other again. There was also a growing recognition, however, that British and French interests might be better served by settling their disputes rather than fighting over them. Voices in their diplomatic establishments argued that it was time to defuse tensions.[4]

King Edward VII, on the throne since the death of his mother Queen Victoria in 1901, played a part in this rapprochement. Already more than 60 years old, Edward had spent considerable time in France, his favourite foreign destination. In his adolescence, during a visit to Paris with his strict and overbearing parents, he told the less constrained Napoleon III that he wished the French emperor were his father. For Edward, who was fluent in French, France represented an escape not just from his prudish parents, but from the social strictures they embodied and espoused. France's less repressed attitudes allowed Edward to indulge his taste for carousing and womanising.[5] During the Boer War, this reputation had prompted abusive French cartoons depicting him as a sozzled and obese wine barrel.[6]

Yet Edward was more than a hedonistic philanderer. He was also a charming and skilled diplomat, and he put these talents to good use for his country during the 1903 state visit to Paris. Two historians recount that, in advance of what they deem 'the most important royal visit in modern history', many Parisian Anglophobes had planned to bay at Edward about Fashoda and South Africa, but in the event the French crowds (mostly) cheered '*Vive notre roi!*'[7]

A monarch's personal charm was not, of course, the sole factor in reconciling two national enemies and rivals. Diplomatic conversations and negotiations continued for another year, lent greater urgency by the outbreak of war in early 1904 between Russia and Japan, France and Britain's respective allies. Both Paris and London wanted to avoid being ensnared in conflict with each other. In April 1904, they agreed an *entente cordiale*: not a military alliance, but an understanding to address remaining colonial disputes. Three years later, concerned that Russia's weakness after its defeat by Japan might allow Germany to dominate the European continent, London signed a convention with St Petersburg that put the great game of their imperial rivalry on hold. Kaiser Wilhelm II, Edward's nephew, was convinced that his uncle was sewing up Europe against him in order to contain Germany's historic destiny.[8]

II

Now *that* was a state visit. Some have argued that the alignment endorsed by the Parisian crowds did not end up serving Britain – or, in fact, the entire human race – very well. A subsequent world war featuring the British Empire should have been avoidable, and the failure to avoid it raised the curtain on a twentieth-century horror show.[9] It is debatable. What cannot be doubted is that King Edward's trip inaugurated a momentous Anglo-French strategic convergence.

By such standards we might try to assess the long-delayed but finally consummated state visit of US President Donald Trump to the United

Kingdom in June 2019. Based on past performance, the president's decorum on this trip arguably exceeded expectations (though he did take time to call London's Muslim mayor a 'loser'). The real problem was that the entire rationale for the visit involved transparent layers of illusion. Far from convergence, the Trump state visit was a farcical expression of strategic fantasy. It represented a determination to inhabit the past, to hark back to a period of shared Anglo-American adversity and common purpose throughout much of the twentieth century.

This is not to suggest that the US–UK alliance lacks substance. The two countries are and will continue to be important allies across many domains, including the vaunted intelligence partnership. In 2019, however, there is a specific Brexiteer's concept of a 'special relationship' that approaches nonsense.

Throughout the past 300 years, Britain weighed repeatedly in a continental balance of power to prevent the emergence of a hegemon, whether that be Louis XIV, Napoleon, Wilhelm II, Adolf Hitler or Joseph Stalin. Now Britain has decided to withdraw from the European Union, abandoning a vital vehicle for British power to France and Germany. And with the absurd demands from hard Brexiteers for how departure should be organised – including their disregard for the EU's crucial role in Northern Ireland's peace – they have effectively isolated Britain from Europe, uniting the EU 27 against it.[10]

The initial invitation for a Trump state visit came in January 2017, during a period of maximum British self-deception over the supposed deliverance of an American trade deal to compensate for the new barriers to be erected between Britain and the EU, its largest and closest economic partner. The idea is economically illiterate on multiple levels. Firstly, Britain by itself will not have anything like the economic clout that it has hitherto enjoyed as a member of the largest and richest economic grouping in the world; one thing that the EU does, and does well, is trade deals. Secondly, and relatedly, the laws of economic 'gravity' – the combined mass and proximity of neighbouring economies – dictate that economic relations between Britain and continental Europe will remain far more important than those between Britain and the US.[11] The *Financial Times* has reported on a 2018 UK government study estimating that 'a US free trade agreement would increase UK GDP by only 0.2 percent after 15 years, a tiny fraction of the 2 to 8 percent costs of Brexit during that time'. Moreover, since the UK does roughly three times more trade with the EU than with the United States, 'to compensate for any fall in UK–EU trade, UK–US trade would have to grow by a much bigger proportion. If Britain's imports and exports to the bloc dropped by 10 percent, it would require a 37 percent increase in trade with the US.'[12] This will not happen for political as well as economic reasons: the British public will not accept, for example, a substitution of American for EU food standards on such matters as chlorine-washed chicken and hormone-injected beef.

Theresa May had conveyed the invitation for a Trump state visit in person. She was the first foreign leader to meet with the new American president, and their awkward hand-holding conveyed a sense of diplomatic desperation: committed to leaving the EU, Britain must embrace the United States tightly, no matter how often its leader embarrasses, undermines and contradicts British policy and British interests. Anyway, Trump was not very good at holding hands.

III

Since the pro-Brexit argument waves the flag of 'Global Britain' anchored by a special relationship with the United States, it is probably worth asking what Americans other than Trump think of the idea. And the answer, in consistent formulations of the American interest by American strategists, statesmen and stateswomen since the Second World War, is not much.

The Americans were active promoters of European integration since well before the Marshall Plan, which was very much premised on the idea. There was some early debate in the Harry Truman administration about how deeply Britain should be involved in that integration, with George Kennan in 1950 taking the view that Britain belonged more naturally in an Anglo-Saxon community with the United States and Canada; he worried, among other things, that British diffidence about a European construct would slow down its development. Kennan ran into opposition, however. His friend Charles Bohlen, for example, then number two in the US

Embassy in Paris, argued persuasively that close British involvement was necessary to assuage French and others' fears of German domination.[13]

There was also the argument that Britain was no longer powerful enough to stand apart from continental Europe. In 1962, Dean Acheson, the former secretary of state under Truman, gave a speech at West Point. He was talking not about Brexit but rather *Brenter* – that is, whether the UK should join what was then the Common Market. One sentence became famous: 'Great Britain has lost an empire and has not yet found a role.' But Acheson had more to say. 'The attempt to play a separate power role – that is, a role apart from Europe, a role based on a "special relationship" with the United States, a role based on being head of a "commonwealth" which has no political structure, or unity, or strength – this role is about played out.'[14]

Acheson was an Anglophile to an extent that had caused him trouble with Congress while he was secretary of state. But he was also a cold-blooded realist when it came to matters of power, and he wanted to assert clearly that Britain's power was fading and that it needed to latch itself to the precursor of the EU precisely to restore some of that power and to preserve its effective autonomy.[15]

Though there were times when US administrations appeared ambivalent about European ambitions, they almost always came around, and they certainly maintained that Britain within the EU was better for American purposes than Britain outside it. In the transatlantic acrimony over its Iraq invasion, the George W. Bush administration played at exploiting divisions between 'old' and 'new' Europe. Yet the administration in its second term recognised the importance of rebuilding good relations with Brussels, the destination of Bush's first foreign trip after his second inauguration.

The Barack Obama administration embraced British unity with Europe as well. Philip Gordon, Obama's assistant secretary of state for European and Eurasian affairs (and a former editor of this journal), was speaking to London journalists in 2013 when one of them asked about the prospect of a referendum on leaving the EU. His answer: 'We have a growing relationship with the EU as an institution, which has an increasing voice in the world, and we want to see a strong British voice in that EU. That is in

America's interests. We welcome an outward-looking EU with Britain in it.'[16] This statement caused a great rending of garments and gnashing of teeth in Britain's Europhobic press. Obama himself travelled to London, at David Cameron's request, in 2016 to more or less repeat what Gordon had said, causing Boris Johnson to observe that Obama's father was Kenyan so the president no doubt disliked Britain.

The Obama administration believed that Brexit would be damaging to US–UK relations for exactly the same reason that Acheson wanted Britain to join the Common Market: because separation from Europe would diminish Britain on the world stage and render Britain more inward-looking and self-absorbed. Of course, the Obama administration could not begin to imagine the spectacle of self-obsession and self-harm that has actually ensued.

The notion that a 'Global Britain' with a reinvigorated special relationship with America would somehow compensate for its loss of influence in Europe was never plausible, but became downright incredible insofar as the referendum coincided with the emergence of a far less benign global environment. The Trump presidency, hostile to the EU and broader liberal order, has naturally welcomed Brexit. But it is hard to see this embrace as particularly encouraging for Britain.

In the most benign scenario, Brexit will mean a weaker Britain, and a poorer one relative to expected growth had it remained in the EU. This would render Britain a less valuable ally for the United States. That would not be a disaster in itself, but it is discouraging at a time when greater rather than corroded transatlantic solidarity is needed against the rebound and rise of authoritarian powers such as Russia and China. In any event, given the crisis of both American and British politics and government, the most benign scenario is not something we should count on.

Notes

1   Robert and Isabelle Tombs, *That Sweet Enemy: The French and the British from the Sun King to the Present* (London: William Heinemann, 2006), esp. pp. 339–65.

2   *Ibid.*, pp. 407–22; and Graham Allison, *Destined for War: Can America and China Escape Thucydides's Trap?* (London: Scribe, 2017), pp. 61–2.

3   Tombs, *That Sweet Enemy*, pp. 432–7.

4   Allison, *Destined for War*, pp. 72–3; and Tombs, *That Sweet Enemy*, pp. 436–8.

5   Robert K. Massie, *Dreadnought: Britain, Germany and the Coming of the Great War* (London: Vintage Books, 2007), pp. 13–17; and Tombs, *That Sweet Enemy*, pp. 400–2.

6   See Fabrice Serodes, *Anglophobie et politique: de Fachoda à Mers el-Kébir: visions françaises du monde britannique* (Paris: Harmattan, 2010).

7   Certain French nationalists, recognising Britain's importance in countering Germany, had warned their followers against protesting Edward's visit. Tombs, *That Sweet Enemy*, pp. 438–42.

8   Edward, declared Wilhelm in front of an audience of hundreds, was 'Satan. You cannot imagine what a Satan he is!' Allison, *Destined for War*, pp. 72–7; and Tombs, *That Sweet Enemy*, pp. 437–42.

9   See Niall Ferguson, *The Pity of War* (London: Allen Lane/Penguin Press, 1998).

10   See Jonathan Stevenson, 'Does Brexit Threaten Peace in Northern Ireland?', *Survival*, vol. 59, no. 3, June–July 2017, pp. 111–28.

11   See Paul Krugman, 'Brexit Meets Gravity', *New York Times*, 10 July 2018, https://www.nytimes.com/2018/07/10/opinion/brexit-meets-gravity.html.

12   Chris Giles, 'Would a Trade Deal with Trump Boost Brexit Britain?', *Financial Times*, 4 June 2019, https://www.ft.com/content/40d74c90-85e5-11e9-97ea-05ac2431f453.

13   These insights into the Truman-administration debate are from a chapter by Avis Bohlen, in her draft biography of Charles Bohlen, which she has generously shared with the authors.

14   Dean Acheson, 'Our Atlantic Alliance: The Political and Economic Strands', speech delivered at the United States Military Academy, West Point, New York, 5 December 1962, in Douglas Brinkley, 'Dean Acheson and the "Special Relationship": The West Point Speech of December 1962', *Historical Journal*, vol. 33, no. 3, 1990, pp. 599–608.

15   *Ibid*.

16   George Parker, Jim Pickard and Richard McGregor, 'Stay at Heart of Europe, U.S. Tells Britain', CNN, 10 January 2013, https://edition.cnn.com/2013/01/10/business/us-uk-euro-plea/index.html.

Correction

Article title: Mad Momentum Redux? The Rise and Fall of Nuclear Arms Control
Author: Arbatov, A.
Journal: *Survival*
Citation details: Volume 61, Number 3, June–July 2019, pages 7–38.
DOI: https://doi.org/10.1080/00396338.2019.1614785

p. 14

The final sentence of the final paragraph has been amended to read:

Russia is vaguer on the notion of limited nuclear warfare, but some unofficial sources relate it to tactical nuclear platforms, the boost-glide *Avangard* system and various sub-strategic systems.

p. 16

The second full sentence of the first paragraph has been amended to read:

China has also joined the anti-satellite arms race, having tested its system in 2007, and India conducted its first test in 2019.

p. 29

The penultimate sentence of the first full paragraph has been amended to read:

After satellites detect a missile launch 60 to 90 seconds later, the next time radars will see a hypersonic glider will be three to four minutes before impact, which does not leave time for authorisation of a launch-on-warning strike.

Survival | vol. 61 no. 4 | August–September 2019 | pp. 191–192   DOI 10.1080/00396338.2019.1630156